Photograph by Mick Bradley

Susan Magarey AM, FASSA, PhD, was made a member of the Order of Australia for pioneering Women's Studies as a field of academic endeavour.

Her publications include four books: the prize-winning biography of Catherine Helen Spence, *Unbridling the tongues of women* (1986) now being re-published; *Passions of the first-wave feminists* (2001); *Looking Back: Looking Forward. A Century of the Queen Adelaide Club 1909-2009* (2009); and, with Kerrie Round, *Roma the First: a Biography of Dame Roma Mitchell* (2007, second, revised, imprint 2009). She has edited eight collections of articles – including *Women in a Restructuring Australia: Work and Welfare* (1995) with Anne Edwards, and *Debutante Nation: Feminism Contests the 1890s* (1993) with Sue Rowley and Susan Sheridan – and was for twenty years (1985-1995) the Founding Editor of the triannual journal *Australian Feminist Studies*.

She is the Founder of the Magarey Medal for Biography and a member of the Board of History SA. She is writing a history of the Women's Liberation Movement in Australia. For fun, she swims, gardens, cooks and listens to classical music. She describes her life in the words of Australian poet Jennifer Maiden: 'Ambivalent, ambidextrous, ambiguous, androgynous, amorous, ironic'. In her next life she will be a trapeze artist.

Catherine Helen Spence. Image courtesy of the State Library of South Australia, SLSA: B3675.

Unbridling the Tongues of Women

*A biography of
Catherine Helen Spence*

SUSAN MAGAREY

Published in Adelaide by

University of Adelaide Press
Barr Smith Library
The University of Adelaide
South Australia
5005
press@adelaide.edu.au
www.adelaide.edu.au/press

The University of Adelaide Press publishes externally refereed scholarly books by staff of the University of Adelaide. It aims to maximise the accessibility to its best research by publishing works through the internet as free downloads and as high quality printed volumes on demand.

Electronic Index: this book is available from the website as a down-loadable PDF with fully searchable text. Please use the electronic version to complement the index.

© Susan Magarey 1985, 2010

First published 1985 Hale and Iremonger, Sydney
Republished 2010 by University of Adelaide Press with a new Introduction

This book is copyright. Apart from any fair dealing for the purposes of private study, research, criticism or review as permitted under the Copyright Act, no part may be reproduced, stored in a retrieval system, or transmitted, in any form or by any means, electronic, mechanical, photocopying, recording or otherwise without the prior written permission. Address all inquiries to the Director at the above address.

Subject Keywords
Women authors - Australian Biography - Women in Public Life Australia - Women's rights Australia History

For the full Cataloguing-in-Publication data please contact National Library of Australia: cip@nla.gov.au

ISBN 978-0-9806723-0-5 (electronic)
ISBN 978-0-9806723-1-2 (paperback)

Book design: Céline Lawrence
Cover concept: Fiona Cameron. Drawing by Hugo Shaw

Preface

During her long life Catherine Helen Spence sought to make her voice heard in a world dominated by men. She penned editorials, delivered sermons and spoke at public meetings both in Australia, in the United States and in Britain. Both by her own example and in her support for women's cause, she sought 'to unbridle the tongues of women'. Although she was well-known in her day, indeed renowned as the 'Grand Old Woman of Australia' at her death in 1910, knowledge of her life of achievements slipped in subsequent years. When in 1985, Susan Magarey published her prize-winning biography of Spence, *Unbridling the Tongues of Women*, Spence had become largely forgotten. *Unbridling* did more than recover the story of Spence's life and work, it suggested new approaches to Australian history. It was the first biography of a first-wave Australian feminist written by a second-wave feminist historian. As such it inspired and set an example of feminist biography and history which has seen a great outpouring of feminist historical and literary scholarship in biographies of Australian feminist activists and of Australian women writers; Spence herself was of course both a writer and a political activist. *Unbridling* must also be located as an influential early text in the development of Australian feminist history in the last three decades. In this and her other work, Susan Magarey has achieved much in the on-going campaigns to ensure that women's voices and perspectives are heard in public debate.

It is important that women's issues and women's history be kept to the forefront and it is highly timely that this book should be re-published now. Susan Magarey's new introduction sets the original study in the context of more recent research on Spence. It will bring to a new generation of readers the importance of unbridling women's tongues.

Margaret Allen
17 September 2009
Gender Studies
University of Adelaide

Introduction to the New Edition

Catherine Helen Spence was a powerful and persuasive public speaker. She had, in a sense, been practising speaking for most of her adult life. She recalled a moment in the 1850s when she was in her late twenties – a wonderfully back-handed moment – when she began to sing while she was doing the ironing. Her four year-old nephew 'burst out with "Don't sing, auntie; let me hear the voice of your words."' So she abandoned melody and recited Wordsworth. But this was, as she herself was to observe, exercising her gifts exclusively for 'home consumption'. Law and custom, she continued,

> have put a bridle on the tongues of women, and of the innumerable proverbs relating to the sex, the most cynical are those relating to her use of language. Her only qualification for public speaking in old days was that she could scold, and our ancestors imposed a salutary check on this by the ducking stool in public, and sticks no thicker than the thumb for marital correction in private.

Historian Marilyn Lake has observed, 'Oratory was a masculine performance; womanliness demanded a soft voice and winning smiles'. Perhaps Catherine Spence was the exception which proved the rule.

Once launched in the 1870s, Miss Spence won acclaim and affection for her 'rare gifts of speech and intellect'. At home in Adelaide, a reporter was to praise a sermon he heard her deliver, approving her slight Scots accent, her clear, firm voice and her unselfconsciousness. Another observer exclaimed over her speech to a public meeting: 'Does not Miss Spence speak well and clearly'. Abroad, too, in 1893-4, she elicited enthusiasm. Even in the United States, where a woman speaking in public was not such a rare phenomenon by the end of the nineteenth century, Catherine Spence's public address at the World Congress of Charities & Corrections in Chicago gained, she reported, 'a most attentive hearing, and was frequently interrupted by applause, which is not such a common thing in America as it is in Australia'. A charismatic speaker, she was: further east she presented, she was told, 'the finest political address given in Boston for ten years'.

Catherine Spence knew that she was carving out a new path along which other women would follow her. When she insisted on giving her own lecture to the South Australian Institute, an unprecedented innovation in 1871, she did so, she said, 'to make it easier henceforward for any woman who felt she had something to say to stand up and say it'.

Unbridling the tongues of women: a biography of Catherine Helen Spence began life as a thesis for a Master of Arts degree at the Australian National University, completed in 1971. Subsequently, I was advised to send it to Melbourne University Press, the principal publisher of Australian historical work. It came back with a letter saying that they thought it was very well written, but that there was no market for books about women. This was in 1973, just two years before International Women's Year and the appearance of Anne Summers' *Damned Whores and God's Police*, Beverley Kingston's *My Wife, My Daughter, and Poor Mary Ann*, and later, Miriam Dixson's *The Real Matilda*, so Melbourne University Press missed out on what might have been a small scoop. My thesis was eventually published by Hale & Iremonger in 1985.

At the heart of the researches that I carried out was Catherine Spence's *Autobiography*, a work that she wrote during her last months, sometimes in indelible pencil because she was writing in bed, and, she said, 'A nice state I and the sheets would be in if I used ink'. Following it fairly closely, I depicted her on a journey which brought her, at the celebration of her eightieth birthday in 1905, to the declaration, 'I am a New Woman, and I know it'.

Introduction to the new edition

In Australia the New Woman was a composite figure, associated with the appearance of the bicycle (with women riding astride them), the democratisation of smoking in the form of cigarettes (and women smoking), campaigns for rational dress for women, and, most scandalously, women's challenge to the double standard of sexual morality and their assertion of a specifically sexual autonomy. She appeared tamely enough when Catherine Spence reviewed Olive Schreiner's novel, *A Story of an African Farm* and Mona Caird's *The Wing of Azrael* for the South Australian *Register* in 1889, under the brisk headline 'Why Do Women Wilt?' But the New Woman went on to become a subject of heated controversy in the wake of Ibsen's play, *The Doll's House*, which toured Australasia in 1889-1890; a subject of public lectures in Melbourne during the 1890s; an object of appalled attention in the pages of the radical nationalist journal, the *Bulletin*.

Miss Spence was politically astute. She knew well that, by juxtaposing the visual image of herself – a short, square, white-haired spinster in her eighties – with a stereotype generally considered sexually shocking, she would compel people to attend to what the term 'The New Woman' meant. And she proceeded to give it a meaning that she wanted it to have:

> I mean an awakened woman ... awakened to a sense of capacity and responsibility, not merely to the family and the household, but to the State; to be wise, not for her own selfish interests, but that the world may be glad that she had been born.

This book, *Unbridling the tongues of women*, relates the ways in which Catherine Helen Spence arrived at this definition of herself, this imperative for women.

It is a story that still rewards attention. Now, though, a century after Miss Spence's death, a quarter of a century after this book first arrived in book-shops, that narrative needs some revision. For the past twenty-five years have seen considerable scholarship devoted to the life and works of Catherine Helen Spence: there are newly-identified sources of information, and other, related, fields offer fresh contexts in which to locate her narrative, a story which then takes on different hues from those contextual colours. To make such an affirmation is not to ignore the scholarship that was available at the end of the 1960s. Rather it is to point up the immense increase and great enrichment of scholarship that late twentieth-century feminism prompted around the lives and works of women, a burgeoning which now includes an array of biographies of other first-wave feminists and studies of nineteenth-century women writers, all enhancing our understanding not only of Catherine Helen Spence but also of her times. Here I present a brief account of that scholarship to accompany this new edition of my book.

First: the newly-identified sources of information. One work which prompts a reconsideration of almost every aspect of Catherine Spence's life because it compels attention to her domestic life, 'the core', as historian Peter Cochrane notes, 'that guides or drives or perhaps explains the public life', was something that she wrote herself. But it is not her own. It is her record of her mother's recollections of life in Scotland and early years in Australia. Edited by Judy King and Graham Tulloch, *Tenacious of the Past: The Recollections of Helen Brodie*, published in 1994, elaborates the class-characterisation of her parents' families, and her parents' relationship with each other.

Theirs had been a love-match. At twenty-four, Helen Brodie could have been considered a 'bonnie lass', with dark brown hair and fine blue-grey eyes which were large, clear and expressive, distracting from her short nose, her florid complexion, 'the face round rather than oval', and her 'stout compact figure'. David Spence was twenty-six, tall at five feet ten inches (178 cms) and had a long nose and pale skin; he was going bald already, but a high forehead was in favour at the time. She was a daughter of six or seven generations of tenant farmers and a snob: she had so fine a sense of social gradation as to object to the people she found herself among – retail traders – as 'some degrees lower in position and education than her own circle' when she visited London as a young woman. He had been educated to be a lawyer, a Writer to the Signet, and won favour for his educated voice and manner. Moreover, they shared their progressive liberal politics. The future glowed as they settled into the pretty lowlands village of Melrose.

Sadly, that shine quickly dimmed. Their politics separated them from 'the better class of society', and the townsfolk who formed their primary circle of acquaintance were 'very narrow and very dull'. David Spence's investments were not doing well, and he took to working at night as well as all day, 'going over his books'. Their first child was not born until three years after their marriage. Most importantly for the events that followed, the only one of her children that Helen Brodie was able to suckle was the child who bore her own name, Catherine Helen, the fifth of eight. And she was the child who – as *Unbridling the tongues of women* relates – set about trying to make up for her father's financial difficulties, after the family had suffered

Introduction to the new edition

his financial collapse and emigrated to Adelaide. Catherine Spence rejoiced in her earnings as a seventeen year-old governess, noting, tellingly, 'My mother said she never felt the bitterness of poverty after I began to earn money'.

This became one of the most crucial emotional moments in the lives of both Helen Brodie and Catherine Spence. For it was at about this time that a young man asked Catherine Spence to marry him, and even though she liked him well enough, she refused. One reason for her decision was, she said, 'the Calvinist creed that made me shrink from the possibility of bringing children into the world with so little chance of eternal salvation'. But the other was her newly-achieved ability to help support her mother: 'I was 17, and had just begun to earn money'. It was a choice to remain with Helen Brodie as the other children left to make their ways in the world. After David Spence died in 1846, the partnership that would sustain the households in which Helen Brodie and Catherine Spence lived for the next forty-one years was a partnership between mother and daughter. They were to remain each other's dearest and closest companions for the rest of Helen Brodie's long life.

Catherine Helen Spence
and her mother, Helen Brodie Spence.
Image courtesy of the State Library
of South Australia, SLSA: B7106.

Twenty-five years on, it is imperative to correct a mistake about these events. The James Allen who sought Catherine Spence's hand in marriage was not, as I announced in *Unbridling the tongues of women*, the person known as 'Dismal Jimmy'. James Allen's descendant, Mrs Audrey Abbie, identifies him as the James Allen (c.1816-1881) who shared David Spence's cabin on the *Dumfries*, the ship on which David journeyed to South Australia ahead of the rest of his family. Historian Barbara Wall notes that he associated with the Spence family when they lived at Brownhill Creek. He became a chemist in Hindley Street, Adelaide. He was listed among the seatholders and subscribers of the Unitarian Christian Church in 1865; his daughter, Lavinia, married another Unitarian, AM Simpson of A. Simpson & Son, ironworkers, ancestors of Audrey Abbie. Later, James Allen lived in Unley and was active in political movements. I am grateful to both Mrs Abbie and Dr Wall for correcting this blunder.

Catherine Spence's own account of her refusal of James Allen is certainly present in *Unbridling the tongues of women*. But it has little of the emotional intensity that a reading of Helen Brodie's recollections imparts to that narrative. Such intensity, together with a fresh consideration of the various households that Catherine Spence formed in the course of her life, brings a different aspect of Miss Spence's personality to the fore. Ambitious she undoubtedly was, from her very early years; she said so herself, and *Unbridling the tongues of women* follows suit. But she was also immensely generous, an element evident in her relationships with her kin, the members of her households and with her friends. In an article on 'The private life of Catherine Helen Spence' published in 2009, I revised my earlier analysis and argued that generosity was a major driver of her public life as well: she wanted to make the world fairer for everyone.

Another contribution that modifies understandings of Catherine Spence's life concerns the principal source for any narrative of that life, her *Autobiography*. Historian, Helen Jones, published two articles titled modestly, postscripts to 'the Life of Catherine Helen Spence' in the *Journal of the Historical Society of South Australia* in 1987 and 1988. They include two letters to Sydney suffragist, Rose Scott: one from Catherine Spence's niece, Lucy Morice, daughter of Catherine Spence's brother, John; a second from another niece, Eleanor Wren, daughter of William Wren and Catherine Spence's younger sister, Mary. Both were close to their aunt: Lucy Morice shared a number of her socio-political interests, in particular in feminism and in kindergartens; Eleanor Wren, with her brother Charles, lived with her aunt and her

Introduction to the new edition

grandmother, after the children had been left orphans in the 1860s until the late 1880s, at one time being nursed in bed with some kind of back problem for as long as three years, at another copying out all of her aunt's three-decker novel, 'Handfasted', because Miss Spence thought Eleanor's handwriting would give it a better chance of winning a prize than her own. The two letters are about Catherine Spence's death on 3 April 1910, and they reveal disagreements about Auntie Kate's will.

Lucy Spence Morice.
Image courtesy of the State Library of South Australia
SLSA: B58523.

At the core of the trouble was Lucy Morice's belief that control of her aunt's affairs had been wrested from her by Ellen Gregory who, as a member of the household in which Catherine Spence had been living, had found a will written fifteen years earlier which gave such control, instead, to the Wrens. Ellen Gregory was not, as *Unbridling the tongues of women* suggests, a chosen intimate friend of Miss Spence. But she was a cousin of the young Wrens, born in 1852, only about ten years older than they were, and since Catherine Spence felt responsible for her presence in South Australia, she made a place for her in the succession of households that she formed. She called her 'Cousin' when referring to her in letters to the Wrens, 'coz' in her diary. Miss Gregory would go out sewing in other people's households to earn something towards her living, but it was never an independent living; Miss Spence regarded her as one of her own financial responsibilities. Miss Gregory, in turn, provided domestic support for Miss Spence in those households. Catherine Spence noted that she was 'the prop and mainstay of my old age'.

Lucy Morice probably wanted to be the person who completed her aunt's unfinished *Autobiography*. Eleanor Wren wrote asking her if she would undertake that task, but she did not reply immediately: 'I was too ill to think the day I got her letter', she told Rose Scott. She did write accepting the proposal, she said, but before she posted her letter, she received another from Eleanor Wren saying that she had decided that the best person for the job was Jeanne F. Young, Miss Spence's lieutenant in her campaigns for proportional representation. Between them Eleanor Wren, Jeanne Young and the editor of the South Australian *Register*, William Sowden, decided that Mrs Young should complete Miss Spence's narrative, writing in the first person, 'to avoid a break in the story'. Eleanor Wren handed over to Jeanne Young the diaries that Catherine Spence had kept every year of her life, and a 'mass of

Unbridling the tongues of women

Eleanor Wren.
Image produced with kind permission of Mrs Marjorie Caw, 1970.

notes' which Catherine Spence had made as preparation for her own writing, and Jeanne Young valiantly set about the final eight chapters. All of the chapters were published in the *Register*, week by week, beginning in the week that she died. The completed book was published in December 1910. The Libraries Board of South Australia published a facsimile edition in 1975, to mark International Women's Year. Excerpts from it were published in 1987 in Helen Thomson's edited collection of some of Catherine Spence's writings. It was published again, in full, in *Ever Yours, CH Spence* in 2005 with helpful and informative annotations by Barbara Wall.

Readers of the whole *Autobiography* will have no difficulty in distinguishing the hand of Catherine Spence from that of Jeanne Young. Years after its first appearance, novelist Miles Franklin was to write rudely of 'that Young person': 'She doesn't know how to make paragraphs even'. Later still, historian Helen Jones remarked:

> The sections on proportional representation, which dominate this part of the book, are strong and studded with anecdotes. The remainder varies: some parts are thin, lacking background ... [She] ignores other causes, episodes and people of importance.

Any comparison between Jeanne Young's chapters and the richly-textured record that Catherine Spence kept of her work and travels in 1894 could suggest that Jeanne Young, too, may have found Catherine Spence's atrocious handwriting difficult to read – even if she had recognised any of the names of the politically progressive people amongst whom Miss Spence won such affection and admiration.

That record of 1894 is a diary, the only one of Catherine Spence's diaries ever to have been recovered. It seems that Jeanne Young discarded all the others after she had completed her book, *Catherine Helen Spence: a study and an appreciation*, in 1937. It is possible that this diary escaped the same fate because it was especially detailed, and that is probably because it concerns her travels. It begins when Miss Spence is in the east of the United States, following her attendance at the Great World Fair and Congresses held in Chicago from August to November 1893, and it records her activities there, then in Scotland, England, Europe including Italy, and finally back in Adelaide, just in time for the passage of the legislation giving South Australian women the vote in elections to the colonial parliament, and also, the right to sit in the parliament. She uses it as notes from which to compose the articles that she sends back to Australia for publication in the press, a means of earning her living even while she was away from home. She also tries to earn her way while she is in the United States with her lectures, and with her writing: almost every day when she is not actually giving an address, she is writing articles and addresses, as well as letters home, and to her new acquaintances.

The names of these people, and her descriptions of them expands very considerably the reference in the *Autobiography* to Charlotte Perkins Gilman, leading theorist of late nineteenth-century feminism, who organised a women's meeting for Miss Spence in San Francisco when she first reached the United States in May 1893. In the east she meets women suffragists: she goes to visit Hull House, the settlement that Jane Addams and Ellen Starr founded in Chicago in 1889, combining welfare work and teaching by resident female college graduates among the poor and labouring classes who attend meals and classes; Susan B. Anthony invites her to stay in Rochester, New York; in New York she listens to suffrage leader Carrie Chapman Catt addressing a meeting about the achievement of female suffrage in Colorado in November 1893; she attends the Women's Suffrage Congress in Washington DC in February 1894, where Susan Anthony introduces her to the assembled conference. She meets others, too, politically and socially progressive people: descendants of the abolitionists, members of dissenting religions – particularly Unitarians – publishers, journalists, advocates of Henry George's Single Tax, and intellectuals: people willing to hear her speak about proportional representation; people who respond warmly when she gives them copies of the novel, *An Australian Girl* to read, thereby introducing them to her friend, another distinguished Australian author, Catherine Martin; people with whom she can enjoy a game of cards; people who tactfully offer help with sewing, so that Miss Spence's frayed skirts are mended.

In this diary we meet a more vulnerable and less entirely competent woman than her account in the *Autobiography* creates. In the diary we read her telling herself 'It seems as if I was always to have a tremendous scrimmage when I go anywhere'; having trouble with her packing, 'It is terrible work getting so much into these two receptacles'. In Scotland, she accidentally leaves her black box behind. In Italy in October, where she is to meet Catherine Martin and her husband Fred in Siena, she falls asleep on the train to Milan and her purse is stolen. This is a double disaster because it contains the ticket for her black box, which she has had to check into the luggage van. She was sixty-nine when she undertook this journey: it must have required considerable courage, as well as stamina to overcome all of these accidents. Listen to how she writes to her brother about arriving in New York.

> I landed in N.York in the dark – I went to the baggage room to recheck my big trunk – I was directed to a street car which took me straight to Long Island Station. I sat there ... for an hour and a half and I reached Rockville Centre at 11 o'clock and the station was closed – there I was with my Gladstone and my tin hatbox both heavy with a handbag, an umbrella and a parasol – Nobody who came out of the train knew anything about Mrs Sanger [with whom she was to stay] and I felt a somewhat forlorn if not despairing little woman – But out of the darkness came a young man ... He said he knew Mrs Sanger and he was going that way ... Mrs Sanger had been three times to the depot to meet me and had gone to bed. But she knew who it was when the knock came and hastened down to meet me and her welcome was as warm as you could imagine – Now do not you think that – idiot that I am ab[ou]t localities – I managed the trials through arrivals in such cities as ... New York wondrous well.

There are other moments of doubt and anxiety in the diary, too, moments not to have been guessed at from the *Autobiography*. The culmination of her visit to Britain was to be a great meeting at the River House, Chelsea, on 10 July, at which Catherine Spence was to speak in company with the most notable supporters of proportional representation. Unlike the friends whom she made in the United States, these were English people; they might look askance at her Scottish burr, and besides many of them had titles, even if they were predominantly liberal reformers. They included the philanthropist Nathaniel Rothschild, the first Jewish peer in England; John Lubbock, first Baron Avebury; Leonard, Baron Courtney; John Westlake, Professor of International Law at Cambridge University, and his wife Alice, one of the daughters of Thomas Hare, English inventor of this voting system; and Sir John Hall, formerly Prime Minister of New Zealand, subsequently a leader of the women's suffrage cause in the British Parliament. It was a daunting prospect, and her diary shows her becoming more and more anxious as the date approaches.

'I feel strangely stupid', she notes on 3 July. 'Oh! It is a plunge', she exclaims two days later, arriving in London and being 'bothered about luggage' as she goes to stay with the Westlakes: 'This is a very beautiful house for two very busy people', she notes nervously. Four days pass with the Westlakes being too busy for more than a very little time for Miss Spence: 'I think I get low spirited in this great London', she tells her diary. 'I wrote a lot of letters to hunt up my friends but I feel as if there were few indeed that could be depended on'. Finally, on the day of the great meeting itself, she decides that she spoke 'pretty well' but without the humour that lightened up her addresses in the United States. 'How could one be funny with these people', she expostulates to herself. Fortunately for her, and the busy Westlakes, two Australians living in London at the time – Edward and Mary Petherick – take her to stay with them and look after her properly.

That is a story in itself, because at that time the Pethericks were in a turmoil over Edward's bankruptcy and the possibility that he would have to sell his magnificent collection of Australiana. It is Australia's good fortune that, with Mary's help, they weathered this financial crisis, and brought the collection to Australia where it formed part of the basis of the National Library. That story is to be found today in *Ever Yours, C.H. Spence*.

Second: the body of scholarship prompting some revision of this biography. It is to be garnered from a variety of fields: economics, education, literary studies, political studies. One of the most recent publications to have included an entry on Catherine Spence is *A Biographical Dictionary of Australian and New Zealand Economists*, edited by JE King and published in 2007. There it was possible to suggest that, although she had had no formal education in the field, she had, she said herself, a 'turn for economics', and may well have taught much to her brother, John, who rose to prominence as manager of the new branch of the English, Scottish and Australian Bank opened in Adelaide in 1863. This item points to her journalism, dealing with land legislation, wages, industrialisation and taxation, and later, with Henry George and his proposal for combating poverty by drawing all taxation from the land and the land alone – a Single Tax.

It also draws attention to the text about the laws and institutions of the colony that she was invited to write for school students, *Laws We Live Under*, published in 1880. This, the first economics text for Australian secondary schools, included general principles of political economy, an explanation of wealth and a clear, if careful, endorsement of free trade rather than protective duties. Set this work amidst the research that historian Alan Atkinson is carrying out on the pedagogical reforms introduced into Australian schools between about 1870 and 1890, in particular his analysis of the – innovative – inductive – method of teaching geography in South Australian schools, and it resonates with precisely the same principles, adapted to a different subject area. As Catherine Spence was to write:

> It was to be simple enough for intelligent children in the fourth class; 11 or 12 – it was to lead from the known to the unknown – it might include the elements of political economy and sociology – it might make use of familiar illustrations from the experience of a new country – but it must not be too long.

John Anderson Hartley.
Image courtesy of the State Library of South Australia
SLSA: PRG280/1/4/510.

Such a context for her book could suggest the desirability for further research on Spence's friendship with John Anderson Hartley who, as head of the South Australian Education Department, commissioned it, among the host of other reforms that he introduced to Australian schools. For, Atkinson argues,

In many ways, South Australians were always more willing than neighbouring colonists to see themselves as part of a community of provinces. They were more ready, for instance, than either Victorians or New South Welshmen to make formal and detailed comparisons between their school systems and those of their neighbours.

Accordingly, they, and Catherine Spence with them, were ready to imagine that community of provinces as a nation, earlier than the colonial educators of Victoria or New South Wales. Those older colonies only began to lay the foundations for a nationalism that extended to the continent, a nationalism that would make federation possible, in the late 1880s. Would it be possible to make a case for South Australia taking a lead in assent to federation because the population had already learned to imagine a continental community as a nation, not only from their teachers of geography but also from the carefully inductive economics they had imbibed from Miss Spence?

It would not be difficult. Another relatively recent publication containing an item on Catherine Spence is *The Centenary Companion to Australian Federation* edited by Helen Irving, published in 1999. That entry notes that Spence considered federation inevitable as early as 1877. Federation would, she declared, 'give to Australian politics that dignity and consistency which have been so woefully lacking in the past'. She was arguing for a broader consideration of ways of strengthening bonds between Britain and her colonies, ways which included the possibility of the colonies gaining representation in a reformed House of Lords. She invoked the 'bonds of race and language, the common traditions which we have inherited … and the best interests of both colonies and mother country'. Of course, her principal concern was to introduce elections using proportional representation. To that end she urged, 'Let all Australians, then, endeavour to lay aside every petty jealousy, and heartily combine in one great aim for the federation of the Dominion of Australia'.

In such a context, her willingness to nominate for election to the Adelaide Federal Convention in 1897 – the path-breaking move which made her Australia's first female political candidate – resonates with an allegiance to empire quite as much as it invokes her determination that only proportional representation would provide what English political theorist, Anne Phillips, has termed 'mirror' representation, that is representation of all the different groups in a population. Catherine Spence's commitment to 'effective voting' was, at its core, a commitment to what would increasingly be seen as a morality as distinct from politics, and a quite wonderfully optimistic morality. If equality 'is actual representation of the citizens' in a 'pure democracy', she argued, then 'truth and virtue, being stronger than error and vice, and wisdom being greater than folly, when a fair field is offered – the higher qualities subdue the lower and make themselves felt in every department of the State'.

That context – her allegiance to the British empire, the project of colonisation, establishing centres of progressive and intelligent civilisation around the world – shows Catherine Spence as unable to imagine the change in attitudes to separating children from their parents that has taken place between her years with Caroline Emily Clark and the Boarding-Out Society and those years, more than a century later, in which today's readers of this book, like me, watch with relief as Prime Minister Kevin Rudd apologises to the 'stolen generation' of Aboriginal children forcibly removed from their families. The chapter 'Edging out of the domestic sphere' in *Unbridling the tongues of women* offers a somewhat strident defence of this aspect of Spence's work against historian Kay Daniels' critique of its capacity for class oppression. But it fails altogether to question Spence's assumption – common enough at the time – that any children would benefit by being compulsorily separated from their kin.

Similarly such a context shows Catherine Spence as unable, for most of her life, to imagine the conceptual changes that have emerged in the late twentieth and early twenty-first centuries' consideration of 'whiteness' and 'Englishness' as susceptible to question (though her determination to emphasise the virtues of Scots as colonists functions well in dis-aggregating 'the British'). Both challenges reverse the traditional direction of attention and concern, rendering problematic the conventionally taken-for-granted. 'Whiteness', then, rather than, say, 'Aboriginality' becomes a focus of attention, and that not only brings race relations to the centre of analyses of the history of colonisation in Australia, but also renders the white colonisers and their activities a subject requiring explanation. Similarly, a shift from national to trans-national historical analyses, an approach which, in the words of one of its principal exponents, American feminist historian Antoinette Burton, 'conceives of nations as permeable boundaries, subject to a series of migrations, diasporic contests and re-configurations, not just after colonialism but throughout its history', can de-centre Britain as the heart of empire and make 'Englishness' as much a subject of investigation as might be identity in colonial societies. Catherine Spence's first novel, *Clara Morison*, depicts Aboriginal people in South Australia as lazy, dishonest, backward and primitive, as I pointed out in an article published in 1995. Historian Janette Hancock elaborates this perception in an article published in 2003, including *The Laws We Live Under* in her analysis, and observing that confronting such challenges is 'a necessary step towards any reconciled history', a move essential to twenty-first century race relations in Australia. Yet, even Jeanne Young was compelled, from her reading of Catherine Spence's handwritten notes, to add to the 'American' chapter of the *Autobiography* a confession of a new perception borne in upon Miss Spence while staying in the Boston household of William Lloyd Garrison, son of the famous Abolitionist. In this house, she wrote:

> I began to be a little ashamed of being so narrow in my views of the coloured question. Mr Garrison, animated with the spirit of the true brotherhood of man, was an advocate of the heathen Chinee, and was continually speaking of the goodness of the negro and coloured and yellow races, and of the injustice and rapacity of the white Caucasians.

Those committed to reconciliation will not approve of her terminology. But the sentiment represents a major shift in assumption and attitude by this extraordinarily intelligent sixty-nine year-old.

Introduction to the new edition

An ability to be persuaded to such a change of mind, coupled with the range of Catherine Spence's reading and thinking, establishes her firmly in the forefront of intellectual life in Australia. So, too, do the series of articles that she wrote for the South Australian *Register* in 1878, the articles which so pleased her editor that he published them as a pamphlet titled *Some Social Aspects of South Australian Life*. Melbourne intellectual, Henry Gyles Turner, praised it as an 'excellent contribution to the social history of colonial life'. They are certainly that. But they are also much more. They present comparisons with Britain, France and the United States, and other Australian colonies; allusions to Dickens, Thackeray, Browning, Thomas Hood, George Eliot and GH Lewes, Ouida and Balzac. She refers to the *Spectator*, the *Quarterly Review*, the *Cornhill Magazine*, the *Nineteenth Century*, and the *Art Journal*. She writes about the biography of Lord Macauley. She quotes political economists WR Greg and Harriet Martineau and political philosopher John Stuart Mill, to say nothing of two early stalwarts of the English campaigns for rights for women: Millicent Fawcett and Elizabeth Garrett Anderson. Her Australian references include the *Age* and the *Argus*, Henry Hayter, the statistician who would be appointed government statist in Victoria in 1881, and, from the pages of the *Melbourne Review*, the doctor who would become the leading gynaecologist in Melbourne in the 1890s, the evocatively-named Walter Balls-Headley. She was a 'public intellectual' a century before the term was coined.

A public intellectual, and one who deserves a place on an international stage, literary critics have now decided. The 1970s and 1980s saw a revival of Catherine Spence's fiction: all but two of her novels were either published for the first time or reprinted, and new critical assessments described her as an Australian founder of traditions of realist fiction, or 'feminine … writing', or inaugurating 'the line of middle-class novels of society developed later by Rose Praed, "Tasma", Henry Handel Richardson …'. Writing after *Unbridling the tongues of women* had appeared, literary historian, Elizabeth Perkins, determined that Spence's first novel, *Clara Morison*, was 'the first colonial work that may fairly be compared with that of George Eliot or Elizabeth Gaskell', and literary critic Fiona Giles expanded that range of comparisons to locate Catherine Spence's work in the development of realist fiction in Europe.

Spence has a place in another international tradition, too, this one of feminist writing. *Unbridling the tongues of women* notes that Spence's novel, *Handfasted*, and her short story *A Week in the Future*, were both important innovations in their time. Indeed, *Handfasted* was so far ahead of its time that it was not to achieve publication until 1984, almost a century after it was written, in an edition edited by literary critic, Helen Thomson. Another literary scholar, Nan Bowman Albinski, added a further feminist detail to the story of Catherine Spence's life in an article about *Handfasted* when she pointed out that north American writer, Annie Denton Cridge, published a 'striking feminist role reversal satire' in 1870 in which women 'consolidate' their monopoly of public life with their oratorical abilities and eloquence; one of the heroines of *Handfasted* is a notable speaker in a predominantly oral culture. Whether Catherine Spence had read Cridge's work or not, she was to correspond with this feminist author's son, Alfred Cridge, 'felt at home' with him immediately when she met him in San Francisco, and spent time in his company, both in the west and in Chicago, during her trip to the United States in 1893-4.

Unlike *Handfasted*, *A Week in the Future* did gain publication during Spence's lifetime; it appeared as a serial in the *Centennial Magazine* in 1889, but it was not produced as a book until 1987. Its inspiration was a work called *Scientific Meliorism and the Evolution of Happiness* by Scotswoman Jane Hume Clapperton, published in 1885. Catherine Spence reviewed it for both the *Adelaide Observer* and the South Australian *Register* in 1887 and, as historian, Lesley Llungdahl has demonstrated, in her own work borrowed so extensively and freely from Clapperton's that some passages are direct transcriptions. This apparently caused no difficulty between the two Scottish-born authors: neither claimed originality for their ideas and Miss Spence was to spend a happy few days staying with Miss Clapperton – a member of the intellectually exclusive and socially radical Men and Women's Club and of the Malthusian League in England – when she was in England in 1894.

The delay in these works achieving both publication and recognition is surprising in the light of their intellectual scope, and of the interest that has grown during the later decades of the twentieth century in specifically feminist utopian fiction or feminist future-vision novels. The works of such writers as Marge Piercy, Ursula Le Guin and Joanna Russ in the United States in the 1970s-1990s are usually seen as later manifestations in a tradition that began with Charlotte Perkins Gilman's *Herland*, first published in 1915. Spence's plot has none of the narrative drive of Gilman's, but the utopian society that she depicted is far more realistic, and was published a quarter of a century earlier. Now, finally, she can take her place at the beginning of that international tradition of feminist future-vision fiction, another manifestation of herself as a 'New Woman'.

Introduction to the new edition

This New Woman was, of course, a feminist. Some have contested such a view, pointing to a passage in the *Autobiography* in which Jeanne Young, ventriloquising Catherine Spence, commented on the women's suffrage movement in South Australia, arguing for the greater importance of elections using proportional representation:

> Though sympathetic to the cause, I had always been regarded as a weak-kneed sister by the real workers. I had failed to see the advantage of having a vote that might leave me after an election a disenfranchised voter, instead of an un-enfranchised woman.

There were several differences between the views and commitments of Miss Spence and Mrs Young as we made clear in *Ever Yours*. I would maintain that this is one of them. For as well as supporting the campaign for votes for women and trying to establish a local branch of the National Council of Women, to say nothing of the protests against unjust constraints on opportunities for women which her novels dramatise, Catherine Spence was capable of a delightfully – and revolutionary – feminist joke. Barbara Wall found it in a story for children, one of many that Catherine Spence wrote, this one published in the *Adelaide Observer* on Christmas day, 1886. It is called 'The Hen's Language'. In it, one Dr. Polyglot decides to learn the languages of the poultry yard. Once he has done that, he approaches his cocks and hens and, to encourage conversation, asks them all to say what they would like. The cocks 'who are always bold forward birds' respond first, each individually:

> A handsome yard to me then give,
>   As large as this or bigger,
> With fifteen handsome hens to live
>   And cut a splendid figure…

The hens strike in, indicating that the males do not 'perfectly' represent the rights and aspirations of the female. On the contrary. It is, of course, good 'to have much food' for themselves and their chickens.

> But cocks must fight
> To keep all right
> So do not pen
> Us up in flocks;
> Why not one hen
> To fifteen cocks?

Of course, Catherine Spence, like everyone else, knew that 'one cock suffices to keep fifteen hens in fertile eggs and chickens', observes Barbara Wall; this story is not about the mechanics and economics of the fowl-yard. Rather, what the cock is talking about is 'pleasure and power'. 'And if the mainspring of life is pleasure and power, then why not, as the hen sings, one hen to fifteen cocks? It is a joke of course, but a remarkable joke for a woman to publish in a newspaper in 1886', writes Wall.

That was the year in which Edward Stirling – one of Miss Spence's pupils in his youth – introduced into the South Australian House of Assembly his Bill in favour of enfranchising women. The Woman Suffrage League had formed and begun its campaign within the following two years. When, towards the end of 1894, a new Bill to give women the vote was before the South Australian parliament, Catherine Spence's ship finally arrived home in Adelaide. Rose Birks, Treasurer of the Woman Suffrage League, hastened to Glenelg to find her and urge her to speak to various members of the parliament, proposing that there be a party at which Miss Spence should speak 'to show that we are in concert about the reform'. The author of that cheeky challenge to the patriarchal assumptions of the fowl-yard, promised all her help: 'Mrs Birks thinks I have come back in the nick of time', she told her diary.

There were, of course, efforts to commemorate 'The Grand Old Woman of Australasia' soon after she died in April 1910. The *Autobiography* was supplemented by a portrait painted posthumously by no less a talent than the artist later known as Margaret Preston; it hangs in the Art Gallery of South Australia. A scholarship to support women's sociological research was founded and, after a time during which its funds had shrunk too far for it to be awarded, it is once again healthy and supporting women's research. But more recent years have seen Miss Spence far more thoroughly recognised. A statue was commissioned for the sesqui-centenary celebrations of the foundation of the colony of South Australia in 1986; sculpted by Ieva Pocius, it stands in Light Square. A wing of the State Library of South Australia has been named after her. A street in Adelaide is named after her, and there is a plaque in front of the library on Norwood Parade in the local council district where she last lived. In 2001, her picture appeared on Australian five-dollar notes to mark the centenary of federation, a national celebration.

Now, a century after her death, Catherine Spence also appears far less alone than she did when I first began researching her life. There were other women who would become powerful speakers later in the same period: Mary Lee and Elizabeth Webb Nicholls in South Australia; Louisa Lawson and Rose Scott in New South Wales; Vida Goldstein not only in Victoria but also in both Britain and the United States. And those examples could be multiplied. She was one of a considerable number, speaking out of turn, breaking the rules – unbridling the tongues of women.

She was also a very considerable intellect, an international talent, and – more than has gained acknowledgement before – she had great charm. 'Yesterday', wrote Audrey Tennyson in 1901, we had 'the famous old Miss Catherine Spence' to visit. Lady Tennyson, wife of Hallam – the second Baron Tennyson who was, at the time Governor of South Australia – and daughter-in-law of England's famed poet Alfred Tennyson, found her guest enchanting.

> She is a most clever bright kindly sympathetic old lady, well read, full of fun, very tiny, with a look of the dear Queen & much her height, aged 75, but brisk & energetic as ever. … She & Hallam made great friends. She rushed at him when he came into the room, clasped his hand in both of hers & said, 'To think that I should ever clasp the hand of your Father's son – I am right glad to do it'.

Susan Magarey
Kent Town
October 2009.

References*

Nan Bowman Albinski, '*Handfasted*: An Australian Feminist's American Utopia', *Journal of Popular Culture*, vol.23, no,2, Fall, 1989.

Margaret Allen, 'Biographical Background' in *Catherine Martin, An Australian Girl*, ed. Rosemary Campbell (University of Queensland Press), St Lucia, 2002.

Alan Atkinson, 'Speech, Children and the Federation Movement' in Joy Damousi and Desley Deacon (eds), *Talking and Listening in the Age of Modernity* (ANU E-Press) Canberra, 2007.

Antoinette Burton, *At the Heart of the Empire: Indians and the Colonial Encounter in late-Victorian Britain* (University of California Press), Berkeley, 1998.

Carol Fort, 'John Anderson Hartley (1844-1896)', in Wilfrid Prest (ed.) with Kerrie Round and Carol Fort, *The Wakefield Companion to South Australian History* (Wakefield Press), Kent Town, 2001.

Fiona Giles, 'Finding a Shiftingness: Situating the Nineteenth-Century Anglo-Australian Female Subject', *New Literatures Review*, 18, 1989.

Janette Hancock, '"Me, Myself and Others": A New Look at Catherine Helen Spence', *Lilith: a feminist history journal*, no.12, 2003.

Alexandra Hasluck (ed.), *Days: The Australian letters of Audrey Lady Tennyson to her mother Zacyntha Boyle, 1899-1903* (National Library of Australia), Canberra, 1978.

Helen Jones, 'A Postscript to the Life of Catherine Helen Spence', *Journal of the Historical Society of South Australia*, 15, 1987.

Helen Jones, 'A Further Postscript to the Life of Catherine Helen Spence', *Journal of the Historical Society of South Australia*, 16, 1988.

Nick Jose (ed.), *Macquarie PEN Anthology of Australian Literature* (Allen & Unwin), Sydney, 2009.

Judy King and Graham Tulloch (eds), *Catherine Helen Spence: Tenacious of the Past: The Recollections of Helen Brodie*, (Centre for Research in the New Literatures in English & Libraries Board of South Australia), Adelaide, 1994.

Marilyn Lake, 'Sounds of History: Oratory and the fantasy of male power' in Joy Damousi and Desley Deacon (eds), *Talking and Listening in the Age of Modernity* (ANU E-Press), Canberra, 2007.

Lesley Durrell Ljungdahl (ed.), *Catherine Helen Spence: A Week in the Future* (Hale & Iremonger), Marrickville, 1987.

Susan Magarey (ed.) with Barbara Wall, Mary Lyons and Maryan Beams, *Ever Yours, C.H. Spence: Catherine Helen Spence's An Autobiography (1825-1910), Diary (1894) and Some Correspondence (1894-1910)*, (Wakefield Press), Adelaide, 2005.

Susan Magarey, *Passions of the first wave feminists* (UNSW Press), Kensington, 2001.

Susan Magarey, 'Catherine Helen Spence's Journalism: Some Social Aspects of South Australian Life, By A Colonist of 1839 – C.H. Spence' in Margaret Anderson, Kate Walsh and Bernard Whimpress (eds), *Adelaide Snapshots 1850-1875* (Wakefield Press), Kent Town, 2010, forthcoming.

Susan Magarey, 'The Private Life of Catherine Helen Spence, 1825-1910' in Graeme Davison, Pat Jalland and Wilfrid Prest (eds), *Body and Mind: Historical Essays in Honour of F.B. Smith* (Melbourne University Press), 2009.

Susan Magarey, 'Catherine Helen Spence (1825-1910' in J.E. King (ed.), *A Biographical Dictionary of Australian and New Zealand Economists* (Edward Elgar), Cheltenham/Northampton, 2007.

Introduction to the new edition

Susan Magarey, 'Secrets and Revelations: A Newly Discovered Diary', *Bibliofile*, vol.11, no.2, August 2004.

Susan Magarey, 'Spence, Catherine Helen (1825-1910)' in Helen Irving (ed.), *The Centenary Companion to Australian Federation* (Cambridge University Press) Oakleigh, 1999.

Susan Magarey, 'Catherine Helen Spence And The Federal Convention', *The New Federalist: The Journal of Australian Federation History*, no.1, June 1998.

Susan Magarey, 'Catherine Helen Spence – Novelist' in Philip Butterss (ed.), *Southwords: Essays on South Australian Writing* (Wakefield Press), Kent Town, 1995.

Susan Magarey, 'Why Didn't They Want to be Members of Parliament? Suffragists in South Australia', in Caroline Daley and Melanie Nolan (eds), *Suffrage and Beyond: International Feminist Perspectives* (Auckland University Press/Pluto Press Australia), Auckland/Annandale, 1994.

Susan Magarey, 'Catherine Helen Spence', *Constitutional Centenary: The Newsletter of the Constitutional Centenary Foundation Inc.*, vol.2, no.2, May 1993.

Susan Magarey, 'Sex vs Citizenship: Votes for Women in South Australia', *Journal of the Historical Society of South Australia*, no.21, 1993.

Susan Magarey, 'Feminist Visions across the Pacific: Catherine Helen Spence's Handfasted', *Antipodes: A North American Journal of Australian Literature*, vol.3, no.1, Spring 1989.

Patrick Morgan, 'Realism and Documentary: Lowering One's Sights' in Laurie Hergenhan, Bruce Bennett, Martin Duwell, Brian Matthews, Peter Pierce and Elizabeth Webby (eds), *The Penguin New Literary History of Australia* (Penguin), Ringwood, 1988.

Elizabeth Perkins, 'Colonial Transformations: Writing and the Dilemma of Colonisation' in Laurie Hergenhan, Bruce Bennett, Martin Duwell, Brian Matthews, Peter Pierce and Elizabeth Webby (eds), *The Penguin New Literary History of Australia* (Penguin), Ringwood, 1988.

C.H. Spence, 'Two theories for the working of bi-cameral legislatures', *Melbourne Review*, no.4, 1879.

C.H. Spence, *Federal Convention elections and effective voting*, leaflet, reprinted from the *Weekly Herald* [1897], National Library of Australia, Australian Politics pamphlets.

'S': 'A Colonist', 'Australian Federation and Imperial Union', *Fraser's Magazine*, October 1877.

Catherine Helen Spence, *Handfasted*, edited, with a preface and afterword by Helen Thomson (Penguin Books, with the assistance of the Literature Board of the Australia Council), Ringwood, 1984.

Helen Thomson (ed.), *Catherine Helen Spence* (University of Queensland Press), St Lucia, 1987.

Helen Thomson, 'Love and Labour: Marriage and Work in the Novels of Catherine Helen Spence' in Debra Adelaide (ed.), *A Bright and Fiery Troop: Australian Women Writers in the Nineteenth Century* (Penguin) Ringwood, 1988.

Barbara Wall, 'The Hen's Language', typescript, in the author's possession.

Barbara Wall, 'Catherine Helen Spence: a bibliography': State Library of South Australia home page/ South Australiana/Subject Websites/Catherine Helen Spence/Barbara Wall.

* For help, over many years, and especially with this introduction, I would like to thank Margaret Allen and Barbara Wall. I am deeply grateful to my old friend Hugo Shaw for the picture that adorns the cover. As always, I am indebted to Susan Sheridan for quality control. Readers will discern in the pages of this book an ongoing debate with historian Kay Daniels. I am grateful to Kay for much more than the discussion here – including years of friendship, and I am very sad that her untimely death deprived us all of her brilliant intellect, her wit, her scholarship – and her fabulous cooking.

Catherine Magarey
16 September 1948 - 2 May 1972

Contents

Abbreviations *2*

Acknowledgments *3*

Introduction *5*

1 Acquiring a room of her own *23*

2 The line of least resistance *43*

3 Faith and enlightenment *63*

4 Edging out of the domestic sphere *77*

5 Learning for the future *93*

6 Round woman in her round hole *105*

7 Prophet of the effective vote *121*

8 The New Woman of South Australia: Grand Old Woman of Australia *141*

Endnotes *165*

Bibliography *191*

Index *207*

Abbreviations

ANL	Australian National Library in the text of chapter seven, it also means Australian National League
AUC	Adelaide Unitarian Congregation
FPPU	Farmers' and Producers' Political Union
LBSA	Libraries Board of South Australia
LDU	Liberal and Democratic Union
ML	Mitchell Library
Register	South Australian *Register*
SA	South Australia
SAA	South Australian Archives
[SA]	local legislation in South Australia
UCC	Unitarian Christian Church
UCCC	Unitarian Christian Church Committee
ULP	United Labor Party
UTLC	United Trades and Labour Council

Acknowledgments

So many people have helped me with this book that it should probably be regarded as a collective enterprise. Even so, there are particular debts that I should like to acknowledge.

Many South Australians offered me time and information when I was first carrying out research on Catherine Spence. I would like to thank especially Mrs A. A. Abbie, Mrs R. N. Beckwith, Mrs C. Barham Black, Miss M. E. Crompton, Miss Phyllis Crompton, Mrs Nancy Jones, the Reverend Allen Kirby, Mr Patric Morice, Mrs Rose Moore, Mr Moxom Simpson and Miss E. G. Walker. To Mrs Marjorie Caw I owe more than I can adequately acknowledge here.

I am grateful, too, to the staff of the South Australian Archives and Newspaper Reading Room, and to the staff of the Petherick room in the Australian National Library, particularly to Mrs Pauline Fanning. I first began reading about Spence at the suggestion of Manning Clark, and under the guidance of Douglas Pike and Barry Smith. I wish to thank them, and Kathleen Woodroofe, for comments on my work which encouraged me to take it further. That, however, was some time ago. Two friends – Eric Fry and John Merritt – gave me the support and challenge that I needed to take up again the questions that Catherine Spence's story raised for me.

Many of those questions arose from discussions current in the Women's Liberation Movement in Canberra throughout the 1970s. I learned more from them, I believe, than I have so far learned from any other experience. I would like to thank everyone who was involved in the Women's Studies Program at the Australian National University from 1978 to 1983 for all they taught me. My feminist friends have lived with my work on Catherine Spence for as long as we have known each other, offering constructive comment and asking difficult questions. I owe Kay Daniels a particular debt, and for more than the continuing debate that will be found in these pages. I am especially grateful to Ann Curthoys and to Margaret Power for presenting me with issues which I may never be able to solve. Most of all, I want to record here my gratitude to Daphne Gollan and to Julia Ryan for their part in forming my ideas about a great many more subjects than the life of Catherine Spence, and to Susan Sheridan for, among many other things, teaching me all over again how to read.

For support, encouragement, and scepticism enough to prove a real goad, I will always be thankful to Myra Troy.

This book would never have appeared without the hard work of Leeanne Greenwood, Maribelle de Vera, Christine Wise and Jenni Knobel; the financial assistance of the Faculty of Arts at the Australian National University; the helpful suggestions of Anna Davin and Marjorie Scales; and the monumental patience of Sylvia Hale. I am grateful to them all.

Introduction

In November 1839 a passenger ship, *Palmyra*, sailed slowly up a creek until it reached a jumble of temporary buildings that constituted a port. Surrounded by dismaying mangrove swamps, the passengers disembarked and organised themselves and their possessions into port carts. Their drive, along a dusty road through sparse, sunburnt grass, in a wind blowing directly from the north as though from a furnace, eventually jolted them across a meagre river into a settlement of broad, straight streets, lined with tents, interspersed with houses of brick, wood, earth or stone. This was Adelaide – the centre of a three-year-old British colony established on the coastal plain of Gulf St Vincent in South Australia. Among the passengers scrambling out of the port carts was a red-headed young woman, undoubtedly sunburnt, and appalled by her surroundings. 'When we sat down on a log in Light square, waiting till my father brought the key of the wooden house in Gilles street, in spite of the dignity of my 14 years just attained, I had a good cry'.[1] This was Catherine Helen Spence.

Nearly three-quarters of a century later, in October 1905, in a church schoolroom in Adelaide, a public gathering celebrated Catherine Spence's 80th birthday. At that party, South Australia's chief justice proclaimed her:

> the most distinguished woman they had had in Australia … There was no one in the whole Commonwealth, whose career covered so wide a

ground. She was a novelist, a critic, an accomplished journalist, a preacher, a lecturer, a philanthropist, and a social and moral reformer.

Spence responded:

> I am a new woman, and I know it. I mean an awakened woman ... awakened to a sense of capacity and responsibility, not merely to the family and the household, but to the State; to be wise, not for her own selfish interests, but that the world may be glad that she had been born.[2]

At that time, the 'new woman' was scarcely ten years old in Britain and hardly known in Australia. Yet there, in that outpost of Britain's empire, a short, stout 80-year-old with silver-grey hair claimed that her beliefs and her achievements placed her in the forefront of the 'woman movement' that was sweeping the western world.

By 1905, white South Australia was only a little younger than Catherine Spence. Adelaide had grown from the incongruous combination that she had first encountered, of planned streets and haphazard house-building, into a 'Garden City'.[3] It had long ceased to be a walking town: its paved roads, lit by gas which was about to yield place to electricity, led out of the central square, past the parklands to the suburbs into which the people had spilled as their numbers grew. The population had increased from 10,000 or so in 1839 to over 350,000 in 1901.[4] The indiscriminate assemblage of tents, working people's cottages and investors' houses had yielded place to the clear distinction between the small, crowded dwellings of the industrial suburbs to the west, the great and lesser mansions of North and South Adelaide and East Terrace, and the modest respectability of the suburban houses spreading to the north and east of the city. Adelaide had become a thriving centre of commerce, cultural exchange, and government.[5] Midway along one side of its central square, across King William Road from its formal, official link with Britain (Government House) and diagonally across an intersection from the Adelaide Club (the centre of South Australia's local rulers), stood a grey stone, columned parliament house. No longer the rawest colonial experiment of Britain's government and free enterprise ideologues, by 1905 South Australia was a member of the new, independent Commonwealth of Australia. Its governments continued to safeguard the interests of its external investors, but by then they were protecting, as well, those of its own ruling class. Such preservation was neither blatant nor simple. Just as South Australia had, like the other Australian colonies, developed its own Westminsterstyle parliamentary

Introduction

democracy, so it had developed an economy and social order polarising between the interests of capital and labour, with parliamentary parties newly formed to contest those interests. But the slow emergence of welfare states in the 20th century followed from not only the struggles between capital and labour, but also those between a patriarchal ordering of social relations and an active feminist movement. South Australia, in 1905, could hardly be described as a welfare state but it had, for the first time, a Labor premier, and its women had been voting in parliamentary elections for nine years. So South Australia, too, had some claim to being in the vanguard of the 'woman movement'.

Of course, Catherine Spence's feminism was woven from far more strands of thought and activity than those which led to the successful campaign for female suffrage in South Australia. Likewise, that colony's admission of women to formal citizenship depended on a much wider range of factors than Spence's participation in its public life. But the two are, nevertheless, related. One of the purposes of this book is to explore that relationship: to explore not only the forces shaping Spence's life, and not only what she made of the constraints and opportunities that she encountered, but also the relationship between that story and the story of South Australia. Indeed, only by doing so is it possible to consider both in their totality: an account of South Australia's past which did not include women would be an account of changes in only half a society, and Spence considered that one of the most important formative influences in her life was that 'we took hold of the growth of South Australia and identified ourselves with it'.[6] The rhythm of her life – its periodisation – did not, however, directly match any conventional periodisation of South Australia's public events. An exploration of Spence's life will, I hope, suggest one new approach to South Australia's history, indeed, to the history of Australia.

Spence's public achievements have won public recognition during the 70-odd years since her death. The South Australian government of 1911 established the Catherine Helen Spence scholarship in sociology; the first Spence scholar, E. Dorothea Proud, went to the London School of Economics to undertake a thesis on employers' experiments for improving working conditions in factories.[7] A recent South Australian government named an electoral district after Spence.[8] A section of a school in Adelaide also bears her name. Elizabeth Gunton compiled a bibliography of Spence's works for the South Australian Libraries Board to publish,[9] and the Board also reprinted Spence's autobiography in 1975, the year designated International Women's Year by the United Nations. Far less known outside South Australia by now, Spence nevertheless appears in the pages of Australian histories as different as H. M. Green's *History of Australian Literature* and Geoffrey Blainey's *A Land Half Won*.[10]

Such attention is an acknowledgment of her cultural and political significance in Australia's history. But it is also, often, an acknowledgment of the work of an exceptional woman, and from that she can suffer at the hands of both her admirers and her detractors. Blainey's chapter on Spence is called .'The Veiled Maid of Adelaide'. There is usually implicit in such acknowledgment the patronising attitude expressed by Samuel Johnson when he likened a woman preaching to a dog walking on its hind legs – 'it is not done well; but you are surprised to find it done at all'.[11] Yet it is impossible to ignore the fact that negotiating her way to a public career in the pulpit, in the press and on the platform in a period when 'a woman's ethic' was 'duty and renunciation'[12] constituted Spence's most remarkable achievement. Like Mary Wollstonecraft, Florence Nightingale, Rose Scott, Vida Goldstein – to pick fairly random examples – she presents us with not one subject but two.[13] As a novelist, journalist and electoral reformer she deserves no manner of condescension because she was a woman. But her years of anonymity as a journalist and the nature of her earliest overt engagement in public life show how constantly she was reminded, as we are, of her gender, and of the patriarchal ordering of gender relations that should circumscribe what she could think, say and do. 'No-one', she announced in 1893 as she departed, unaccompanied, for the United States, 'has gone out of "woman's sphere" more than I have during the last twelve years … and yet I believe I am as womanly as ever'.[14]

Early developments in capitalism in Britain had begun defining social existence into the 'separate spheres' of public life and domestic life long before Catherine Spence was born. During the period in which British colonists were establishing a foothold in South Australia, that definitional distinction was becoming synonymous with a distinction between the world of men and the world of women. One of the principal signs of a man's prosperity, among middle-class Britons, was his ability to support a wife and children who did not, themselves, need to venture into the public sphere to contribute to the household's income. Campaigns to exclude working women (and children) from particular kinds of paid work – in coal-mines and textile factories – were establishing gender divisions in the paid labour market, and contracting the range of occupations in which working women could earn wages. One of the avenues to a wage for women that expanded, rather than contracted, was domestic service. That, and the increasing idealisation of the middle-class domestic sphere as a haven in a heartless world for men, reinforced the distinction between public and domestic *as* a distinction between the masculine and feminine. Such developments were in their infancy at the time when the Spences set sail from Britain for South Australia. But as new plants in new soil, they found careful nurture in the colony. The separateness of the worlds of men and women remains part of our inheritance from them today.[15] The public sphere – the factory, the workshop, the market place, the stock exchange, the instrumentalities of the state, the organisation of much leisure and most cultural, intellectual and spiritual pursuits – has been dominated by men, and has been seen as the preserve of men. The domestic sphere – the household, socially-approved sexual relationships, care and rearing of children, service for a male breadwinner, housework – has similarly been dominated by masculine interests, but has been seen as the domain proper to women. Even in the late 20th century, dual labour markets based on a gender division of labour in households demonstrate the persistence of the 'separate spheres' of the feminine and the masculine.[16] Spence's statement indicates the constraints imposed by a patriarchal gender order which could make a woman's activity in the public sphere 'un-womanly', and 'un-womanly' behaviour discreditable. But it also signals the extent to which Spence challenged the social organisation that would confine her to the domestic – the woman's – sphere.

The issues that her story raises speak directly to our own times. Questions about individual fulfilment, personal liberation, social radicalism, are also questions about changes in the social order that will dissolve the distinction between the separate spheres. They reverberate as profoundly in our lives as they did through hers. There has only been one full-length biographical study of Spence published since her autobiography appeared in print in 1910,[17] and that, Jeanne Young's *Catherine Helen Spence: a study and an appreciation*, was published almost half a century ago.[18] The resurgence of feminism that began in the late 1960s makes it time to attempt a fresh acquaintance.

Jeanne Young celebrated Spence 'not as a "Woman Pioneer" of South Australia only, but as … a "Pioneer Woman" of the world, opening new paths for her sisters to tread.'[19] The claim was an appropriate recognition of the achievements listed at her 80th birthday party. One of the achievements not mentioned was the making of the woman capable of doing so much. It is not possible to reach a complete understanding of that process. Unlike Katherine Mansfield or Virginia Woolf, Spence left no journals or letters recording in full her flickers of mood or storms of emotion. Her short autobiography does not, as do Simone de Beauvoir's volumes for instance, detail a post-Freudian explication of stages in her interior growth and shifts in ideas and relationships. Spence's papers and writing constitute a predominantly external record. But it is still possible to make acquaintance with the individual who, in the later years of her life, won affection and esteem not only through her achievements, but also by the impact of her person and personality.

In an age which depicted feminine beauty in terms of the fragile, fair, slender and weak, Spence could not have been considered beautiful. She was short and broad: photographs indicate that she was little more than five feet tall, plump in her 20s, later distinctly stout. Short-waisted, round-shouldered, and short-necked, with a large jaw, heavy features and a prominent wart, she was undoubtedly considered plain when she was young. But later photographs show, and her later friends remembered her face 'as one of grand and rugged strength', dominated by grey eyes which were 'alert, eager and almost searching.'[20] People found her colouring more appealing as she grew older. She had fair skin and hair which offended her when she wore it in carefully-arranged ringlets by being 'red, but not auburn'. As she grew older it turned a beautiful silvery grey.[21] Her lack of conventional beauty occasioned her some distress when she was young. She confided to her diary,

> I do believe my face is an honest one, and, vanity whispers, a pleasant one to look upon. Yet who is pleased to look upon it but my own relations, to whom looks are a matter of indifference. Children like my face, that is one comfort.[22]

But once she had determined that she was to be a spinster, she became as resolutely indifferent to her looks as she was to her dress. Her biographer Jeanne Young recalled, 'It was the accepted belief among most people that "blue stockings" need not worry about dress, and her appearance when she was first pointed out to me as the "great Miss Spence"… tended to confirm this belief. Her niece was accustomed to guarding against this appearance. When seeing Catherine Spence and Jeanne Young off on a train she asked, laughing, 'Please see that Aunt keeps her bonnet on straight.'[23] Spence's dress, like her looks, troubled her when she was young: recalling her first years in South Australia she reflected, 'When a girl is very poor, and feels herself badly dressed, she cannot help feeling shy, especially if she has a good deal of Scotch pride.'[24] She continued to be careless about her clothes, probably as much because her financial resources were always meagre, as because she had other things on her mind. Her dress became more conventional after her visit to the United States in 1893-94, where a friend told her 'a speaker would need to be an Abraham Lincoln in all other respects to render carelessness in dress, on the platform negligible.' She returned, Jeanne Young observed, 'not only a clever and versatile speaker, but a quite attractively dressed woman'.[25]

She had a sweet voice, which was also described as 'rather carrying' and 'pronouncedly Scotch and virile'; she retained her Scots accent all her life.[26] Her speaking manner was engaging, formed by relating fairy stories or reciting poems to her small nephews and nieces with dramatic vocal sound effects.[27] She may have been particularly conscious of her voice. After describing George Eliot's as 'singularly musical and impressive' she remarked 'I am more susceptible to voices than to features or complexion.'[28] On the platform she relied on her voice rather than on the gesticulation that was then an important accompaniment of platform speaking. She recalled, 'I had a lesson on the danger of overaction from hearing a gentleman recite in public "The dream of Eugene Aram" in which he went through all the movements of killing and burying the murdered man.' She preferred the informality she established by speaking naturally in a public forum. 'However little action I may use I never speak in public with gloves on. They interfere with natural eloquence of the hand.'[29] Her insistence upon informality and natural behaviour, as Jeanne Young observed, 'constituted, perhaps, her greatest charm', and she knew it. But her determination to speak ungloved might also have been because she had delicate hands … of which she was rather proud.'[30]

She was skilful with her hands. Another niece recalled that 'she did beautiful work. I have a pelisse and cape which she made for me when I was a baby, with very elaborate open work … called broderie Anglaise, and a point lace collar made when she was 80.' She considered such work important, and for more than the pleasure of doing it: much of the foundation of her education took place listening to her teacher reading aloud to a class of girls learning needlework; in a late novel she depicts education in an arcadian, non-literate, society proceeding through knitting and crocheting, the pieces made becoming the memory triggers in an oral culture.[31] However, the products of such work both in the novel and in her life, were not always works of art. Her niece remembered, too, 'a pair of bright scarlet stockings … made of such prickly wool that they were not worn at all willingly.'[32] Catherine Spence, while being far from inclined towards hair shirts, probably would have endured the stockings – she seems to have been almost indifferent to physical discomfort.

She wore calico underclothes, 'no woollies except a flannel petticoat' even in winter, and her photographs suggest that she usually endured the chronic discomfort of corsets. She took a cold bath every morning, winter and summer. This all argues good circulation and an excellent constitution which probably contributed greatly to her remarkable energy and endurance. Lucy Morice found her aunt's energy amazing:

> On one occasion she was going to lecture at Peterborough … that necessitated catching a train at about 7a.m., and as she was then living in an outlying suburb meant very early rising, and a long tramride in a horse-drawn car. She would get to the township in the afternoon, be met and entertained by some (perhaps) sympathiser … attend the meeting, lecture and conduct a demonstration, and probably get to bed about midnight! Leave the next morning by an early train, and on the occasion I have in mind, go off to speak at Port Adelaide in the evening – a marvellous feat of endurance, but for a woman nearing the eighties it was indeed a wonderful triumph of physical and mental strength and courage.[33]

Her energy came at least partly from her 'usually robust health',[34] but also from the intensity of her concern for her work. When she was 78 she was confined to bed for some months with an unspecified illness which threatened to curtail all her activities. 'But' wrote Lucy Morice, 'after a few months of inactivity she determined that she would not be daunted by physical disabilities, and so she carried on … disregarding the fatigue and distress to which she was liable during the last seven years of her life.'[35] Her intensity and energy sometimes persuaded her friends into ventures against their better judgment. The daughter of one old friend related a story about Miss Spence helping her mother find a washerwoman. After three unsuccessful attempts at employing Miss Spence's candidates, her mother decided that 'a philanthropist, though she had the best will in the world was not the person to go to for help when any work was wanted.'[36] Lucy Morice observed, 'My Mother was inclined to consider that Kate's demands upon my father's purse for her pet schemes or necessitous "cases" were excessive', though she added 'but Auntie Kate never wanted anything for herself although she was never even moderately well off'.[37] Other recollections present her as absent-minded – she left for America without her purse[38] – and prone to awkward situations. She recalled one on her first campaign for proportional representation:

> I had no advance agents to announce my arrival, and at one town in the
> north I found nobody at the station to meet me. I spent the most miser-

Introduction

able two and a half hours of my life waiting Micawber-like for something to turn up; and it turned up in the person of the village blacksmith. I spoke to him and explained my mission to the town. He had heard nothing of any meeting …'Well', I said … 'if you can get together a dozen intelligent men I will explain effective voting to them'. He looked at me with a dumbfounded air, and then burst out, 'Good G–, madam there are not three intelligent men in the town.'[39]

'One of her admirers ... remarked on hearing of some of her misadventures, "Oh, I wish Miss Spence did not do things like that. It does give the Mothers such cause to blaspheme";[40] a comment redolent with the values and attitudes amongst which Spence lived. Such reactions tally with those of her niece; Lucy Morice's regard for her aunt was ambivalent. The tone of her memories of Auntie Kate wavers from amusement to admiration and genuine affection. While Lucy was growing up, her father, Spence's brother, was becoming a wealthy and prominent figure in Adelaide. Shortly before she was married, Lucy Spence was considered an heiress.[41] She may have echoed her mother's resentment at Kate's reliance upon her brother's interest and generosity. But she also admired her aunt for her courage, energy and sympathetic concern for other people. And she loved her for the stories she remembered being told as a child, for her good humour, simplicity and generosity.[42] These were the qualities emphasised by Catherine Spence's biographer, Jeanne Young.

Jeanne Foster Young.
Image courtesy of the State Library of South Australia SLSA: 26285/211.

Jeanne Young met Spence in 1897 when she was barely 30 and Miss Spence was seventy-one. She, like several other friends of Spence's old age, sought her friendship because she admired Miss Spence and her work and wished to share it.[43] A few months after making her acquaintance, Jeanne Young suggested that Spence should offer herself as a candidate for election to the 1897 Federal Convention:

> 'My dear', she protested, 'I fear that I am too old'. I laughed. 'Curiously enough, we all regard you just as one of us. The only difference is, that while we are young and inexperienced, you have had years of experience, and you have the knowledge of men and things which we younger ones still lack'[44]

As this suggests, there was, in their friendship, something of the relationship between teacher and disciple. Jeanne Young acknowledged it indirectly when she wrote 'Had my tastes been merely literary or social, Miss Spence would assuredly have found nothing to bind us together. It was the combination of these, with my deep interest in public affairs that welded the links in our chain of friendship.'[45] Yet her admiration and her proselytism did not prevent her offering a clear-eyed portrait of her mentor.

Catherine Spence could be aggressive, self-important, tactless and intolerant. She 'resented most intensely the modern tendency to drift into "weak fashionable expressions" – as she termed them – such as "nightie", "comfy", and "handky" '; she was so ready to take someone to task for the supposed use of vulgarism of the day that she severely admonished a speaker for using the expression 'somebody was poorly', only to discover that he had actually said 'somebody was poorly clad'. She attacked manners she disliked:

> being asked by an official of a Board, of which she was a member to autograph a book she had written … she did so very pleasantly, but when having extended to another official the offer to do his copy also, she was met with the quasi-condescending reply, 'I don't mind if you do', she lost patience, and said imperatively [sic], 'Do you want me to sign it, or do you not?'

Sometimes her assertiveness proved useful. At a meeting, a member of parliament asked her 'a little offensively, – "Miss Spence, what do you and Mrs Young get out of this?" "Get", she said scornfully, "we get all that is left over after lecturing for nothing, and paying our own expenses".' Her impatience arose Jeanne Young considered, from the fact that, 'feeling herself to be "something worthwhile" to the world … there need be no attempt to veil her knowledge of, and belief in, herself.'[46] Her absorption in her own concerns sometimes made her unperceptive and tactless. At tea tables in Adelaide one can still hear an account of her taking a seat on a tram beside the daughter of one of her acquaintances, and embarrassing the child by relating anecdotes about her family loudly enough for all the passengers to hear.[47] Jeanne Young recounted a story about taking Miss Spence to afternoon tea at Lady Bonython's:

> there were already several callers present. Among them was the mother of one of the girls who had belonged to the Girls' Literary society of which Miss Spence had been president. This girl had recently made an excellent marriage. 'Oh, how is So-and-So?"' Miss Spence asked the mother in her cheerful way. She is perfectly well, and radiantly happy', was the prompt response. 'Well, there is no accounting for tastes', rejoined Miss Spence laconically.
>
> A rather deep silence fell upon the assembly at this remark. With sudden inspiration, and knowing well Miss Spence's remoteness from social life, Lady Bonython rose to the occasion: 'Perhaps, Miss Spence', she said, 'you did not know that So-and-So is married?'
>
> 'Good Heavens, no', said the astonished lady, 'I thought she was still training to be a nurse, and I never could understand the craving so many young people have to take up nursing. I should hate it.'[48]

Spence was, by her own account, 'out of society' and undoubtedly glad to be so. As Jeanne Young remarked, 'Like most intellectual people, nothing annoyed her more than to be called upon to talk mere "persiflage"'. Among people who shared her conversational inclinations she could be delightful. Kerr Grant, later professor of physics at the University of Adelaide, wrote, 'I still recall vividly the impression of keen intelligence and intellectual vigor made by her vivacious and attractive personality.'[49] She could relax: she liked a glass of wine or a little whisky at bedtime, and she always enjoyed card games.[50] Young remembered, 'on those very informal occasions at my home we learned to love her, for it was then that she became so joyously youthful, so aggressively human in her intolerance, but so divinely merciful in her never-failing expressions of love for humanity.'[51] One of her greatest charms was her sense of humour. It was like that of Bret Harte's version of Aesop's *Fables*, which she gave to a friend for Christmas:[52] it had an edge, albeit a fairly blunt one. One of her favourite jokes was against herself, and she told it often. She arrived at a meeting to find that she had not been notified of several earlier meetings. She complained that she 'did not want to be merely an ornamental member' of that Board. Its chairman replied, 'Oh, Miss Spence, no one would ever accuse you of being that.' She was laughing before he realized what he had said. As she left, she encountered the chairman's business partner and, chuckling, told him of the *faux pas*. 'Looking at her very gravely, he said at the end of the recital, "Well, Miss Spence, I am surprised. I really thought Charlie had more tact."'[53]

Her humour, her deep concern and generosity, her courage, and her formidable energy, were the qualities which made her impact so strong. Even people who found her a nuisance admired her: C. C. Kingston, whom she regarded as spineless and whom she badgered with telegrams during the 1895 Premiers' Conference in Tasmania, treated her with goodhumoured courtesy and appointed her a member of the government's Destitute Board.[54] At one meeting of the board, its members were discussing how to punish some of the inhabitants of the Destitute Asylum. They had been allowed out to witness a public function and had returned very much the worse for the hospitality they had met with on their peregrinations. 'Miss Spence stood up for them stoutly. "Poor old things! What harm did it do once in a way!"'[55] Such qualities won her many friends, though – partly because she was so single-minded about her work – few very close ones.

She had, her autobiography suggests, a particularly warm and supportive relationship with her mother. She recorded her mother's pleasure in her earnings as a governess, her mother's acceptance of the parting of their paths over religion, and offered tribute to her mother's sound judgment, accurate observation and kind heart. As the unmarried daughter who remained at home to look after her mother, Catherine participated in the realisation of Helen Brodie's 40-year-old dream – to design the house that she would live in – not in Scotland, but in Trinity Street, College Town in Adelaide. A substantial house of about 12 rooms with huge windows looking out onto the lawns, and trees, it was probably considered comfortable but unpretentious when it was built. And that house, to which they moved in 1870, included a little study in which Spence could work, delighting in being with her books and pigeon holes with her 'dear old mother sitting with her knitting on her rocking chair at the low window'. She treasured her mother's memory of the social changes she had witnessed, taking time off from her own work to record Helen Brodie's recollections of her life. And she knew, she said, that her mother was interested in everything she did: Spence read her manuscripts to her mother, and drew support from her 'untiring sympathy'.[56]

Her mother's support might have been stronger than would have been required by the circumstance of their mutual dependence in a household where, for some considerable time, they also shared the care of Spence's orphaned niece and nephew. Spence thought that she was, herself, very like one of her mother's unmarried sisters, Mary Brodie. Spence's mother thought so too. And since Spence observed that between Helen and Mary Brodie 'there was a love passing the love of sisters', it seems likely that mother and daughter were particularly close.[57] Such intensity can create unwanted fetters. At the age of 95 Spence's mother fell over and, as a result, had to spend the last 13 months of her life in bed. Spence, herself in her 60s, nursed her throughout that time: her mother, she said, 'wanted me with her always'. She was saddened by the 'gradual decay of the faculties which had previously been so keen: Helen Brodie Spence's quiet and painless death in December 1887 must have been a relief: in recalling it, Spence also remarked, 'Henceforth I was free to devote my efforts to the fuller public work for which I had so often longed, but which my mother's devotion to and dependence on me rendered impossible'.[58]

She did not plunge immediately into a public life. The long strain of her mother's illness and death had, she recalled, affected her health.[59] In the beginning of the short story that she wrote during 1888, she depicts her heroine in almost exactly her own situation, saying: 'When, after a long, wearing, and painful illness, I closed my mother's eyes – my companionship and occupation both gone at once – I had to consider how I was to take up my life again'.[60] It is possible that Spence had relied, even more than she recognised, on her mother's devotion and tireless sympathy. It is surely suggestive that, in writing her autobiography, an undertaking in which – in a sense – she became the mother of the work's subject, herself,[61] she had not been able to progress beyond the chapter in which she recalled her mother's last illness and death before her own life ended. Jeanne Young surmised, 'It was as if the task of recording one of the deepest sorrows of her own life – the death of her mother – had been too much for the brave heart'.[62]

She appears to have formed only one friendship close enough to have allowed it within the walls of her household, firm enough to have withstood the vicissitudes of time. When she was London in the mid-1860s, she visited relatives of her brother-in-law, William Wren, and met there a young woman called Ellen Louisa Gregory. According to Lucy Morice, Spence persuaded Ellen Gregory to emigrate to South Australia in the expectation that she would be a comfort to an aunt living there in the country. But the aunt did not find the niece to her liking so in Morice's words, 'Auntie Kate was saddled for life with a protegée who, less than kin, was much resented by my part of the family.'[63] Perhaps Ellen Gregory remained nothing more than a dependent in Spence's household. There are very few references to her to be found in Spence's papers. But even if Spence had first taken Ellen Gregory in because she was concerned at a plight to which she had contributed, 40 years was an improbably long expiation of her mistake. Undoubtedly Ellen Gregory helped in running the succession of households that Spence formed. For many years those households included her mother, and they were seldom without two or three children who had become her responsibility, two of whom were Ellen Gregory's cousins. But Lucy Morice describes one such household as 'a little community', a term evocative in the period of Utopian socialist experiments in equal and co-operative living arrangements, and that suggests greater equality than was likely to have developed if Ellen Gregory had been nothing more than a domestic dependent. The resentment that Morice said her family felt towards this so-called protegée was not extended to any of the other protegés that Spence acquired at various times during her life; it would seem proportionate only if Ellen Gregory's place in Spence's life signified an intimacy considered appropriate only with kin. The very silence in Spence's own record could suggest that she was protecting the privacy of both. It seems highly likely that the two became fast friends and took pleasure in sharing their domestic lives. Ellen Gregory remained with Catherine Spence, 'to be the prop and mainstay of my old age', Spence said, even when, toward the end of her life, she gave up her own household and went to live with the Quiltys. Mrs Quilty had at one time, been a maid in the Spences' household; during the last years of Spence's life she provided her with the two front rooms of her house – as a study and a bedroom – and with her meals. Ellen Gregory went with her and presumably shared all this.[64] When Spence died, she left Ellen Gregory not only all her household furniture, china and linen, but also her best brooch.[65]

All Spence's other friendships had a marked instrumental element, on one side or the other. As a shy adolescent, new to the colony she made friends with three nieces of Catherine Beare and Samuel Stephens, the first colonial manager of the

South Australian Company. The eldest, Lucy, married, had five children and, in 1861, died; the five children, three of whom were quite young, were apparently left almost friendless. Spence had gone to nurse Lucy on her deathbed, and took upon herself the task of finding help for the young Duvals, a function she performed intermittently for the rest of her life. Letters from an uncle in England constituted her their guardian, and, at least initially undertook to remit £100 a year for their support. One of these children, Rose, returned to Miss Spence for help, about two decades later, when she was herself a mother of three small children. She had been widowed, and needed someone to care for the children when she took a job as a clerk in a government department, so she moved to a house near Spence's. Later, she and the children lived for a time with Spence and Ellen Gregory in the 'little community' in East Adelaide. And when Rose died, Spence took her young daughter, Kitty, to live with her, a move which ended tragically in 1904 when Kitty cut her throat in the bath and died.[66]

At the same time as she made friends with Lucy Beare, Spence also made friends with the Stirlings, the Bakewells, and the Taylors – all families with substantial pastoral and mercantile interests in the colony – the first two with numerous children in whom Spence took, she said, much interest. In one household she was 'Miss Spence the storyteller', in the other 'Miss Spence, the teller of tales.'[67] Those families found ways of offering Miss Spence material evidence of their esteem for her. The Stirlings gave her a fare to England and back in 1865, and the Bakewells took her to stay with them when she first arrived in London. John Taylor provided her with the £200 spending money that she took with her on that trip. He was the model for Charles Reginald, the hero of her first novel, and he had taken that novel to England for her in search of a publisher in 1853.[68]

Emily Clark sought an introduction to Spence to congratulate her on her novel; introduced her to the Unitarian congregation in Adelaide; gave her letters of introduction to friends and relatives in England; and drew her into 30 years' work on the welfare of destitute children.[69] Edith Cook shared her opinion about the necessity of secondary education for girls, and as headmistress of the Advanced School for Girls, often invited Miss Spence to give lessons to her students.[70] John Anderson Hartley, Inspector-General of Education in South Australia from 1878 until 1895, became a good friend when Spence offered to help with his work; he supported her campaigns for electoral reform.[71] Alfred Cridge, the American who commented on her dress, with whom she said she felt as at home as with her brother David, was an ardent supporter of her campaign for proportional representation.[72] Alice Henry, like Jeanne Young, shared many of Spence's political views and regarded her as a mentor. Rose Scott and Vida Goldstein looked to her as the pioneer of much that they aspired to themselves.[73] These people were probably her closest friends, outside her household, and her friends were as important to her as she was to them: 'no woman in Australia', she declared toward the end of her life, 'has been richer in friends'.[74] Yet those friendships were characterised by a kind of professionalism: they were important to her primarily as a means of sharing her opinions, her enthusiasms, and gaining support and recognition for her work; any emotional bonds seem to have arisen from this, rather than generating it. Most unusually for a woman of her period, she identified her fulfilment and happiness not with any private and personal relationship, but with her ambition and work, her ideas and ideals.

If her aspirations and her work were her greatest passions, one of her strongest emotions was admiration for people whose work and ideas informed her own. She revered J. S. Mill, Thomas Hare, George Eliot, and later and less expressly Samuel Butler, Henry George, Edward Bellamy, and Charlotte Perkins Gilman.[75] She prized her acquaintance with Mill, Hare and George, recounted her meetings with them, and strove for the implementation of those of their ideas that she had grasped most strongly. In doing so, she encountered the conventions and prohibitions which restricted her achievement, not because she lacked ability, but because she was a woman.

Catherine Spence worked throughout her life to overcome the patriarchal conventions which threatened to thwart her ambition, restrict her self-fulfilment and prevent the achievement of her ends. She protested against social prohibitions chiefly because they hampered her work, work she considered to be directed as much towards the greater welfare of society as towards her own fulfilment. Yet in doing so she expressed, by example as much as by precept, her opinion that women could take a place in the world beyond their households, and accept responsibility in the public affairs of the community. By venturing into such exclusively masculine preserves as journalism and politics herself, she expressed her conviction that women, so inclined, could contribute quite as usefully as men to any field of human endeavour. It was far from easy even to express such a conviction during the 19th century, much less to act upon it. Much of Spence's assertiveness and self-importance probably grew out of the necessity of claiming the hearing and attention automatically accorded to most men. But her self-confidence supported her in such a claim, and by making it on behalf of other women she became Australia's first feminist.

Introduction

Such an achievement had its cost: Spence's life shows, as well, no small measure of doubt, frustration and grief. A fuller understanding of how she perceived herself and her world, and acted upon her perceptions, should illuminate not only our understanding of Australia's past, but also our understanding of the changing position of Australian women. This book's second purpose is to reach such an understanding, for, as Anna Davin has written, 'we must examine the struggle of earlier generations of women to help us win our own.'[76]

1
Acquiring a room of her own

'. . . a woman must have money and a room of her own if she is to write fiction; '
(Virginia Woolf, *A Room of One's Own*)

Catherine Helen Spence was born in 1825, the fifth of eight children of two Scots – Helen Brodie and David Spence.[1] She accounted herself well-born for, she said, 'my father and mother loved each other'. She considered herself well-descended, 'going back for many generations on both sides of intelligent and respectable people'. This was a clear statement of a conviction that she began to reach in her 20s and held firmly by the time she was in her 80s – that sincere affection, intelligence and respectability counted for far more in individual happiness and social harmony than birth, wealth or even piety. But she was not as wholly unworldly as those statements in the opening paragraph of the autobiography that she wrote in her 80s would suggest. She also quoted her father saying that 'he was sprung from the tail of the gentry', while her mother 'was descended from the head of the commonalty'.[2]

Her mother, Helen Brodie, was descended from a long line of East Lothian tenant farmers who had, she boasted, 'always been at the head of their class'.[3] To maintain such a position during the enclosures and onslaught on small holdings of the 18th century, a tenant farmer must have been ready to adopt new agricultural methods and implements. Spence's maternal grandfather had three farms on 19-year leases, which cost him £6000 a year in rents set during the Napoleonic wars, and he had won two silver salvers, awarded by the Highland Society, for having the largest area of drilled wheat sown. Helen Brodie probably grew up in an environment accustomed to innovation; a family of capable and independent-minded women. Spence's grandfather's holdings were drastically reduced when he invested in an unsuccessful attempt to launch an East Lothian bank. When a stroke rendered him incapable of running the one farm that he still held, he turned it over – not to his eldest son – but to his daughter Margaret, who managed the 800 acres profitably for the next 30 years.[4] Spence remembered her aunt as a 'vigorous business-like woman … riding or driving her little gig all over the farm'.[5] Another aunt, Mary, took an independent stance on religion following the disruption of the Church of Scotland in 1843, and instead of remaining with the rest of the family, turned to the Free Church.[6] Helen, herself, had unusually forthright political views: during the debates on the first Reform Bill at the beginning of the 1820s, she wrote two letters to the local press, under the name 'Grizel Plowter', setting forth the advantages of reform.[7] But she did not think of even attempting to retain control of her own financial resources. When she married David Spence in 1815, she brought him a dowry of £1500, believing that 'the wife's fortune should come and go with the husband's'.[8]

Spence's father, William, was the son of a former naval surgeon who retired to practise in Melrose. William Spence appears to have been a gentle, considerate man. The family preserved the story of his getting up early in the mornings to light the fire so that he could take his wife a cup of tea in bed; he would not rouse the maid, 'he said young things wanted plenty of sleep'. It was, said Spence, 'a wonderful thing for a man to do in those days'. His medicine 'trusted much to Nature and not too much to drugs', which meant that his grandson, young John Brodie Spence, passed a painful 11th birthday after having a double tooth extracted.[9] David Spence grew up wanting to be a farmer, but there was no capital in the family to finance such a venture, so he was apprenticed at the age of 15 to the only lawyer in Melrose. He served a three-year apprenticeship – 'five years was required for Writers to the Signet but inferior court practice only required three' – which qualified him to work in a field developing as a specialism of solicitors and attorneys.[10] At the age of 18 he moved to Edinburgh with a friend, earning his living by writing law papers at threepence a page. There, he probably spent much of his time with other members of the legal fraternity who became the most vociferous champions of the Whigs and reform. When he set up as a writer on his own account back in Melrose, he was a declared a 'reformer'.[11] He, too, had come from a household of self-sufficient women: one of his sisters, Mary, established a boarding-school, at which Spence's two elder sisters were educated.[12] However, Spence's parents were reformers, not radicals. They may have been eager to see a limited extension of the franchise. But when they were married, David Spence was making £600 a year, and had £1600 on his books.[13] They set up a household which, by the time they had had eight children, was substantial: they employed three maids to whom they paid the top wage in the district – £8 a year for the cook, £7 for the housemaid, and £6 for the nursemaid.[14] They had no impetus to require radical changes in a social order which offered them such a comfortable living.

They were, moreover, members of the Established Church of Scotland. This, whether Helen and David had any strong religious convictions or not, was essential to David's prosperity. His profession necessarily imposed unbounded trust, and to establish his entitlement to that trust in a Presbyterian society, he must show that he was among the elect.[15] The Spences attended morning and afternoon services in the summer, sat through two successive services in the winter, taught their children the Shorter Catechism, and restricted their Sunday reading to such improving works as Maria Edgeworth's moral tales. They probably held their beliefs seriously: Catherine learned by heart not only the Shorter Catechism and its proofs from the scriptures, but also Watt's hymns which expressed the same doctrine. But she found that doctrine tyrannical and unreasonable, and felt miserably certain that she was already one of the damned. This was, she recalled, the 'only cloud on my young life'.[16]

She was born in Melrose, a small town in a countryside littered with relics of its past history: the ruins of Melrose Abbey, founded by the Cistercians in the 12th century, used as a quarry during the 18th; Hillslap Tower and Langshaw Tower, built during the 16th century, looked over the farms and houses; on the northern peak of the three Eildon Hills, about a mile and a half from Melrose, there were traces of a Roman fort and signal station; and the Eildon Tree Stone was supposed to mark the spot where Thomas the Rhymer, of the 14th-century verse romance, met the Queen of Elfland and was taken with her to Fairyland for seven years.[17] Spence recalled, 'There was not a hill or a burn or a glen that had not a song or proverb, or a legend about it … and my mother knew the words as well as the tunes of the minstrelsy of the Scottish border'. She had her first introduction to politics when she was recovering from measles and the nursemaid took her to hear a Whig campaigner at a gathering around the 16th-century cross in the market place in Melrose.[18]

Melrose parish was also the home of Walter Scott, who had bought Abbotsford, about two miles west of Melrose village, in 1811.[19] He depicted much of the scenery and society around his home in his writing. Spence said, 'There was not a local note in "The Lay of the Last Minstrel" or in novels, "The Monastery", and "The Abbot" [sic], with which I was not familiar before I entered my teens'.[20] That imbued her with a strong sense of tradition. And it was a tradition which included active, independent, forthright women. The Scotswomen of literature are neither particularly subordinate and retiring, nor lofty and remote as in the courtly love tradition; Scott's intrepid Jeannie Deans probably represented the typical Scotswoman for the early 19th century.[21] Spence's reading could only have strengthened the lesson that she said that she learned early from her aunts and her mother, that 'women were fit to share in the work of this world, and that to make the world pleasant for men was not their only mission'.[22] It was a lesson confirmed by her schooling.

The Spences provided all their children with a good education. The boys, William, John and David went to the parish school where they learned reading, writing, arithmetic, Latin and geography; they went on to Edinburgh for more advanced instruction. The girls, Agnes, Jessie, Catherine and Mary, attended a different school because the parish school did not teach needlework. The two elder ones, Agnes and Jessie, went to their Aunt Mary's boarding school in Upper Wooden. Catherine and Mary went to a day school in Melrose, called, said Spence, 'by the very popish name of St Mary's Convent though it was quite sufficiently Protestant'. There, Miss Phinn, who suffered from dropsy and taught from a sofa, offered them 'what was considered the education of a gentlewoman'. Catherine learned piano and fancy needlework, reading, writing, probably arithmetic, French, Italian, music, and a smattering of general knowledge from the books read to the children while they sewed – 'history, biography, adventures, descriptions, and story books'. Her French she knew by eye, but not by ear. She was, she recalled, the only member of the family who could translate French at sight, 'thanks to Miss Phinn's giving me so much of Racine and Molière, and other good French authors in my school days'. But she also found, when she visited Paris when she was in her early 30s, that although she could speak French, 'I spoke it badly, and had great difficulty in following French conversations'. Miss Phinn impressed Spence's mother with her commonsense. She impressed Catherine with the value of learning, and helped her develop confidence in her own abilities. 'I was a very ambitious girl at 13. I wanted to be a teacher first, and a great writer afterwards'. She made her father promise to send her to a new institution in Edinburgh offering advanced education for girls, the year after she turned 13, and around this promise she built her plans and dreams for the future.[23] Her plans, the promise and the security of her stable world, all crumbled when, in

1839, her father's speculation in foreign wheat brought upon the family financial ruin and social disgrace.

David Spence appears to have lost not only all his own money, but substantial investments made by his wife's family as well, buying shares in engrossed wheat. The grain was kept so long that it rotted and the shares became worthless. The discovery of this unusually just reward for greed destroyed both the family's immediate liquidity and the trust and respectability attached to David by the local community, which were essential for his work. A long-standing friend of Spence's sister Jessie was compelled to return some books and music to her by giving them to an intermediary to pass on to an aunt, a proceeding which left her crying as though her heart would break. But she could not write a word to Jessie. Nor did Catherine hear anything from the new friend with whom she had spent a month in Edinburgh over the Christmas of 1838. 'We were hopelessly ruined, our place would know us no more'. In April 1839, Jessie took Catherine to their Aunt Mary's at Wooden to be told of their father's financial collapse: they must leave Melrose, and Scotland, forever.[24]

Apparently plans had already been made. Spence's maternal grandmother, despite that family's losses in David Spence's gamble, had come to the rescue with £500. David had already left Scotland for the newly-founded colony of South Australia where the family had bought an 80-acre section of land. That investment entitled them to free steerage passages for four adults.[25] Spence's eldest sister, Agnes, had died of consumption four years earlier, and her youngest sister, Eliza, had died at the age of two.[26] They decided to leave Spence's younger brother David, with his aunts to complete his education; to spend whatever was necessary to make up the difference between steerage and intermediate fares; and, since Catherine and Mary were too young to count in the quota of adult females required by the colonising authority, to take with them a servant girl. In July 1839, Spence's mother, her older brothers William and John, her older sister Jessie, her younger sister Mary, and Catherine herself, set sail on the *Palmyra* from Greenock.[27] Spence was already burdened with her shattered dreams and her conviction that she was destined for perdition by a tyrannical Calvinist deity. She was armed with nothing but her education and her confidence in her own abilities.

The 80-acre section, the free passages, and the balance in the sexes required of the adults emigrating were all aspects of South Australia's origins in the schemes of early 19th-century British liberal ideologues. Chief among them was Edward Gibbon Wakefield, who, with Robert Gouger, in 1829 outlined the principles of a scheme for 'systematic colonisation'.[28] Wakefield's scheme was, as Marx observed, a rationalisation of capitalist exploitation.[29] To British middle-class liberals, struggling against the power and patronage of Old Corruption in church, state and economy during the heady days of the Reform Act of 1832, it appealed strongly as a proposal for liberty with security. It proposed, by selling land at a 'sufficient price' to engender a social structure that would be both hierarchical and mobile. Within it, all operations of the economy, government, worship, education and culture could be free. No convicts should be sent to such a colony. Equal proportions of women and men emigrating would bring the refining influence of women to life throughout the settlement, and add the stimulus to industry and thrift needed to establish homes for families. Preference for the young, between the ages of 15 and 30, would contribute to the same end. These people were to take part in creating a society in which the pursuit of self-interest would lead to unqualified social harmony. The scheme and the efforts to implement it, in a settlement on St Vincent's Gulf in Australia, suffered a host of false starts and hindrances before it got under way. By that time, Wakefield had washed his hands of the whole affair; but in the northern spring of 1836, the settlers at last embarking from Britain were beginning an experiment which had been significantly shaped by Wakefield's ideas.[30]

David Spence probably learned of the scheme through the colonisation commission's agent at Greenock.[31] It would have appealed to him even if he had not needed to flee from debt and disgrace. His daughter, Catherine, never lost her enthusiasm for its ideals. In her 50s, she looked back to the colony's pioneering days as a time when 'the community of labour and equality of the sexes' meant that South Australia approached a Utopian condition in which there was 'very little difference in the actual circumstances of different classes'.[32] In her autobiography she observed:

> It is sometimes counted as a reproach that South Australia was founded by doctrinaires and that we retain traces of our origins; to me it is our glory. In the land laws and the immigration laws it struck out a new path, and sought to found a new community where land, labour and capital should work harmoniously together.[33]

For much of her life Spence clearly found some kinship with those who would benefit most from the rationalisation of capitalism. Increasingly, though, as she grew older, she held that labour could and should benefit equally. But there was nothing in Wakefield's scheme about equality of the sexes. She had expanded a provision about numbers far beyond its original intention. She was also careful not to stress that experience did not fulfil the hopes of the ideologues.

The early years of the settlement were troubled by the unspecified division of authority between the lieutenant governor and the resident commissioner, strife over financing administration, and – despite all the preliminary wrangling over the 'sufficient price' – speculation in land. By the time the Spences arrived late in 1839, the first two officials had been replaced by George Gawler, who took over the functions of both. He dealt with the difficulties of unemployment, and inadequate provision for establishing the infrastructure necessary for a viable European settlement, by embarking upon a program of government-funded building. He supplied the funds by drawing promissory notes on the British government. New arrivals in the colony with little capital would, temporarily, stand a better chance of winning a living by staying in Adelaide than by moving on into the countryside.[34]

Spence described the situation into which her family moved in 1839 thus:

> There had been a great drought in Australia, and seed cost 20s. to 15s. the bushel ... bread was 2.9d the 4-lb loaf, and it got dearer and dearer, till it got up to 4s ... Wages were very high, and even those who came to South Australia with the determination to farm were terrified to risk putting in such costly seed in a new untried climate.[35]

Like many other early settlers, frightened as well by stories about snakes and 'blackfellows', the Spences stuck to the town. They stayed in a house in Gilles Street for a month, then bought a marquee and pitched it on Brownhill Creek, on the slopes of the south-west end of the Adelaide hills. There they camped for seven months, living mainly on the ton of rice they bought as the cheapest available food, and keeping 15 cows, a pony and a cart, which enabled them to sell milk in the town at a shilling a quart. Winter drove them back into Adelaide: they rented a house, and yards for the cows on West Terrace for £75 a year.[36]

By that time, mid-1840, discussion about ways of raising revenue for local administration and public works had revived the subject of forms of representation for the views of the settlers. In August 1840 Gawler's Legislative Council passed an act to constitute a municipal corporation for the city of Adelaide. On 31 October that year the first election was held. The corporation began by borrowing £250 from the government and committing itself to salaries amounting to nearly £1000.[37] Among the officials that it appointed was David Spence; he was the town clerk, a job that was to earn him £150 a year.[38] It lasted less than three years. News that the British government would not honour Gawler's drafts reached the colony in February 1841; Gawler was replaced by George Grey in May of that year, and Grey set about pruning government expenditure and reinforcing the gradual drift of settlement into the countryside that had begun by the end of 1839. The whole colony suffered a depression that lasted until 1844. In mid-1841, the Adelaide municipal corporation levied rates which should have yielded a revenue of £1333 but the depression meant that the rates could not be collected. The new corporation, elected in October 1841 inherited debts, raised the rates and curtailed the salaries of its staff. Attendance at its meetings declined until, by May 1842, it was difficult to get a quorum. So few people enrolled for the third election, in October 1842, that no vote was taken; the whole body was officially declared defunct in August the following year.[39] David Spence stayed with it until it collapsed. But with the loss of his income, Spence recalled, 'my father lost health and spirits'.[40]

Grey's retrenchments ensured that the depression of 1840-44 was a hard time for colonists like David Spence, who had looked to the forms of publicly-funded employment provided by Gawler's regime for their livelihoods. It was a hard time, too, for many who had expected to make their fortunes. The new branch of a British mercantile firm established by three sons of George Elder survived, but others collapsed. When Jessie Spence married Andrew Murray in November 1841, he was carrying on a drapery business in Hindley Street as a prosperous partner in the firm of Murray and Greig. But the firm collapsed in 1842. Murray found work for, according to Spence, 'a small salary' on a newspaper, the *Southern* (later *South*) *Australian*, that had been founded in 1838.[41]

It was a particularly hard time for young Catherine Spence:

> The years at Brownhill Creek and West terrace were the most unhappy of my life. I suffered from the want of some intellectual activity and from the sense of frustrated ambition and religious despair.[42]

Catherine Helen Spence.

Image reproduced from a photograph in Jeanne F. Young, *Catherine Helen Spence: A Study and an Appreciation* (Lothian Publishing Co. Pty. Ltd.) Melbourne, 1937.

She believed in a deity that signalled pre-destined salvation to the elect through their prosperity; she could not have helped feeling her first experience of economic hardship as a forewarning of damnation. For the Spences, hardship seems to have lasted longer than the depression did. They sold the cows. William and John went off to farm the 80-acre section, probably at Noarlunga, but without success. The rest of the family moved to lodgings in Halifax Street, because they were cheaper.[43] In her first published novel, Spence was to depict a young gentlewoman, newly arrived in South Australia without resources or connections, accepting employment as a maid-of-all-work. Her description of an experience felt as social degradation undoubtedly drew flavour and detail from her own.

Spence's education became, in so altered a world, her refuge, her badge of respectability, her only claim to attention. Neighbours of the Spences in Halifax Street remembered that Catherine, as a girl in her teens, would go through the streets with several books under her arm, often reading as she went. 'We always thought,' one commentator said, 'that she was so vain of her knowledge that she paraded it a great deal more than was necessary',[44] a comment epitomising the attitudes that left her isolated. She may have been making her badge obvious, but she seems more to have been reading to shut out the world. 'The few books we had, or which we could borrow', she wrote, 'I read over and over again. Aikin's *British Poets*, ... and Goldsmith's complete works ... were thoroughly mastered, and the Waverly novels down to *Quentin Durward* were well absorbed'.[45] Her account of the heroine in her second novel, struggling to find congenial conversation among her fellow colonists, and her picture of the hero of a later novel (*Gathered In*), tormented by religious doubt and isolated from anyone who could talk about anything but money, drink and gambling, add depth and detail to the bald statement in her autobiography of her loneliness and frustration.

But her education also became her first personal financial resource. Spence had left Scotland with a testimonial from Miss Phinn saying that 'from the time you could put three letters together, you evinced a turn for teaching – so clear-headed and patient, so thoroughly upright in word and deed'.[46] On board the *Palmyra*, she gathered up the younger children and gave them lessons.[47] But when first in Adelaide she found Miss Phinn's recommendation outweighed by her youth and shyness. The nearest she came to teaching during her first years in the colony was her story-telling to the young Stirlings and young Bakewells, an activity she considered educational, perhaps for them, certainly for herself.[48] But her wish to find work as a teacher probably encountered, too, the difficulties that the depression created for anyone trying to make a living through education. The Independent churchman, T. Q. Stow, whose Classical Academy was one of only 11 pronounced worthy of its name in 1841, was having to farm a lease on the River Torrens to support himself during those years.[49] However, by the time Spence was 17, late in 1843, she had gained employment as a governess to the children of three government officials: the Post-Master General (Henry Watts), the Surveyor-General (E. C. Frome), and Grey's Private Secretary (Alfred Mundy). She taught each family for two hours each day five days a week, and she was paid sixpence an hour.[50] In 1843, the South Australian School Society could not find parents who could afford sixpence a week for school fees. Four years later when free enterprise capitalist development was again winning profits and wealthy colonists formed the South Australian Proprietary School, they fixed its fees at ten guineas a year, equivalent to about four shillings a head a week.[51] Spence was earning 15 shillings a week four years earlier. It is little wonder that she was proud of her income. 'My mother said she never felt the bitterness of poverty after I began to earn money', she boasted.[52]

Spence continued governessing for three years. Then, in 1846, the Spence family's fortunes altered again. Spence's brothers abandoned their attempt at farming. William eventually left South Australia for the west and never returned. John moved back to Adelaide and found work as a clerk in the South Australian Bank, at £100 a year – more than three times Catherine's earnings. David was to arrive from Scotland at about the end of that year, to find work in one of the Adelaide offices administering mining of the newly-discovered copper at Burra, 90 miles north of Adelaide. And Spence decided that, at the age of 20, she could do better than governessing by opening a school. Her sister Mary was nearly 16 years old, and her mother could help. So she set about arranging an establishment like those of her aunt Mary and her own teacher Miss Phinn, on the other side of the world. Her school opened at the beginning of May 1846. Her father, she recalled, 'thought that our difficulties were over'. On 29 May, he died.[53]

David Spence's death, at the age of 57, meant that any expectations that his family had retained, of his fulfilling the conventional patriarchal function of breadwinner, died too. From that time, the Spences looked to their own resources for their livelihoods. Those resources embraced not only the financial help given to them by their aunts in Scotland, but also their households, their friends and their paid work.

The Scottish aunts, Helen Brodie's sisters, were able to provide them with timely and important financial assistance. But it was no fortune that they sent to South Australia. At some time, probably in the 1850s, they despatched £1000 to be invested in the colony, possibly in the South Australian Mining Company – the largest and most secure of the companies formed in the wake of the copper mining boom in Burra in 1846. Early in the 20th century, Spence recalled, 'it was as easy to get 10 per cent then as to get 4 per cent now; indeed I think the money earned 12 per cent at first.'[54] The aunts divided the income from that investment in two: half to be paid to their brother, Alexander Brodie, who had also emigrated to South Australia and settled at Morphett Vale; the other half to be paid to their sister Helen. For Helen and Catherine – the daughter who had remained at home with her – that meant an income of about £50 a year, beginning in about 1858.[55] It was probably a few years before that that Helen's eldest sister died, leaving to her sister and brother in South Australia 'all she had in her power'. Spence did not record the amount, but it was enough for her mother to buy a brick cottage in Pulteney Street and one share in the Burra copper mines. Spence's brother John may have benefited as well; he gave up his job with the Bank of South Australia to go into the aerated water business.[56] The brick cottage was probably the first dwelling that the Spences had lived in, since they left Scotland, as freeholders rather than tenants. For Catherine, the bequest and investment was the 'money and a room of her own' without which it is likely that we would never have heard of her.

For the men of the family, making a living presented no major difficulties. Copper-mining at Burra had restored the profitability of free enterprise capitalism to South Australia in the 1840s, as had the slow extension of the pastoral and agricultural industries. The flight of men and money to the Victorian goldfields in the early 1850s disrupted that stability, but only temporarily: South Australia's wheat-growers and millers profited from the rapidly expanding market for food to become, for a time, the granary of Australia.[57] By that time, William Spence had left for Western Australia. Nothing more is known about his life than that he moved on to New Zealand where he spent the rest of his days, dying unmarried at the age of 80 in 1903.[58] David Spence joined the gold rush in 1851. Spence said little more about him than that he died also unmarried in 1890, when he was sixty-three.[59] But we can be sure that if he, or William, had encountered serious difficulty in making a living, Catherine would have noted it in her autobiography; she makes few bones about other financial difficulties that the family encountered.

John Spence's career most closely illustrates Spence's assertion that 'we took hold of the growth of South Australia, and identified ourselves with it'. It indicates, too, which section of the colony's growth she was talking about: John Spence rose steadily to prosperity and colonial importance. He remained with the Bank of South Australia until 1852, surviving the disruption, not only of the economy, but also of the availability of coin, during the gold rushes.[60] He went into a fizzy drinks business with James Hamilton Parr.[61] He spent some time working for the infant South Australian Railways Department which, in 1856, opened the first government railway to be laid on British soil, running from the city to Port Adelaide.[62] He was employed by the government again, for some years, as official assignee and curator of intestate estates.[63] But he did not continue in his father's South Australian footsteps, even though government employment expanded through the stages which gave representative institutions to the colonists, culminating in the Constitution in 1856. That gave South Australia the most completely Benthamite form of self-government in Australia: the House of Assembly, of 36 members, was to be elected triennially by adult male suffrage, with voting by secret ballot; there was to be no plural voting, and no property qualifications for members. However the democratic power of the lower house was curbed by a Legislative Council of 18 members, to be elected by £25 householders from the whole colony as a single electorate.[64] Clearly, power was to remain in the hands of those colonists who were gaining most from their investments in the colony. Perhaps John Spence could see this. In 1863 he returned to banking as manager of the Adelaide branch of the English, Scottish and Australian Bank, a position he held until 1878. Having retired, he stood, in 1881, for election to the Legislative Council, and while there, achieved office three times during the ministry of J. W. Downer from 1884 to 1887.[65] He also cemented his prosperity during the decade in which drought brought ruin to many South Australian agriculturalists, by speculating extensively, probably in the mining boom following the discovery of large deposits of silver, lead and zinc at Broken Hill in the 1880s.[66] He and Jessie Cumming had been married in 1858, and had four children. The eldest, Lucy, was growing up to great expectations during the 1880s. John Spence died, aged 78, in 1902, his life considered a success story.[67]

For the women, however, winning a livelihood was a different matter. Until the aunts came to the rescue, Spence's mother probably lived on whatever her children could bring in. Even after the legacy enabled her to buy her own house and, perhaps, employ a maid, life in her establishment could hardly have been called sumptuous.

Spence's two sisters gained livelihoods in the way that was most usual and most expected in a patriarchal society, indeed in a way expressly linked to incentives to thrift and industry in Wakefield's plan: they married. Jessie married Andrew Murray in 1841 and over the next 15 years bore ten children, five of whom died in childhood.[68] In 1844 Murray bought the *South Australian* and made himself its editor; it was a conservative paper which took care to support the local representative of the British government on most issues. But it folded in 1851 when he went to Melbourne to become commercial editor of the *Argus*, taking Jessie and the children with him.[69] Jessie outlived Murray, but died in an accident at Gippsland in 1888, when she was sixty-seven.[70] Mary, or May, married in 1855 when she was twenty-five. Her husband, William Wren, was a clerk on the way to becoming a partner of James Boucaut (a lawyer, subsequently three times premier of South Australia). Mary had three children, two of whom survived. But her husband was sickly. In 1864, when she had been married fewer than nine years, Wren died. Mary herself died in 1870, at the age of 40.[71] It appears that Wren left enough for Mary and the children to live on, and Mary left that to the children. When Wren died, Spence, her mother and presumably Ellen Gregory, moved in with Mary and the children, so that they could 'put two small incomes together', and share the work of caring for the children. When Mary died, those children remained with Spence and her mother.[72]

For Catherine Spence, gaining a living was more complicated, for she chose to remain single. In the 1840s and 1850s it was a most unusual choice, particularly in a society whose members had been selected at least partly because of their marriageable ages. Moreover, in a patriarchal culture, spinsterhood carried, as it has continued to carry the stigma of being considered unattractive to men. Spence was not prepared to acquiesce in such labelling; she made it clear that not marrying was a deliberate choice. In her autobiography she recorded that she had two offers of marriage.

> The first might have been accepted if it had not been for the Calvinistic creed that made me shrink from the possibility of bringing children into the world with so little chance of eternal salvation, so I said 'No' to a very clever young man, with whom I argued on many points and with whom, if I had married him, I should have argued until one of us died! I was 17, and had just begun to earn money. I told him why I refused him and that it was final. In six weeks he was engaged to another woman.[73]

Acquiring a room of her own

This smacks of an oft-told tale, with deliberate cheeriness calculated to prohibit probing. Gossip preserved by families of early South Australians identifies the young man as James Allen, an energetic newspaperman who had edited the Adelaide *Times* during the 1840s. He was known to some of the pioneering colonists as 'Dismal Jimmy', probably because of his unpaid labour in the pulpit of the Ebenezer Baptist Church in North Adelaide.[74] The gossip also relates that when he engaged himself to marry only six weeks after proposing to Miss Spence, she was furious. This cannot, now, be anything but speculation. Spence's own account suggests something close to despair engendered by her religion. It also suggests that the triumphant independence she had just achieved, by beginning to earn her own income, made her reluctant to sacrifice that to become anyone's wife, no matter how stimulating the arguments they might have.

The second proposal was made to her when she was 23, by John Alexander Gilfillan, an artist of 55, and a widower with three children.[75] She did not give any reasons for refusing this offer. Her novels suggest two. Margaret Elliot, the self-portrait she drew in her first novel (*Clara Morison*), refers casually to having had two offers, one from a man who thought she had a noble soul, and remarks scornfully that she did not think that much of a reason for marriage. In her fourth novel (*The Author's Daughter*) three of the characters express horror at the prospect of the heroine (Amy) marrying 'that old man' (Lord Darlington). Their repeated assertions that such a marriage would be 'unnatural' suggest that Spence recognised the importance of sexual compatibility in domestic harmony, and, considered it impossible if there was a great difference in the ages of the partners.

More simply, she may have refused both men because she did not love them. In her autobiography, she observed:

> I believe that if I had been in love, especially if I had been disappointed in love, my novels would have been stronger and more interesting; but I kept watch over myself, which I felt I needed, for I was both imaginative and affectionate. I did not want to give my heart away. I did not desire a love disappointment, even for the sake of experience.[76]

Yet, after reading the diary that she kept intermittently at the beginning of the 1850s, Jeanne Young considered that Spence may have 'kept a watch' over her affections at some cost to her peace of mind. She noted that 'From passages in her diary, love affairs to be completed by the happiness of marriage seem not to have been so remote from her imagination in her early years, as we, who knew her only when world affairs had claimed her for their own, had supposed'. The diary suggested that someone had enlisted her affection, only to disappoint her by 'his worthlessness'. In her second novel (*Tender and True*), she depicts the heroine of the sub-plot (Rose Lancaster) undergoing just such an experience: Rosa discovers that the sub-plot's Byronic hero (Miles Davanent), to whom she has given her heart, has a wife and a child, both of whom he disposes of in a thoroughly unfeeling fashion. The theme recurs in various forms, in later novels as well, though without the moral judgement conveyed in *Tender and True*. Perhaps Jeanne Young was right. Perhaps Spence's autobiographical comment was made from the pain-absorbing distance of an old age fulfilled in other ways. Disappointment may have prompted a later diary entry in which Spence wrote, ' "C … and A … contend that if I do really not wish for marriage, I should talk much less about it, for my talking gives to people an entirely wrong impression" '. She went on to admonish herself: ' "Let your ideas never dare to fancy what may happen in case of marriage; that is the forbidden subject. Place the garrett steadily before you and endeavour to train your mind so as to be a useful and amiable member of society and no one's wife, and no one's mother" '.[77]

However, the portrayal of the 'love disappointment' in *Tender and True* carries very little conviction. Indeed, it sails so close to parody that it suggests strongly that Spence was employing a favourite device of romantic novelists with very little imaginative sympathy. Perhaps, then, her diary expressed a positive decision at least as much as a hard-won renunciation of a dream. In an age when, as she has Margaret Elliot tell Clara Morison in her first novel, spinsters were objects of mockery and condescension, it was a formidable resolution. In that novel, the same two characters discuss vocation. Clara's is, Margaret tells her, marriage. Margaret is unsure of what her own is, but she knows it is not marriage: her unwillingness to suppress her own opinions, to defer to any man simply because he is a man, her range of interests and her independence, make her, she recognises, an unsuitable partner for any man in search of a wife.[78] Spence was, during her early years in South Australia, bitterly resentful of the injustice of 'a world made comfortable for the exclusive development of men'. Before yielding to a belief in the inferiority of women, she told her diary, she would discipline her mind, ' "to manly virtues, to manly strength, and to manly studies, that I may learn to live without leaning on anyone" '.[79] This was a clear decision – to face the whole world, not merely part of it, and to face it directly, without any of the constraints, the mediations, or the protections to be gained from having a husband.

This meant that she had, first of all, to find a way of making a living. And that was far from easy. Just as the patriarchal ordering of gender relations ensured that Jessie and Mary could gain their livelihoods by marrying men who would be breadwinners, so the same social order prohibited Spence, as a woman, from becoming her own breadwinner. As Elaine Showalter has observed, 'Victorian women were not accustomed to *choosing* a vocation; womanhood was a vocation in itself'.[80] There is no record of the school that Spence opened in 1846, and it probably did not last long. The colony's reviving economy resuscitated earlier schools and encouraged the foundation of others. She may have had difficulty finding pupils.[81] During the late 1840s, she contributed, anonymously, items to Murray's *South Australian*. But it is unlikely that they earned her anything, and she preserved her anonymity with care.[82] Those years must have been particularly hard for the Spences remaining in their mother's household – for they had only John's and David's salaries to live on. Of course, Spence could have found work as she shows the heroines of *Clara Morison* and *Mr Hogarth's Will* doing, in some kind of domestic service. And she did: in 1850 she reluctantly accepted a live-in post as a nursery governess and house counsellor. But such a position was even more of a check on her independence than marriage would have been, as she was to show in her depiction of Clara Morison's domestic service. It is unlikely that she persisted with it for long; she recorded in her autobiography that she gave up teaching in that year, when she was twenty-five.[83]

The cultural conditions of her life improved. The colony which had been founded with an already-established Literary Association, meeting in London to hear papers like Robert Owen's on 'The Influence of Literature on the Institutions of Nations and the Habits of People', whose first newspaper printed its first issue even before any settlers left Britain, proved culturally richer than Spence's early experience anticipated.[84] As productivity and profits recovered after 1844, the Mechanics' Institute was re-opened, the Book Society and Subscription Library was formed and then amalgamated with the Institute, and – ironically, since the mechanics institutes were supposed to serve the educational needs of the labouring classes – for two years 'the joint conversaziones attracted all the beauty, fashion and respectability of Adelaide'.[85] The Spences, despite their poverty, paid the full annual subscription which enabled them to use the Institute's library and reading room, and Murray passed on to Catherine Spence the newspapers and journals that he received from a reading club.[86] Spence did not immediately throw off her difficulties with her religion but in the households of women and children that she and her mother established, which were financially stable even if they continued to have to look at both sides of a shilling, she did regain some of her childhood's confidence. She set about pursuing the second of the ambitions she had formed as a child in Melrose.

For the rest of her life, Spence attempted to gain a livelihood with her pen. But for over 20 years, from her early 30s until her 50s, her earnings were piecemeal and occasional. Like the narrator in Virginia Woolf's *A Room of One's Own*, her financial security came from an aunt's bequest.[87] And some of her friends were wealthy enough for their generosity to be substantial. In 1854, when she wanted to go to Melbourne to visit the Murrays, she travelled there on a ship consigned to Edward Stirling, by that time a partner in the mercantile firm of Elder Stirling & Company.[88] (Her planned holiday of six weeks became eight months of work; Jessie was unwell and needed nursing and help with the children.[89])

Spence returned to Adelaide on the steamer that was bringing John Taylor back from Britain, carrying with him £30 for Spence for her first novel.[90] In 1865 the Stirlings again provided her with a fare, this time to Britain and back. Edward Stirling had withdrawn from his mercantile partnerships. The family was returning to Britain for their eight children to complete their education; their eldest, Edward Charles Stirling, had won a Westminster Scholarship, and was to read natural science at Cambridge.[91] Perhaps they hoped that Spence would help entertain the younger children. She agreed to go only when she was sure of enough spending money to cover her other expenses. Her friend John Taylor told her he had left her £500 in his will, but would prefer her to benefit from that at a time when she needed it, so she should have £200 immediately to use on her trip.[92] Taylor, who had married one of Stirling sisters, was a banker from Sydney turned financier and pastoralist in South Australia. He left for Britain himself, shortly ahead of Spence and the Stirlings. But he contracted something labelled 'suppressed smallpox' on the voyage and died two days after arriving.[93] Spence reluctantly acquired the rest of his bequest much sooner that she had anticipated.

In the 1870s she became a friend of Joanna and Robert Barr Smith. Robert Barr Smith had taken Stirling's place in the Elders' mercantile firm, which became Elder, Smith & Company, and had grown extremely wealthy: the Barr Smiths' mansion, Torrens Park, was the most lavish and hospitable in the colony.[94] Spence prized their generosity with books: 'What I owed to [Mrs Barr Smith] in the way of books for about 10 years cannot be put on paper'. When she first considered undertaking a public campaign for electoral reform in the 1890s, the Barr Smiths provided her with the funds.[95]

Assistance of this order was important to Spence: being able to spend a year in Britain in the mid-1860s contributed to her self-confidence and to the range of ideas with which she returned. Having the resources to campaign publicly for a cause she had made the foremost mission of her life in the 1890s, brought her to the pinnacle of her achievements. But such assistance was also like cake in the life of one whose daily diet was bread. Spence's economic security came from an aunt's bequest. Her financial independence came from her own effort, and her determination to earn her own living. Having acquired a room of her own, her first achievement was a novel.

2
The line of least resistance

When Spence first began to write she said, 'the novel was the line of least resistance'.[1] She was referring to the world that she had first learned about from her mother and her Scottish school-mistress, in which her everyday environment took on colour and adventure from reading the novels of Sir Walter Scott. She had buried herself in that world during her years as a shy, impoverished adolescent, in strange, uncongenial surroundings. The Spences' membership of the South Australian Mechanics' Institute and its library had enabled her to extend her reading with the work of English writers of her own time. She introduced the hero of her first published novel by presenting him, in the words of the critic Frederick Sinnett, 'talking modern literature, and displaying a highly cultivated mind with a promptitude and pertinacity frightful to contemplate'.[2] The authors he mentioned included not only Shakespeare, Scott and Byron, but also Dickens and Thackeray, whose novels were still reaching the colony in serial instalments in British periodicals at the time when Spence was creating him.

This was a world in which women were already claiming a voice in the public sphere. The 1840s, when the novel was the dominant literary form of writing in English, saw the publication of novels by each of the three Brontë sisters. In 1853 J. M. Ludlow observed despondently 'the fact that at this particular moment of the world's history the very *best* novels in several great countries happened to have been written by women'. By the 1860s, John Stuart Mill could reflect that 'If women lived in a different country from men, and had never read any of their writings, they would have a literature of their own'.[3] Spence may well have formulated her childhood's ambition 'to be a teacher first, and a great writer afterwards' before she knew anything of the women who had written fiction before her. But at about the time that she first had a novel published she began to look to other writers who were women. She 'read and appreciated Jane Austen's novels – those exquisite miniatures'; towards the end of her life she observed, 'so great a charm have Jane Austen's books that I have made a practice of reading them through regularly once a year'.[4] She thought highly of the poems of Elizabeth Barrett Browning.[5] She wrote and spoke of George Eliot and her admiration for her work, wondering at one time how Eliot would have fared had she, like Spence, come to live in an Australian colony.[6] She regarded the 'poems and economic writings' of Charlotte Perkins Gilman as an 'inspiration'.[7] She saw her own life as similar to that of Margaret Oliphant, whose fiction she liked.[8] In her later years she reviewed novels written by younger women as different as her sister colonist Catherine Martin and the South African Olive Schreiner.[9] And she decided that she disliked the Australian Barbara Baynton's *Bush Studies* even more than she had disliked meeting the book's author.[10] If the novel was 'the line of least resistance', then it was because Spence could draw support and encouragement from knowing and approving the work of other women who, in the cosmopolitan world of letters, were subverting the patriarchal dominion over culture by creating a literature of their own.

However, even the mediated indirect public voice that women could find through fiction was still contested in the mid-19th century. The Poet Laureate, Robert Southey, had told Charlotte Brontë that 'Literature cannot be the business of women's life and it ought not to be'.[11] The Brontës published under masculine pseudonyms, and we still know George Sand and George Eliot by theirs. And that was in Britain and France. If the works which achieved print are any guide, there were no more than four women attempting to write novels in all of colonial Australia at that time.[12] In one of the rawest of its outposts, Catherine Spence must have felt entirely alone.

She began her first novel when she was 19 and was working as a governess, but she never finished it. 'My brother's insistence on reading it every day as I wrote it' she remembered 'somehow made me see what poor stuff it was, and I did not go far with it'.[13] Eight years later, she had given up teaching, had gained some experience in journalism with occasional, anonymous contributions to the press, and had learned not to ask John Spence to comment on her fiction until the work was complete. With the encouragement of a friendly neighbour, to whom she read each chapter as she finished it, she concluded the whole novel in time to despatch it with her friend John Taylor as he set off for a holiday in England and France, asking him to submit it to Smith, Elder of London and 'to say nothing to anybody about it'.[14] While she waited to hear the fate of that manuscript she began another. The first, *Clara Morison*, was published in 1854; the second, *Tender and True*, in 1856.

That first burst was followed by another eight years later, in the mid-1860s. Her third novel, *Mr Hogarth's Will*, serialised in the *Weekly Mail* as *Uphill Work* during 1864, was published in 1865.[15] Her fourth, *Hugh Lindsay's Guest*, appeared in serial form in the *Adelaide Observer* during 1867, then as *The Author's Daughter* in 1868. She did not write any more extended fiction after that until the late 1870s, when she produced *Gathered In* in time for Emily Clark to take it on a fruitless search for an English publisher in 1878. That novel was serialised in the *Adelaide Observer* from September 1881 to March 1882; it was not published in book form until almost a century later, in 1977.[16] At the same time as she was writing that work, she must have been writing the short story 'Afloat or Ashore', published in the *Australasian* in 1878. She submitted her sixth novel, *Handfasted* for a competition run by the *Sunday Mail*, but unsuccessfully. That book was not published until 1984.[17] Her last piece of extended fiction, a long short story called 'A Week in the Future' was serialised in the *Centennial Magazine* in 1888-9, then published as a slender volume in 1889. By that time, Spence was in her 60s: her mother had died two years earlier, removing from her a major constraint on her desire to make a more direct intervention in the world of men.

It says much about her sense of vocation as a novelist, and the support she found in knowing that she participated in a cosmopolitan world of women writers, that she continued writing fiction for so long. It says much, too, about the strength of her sense of domestic responsibility and of the perils of venturing outside the domestic sphere, that she persisted in writing fiction at all. The tale of her negotiations with her publishers is a sorry one. Smith, Elder & Company refused *Clara Morison*. Their chief reader, the same William Smith Williams who had declined Charlotte Brontë's novel *The Professor*, wrote Spence a letter similar to the one he had sent Brontë saying that he thought she could do better.[18] John Taylor left the manuscript with another of Spence's Australian friends in London, William Bakewell. He wrote a preface for it and arranged its publication in two volumes, for which Spence was to receive

£40. However, the novel was too long for two volumes, so the publishers abridged it, and reduced their payment by £10 as a fee for the task.[19] Smith, Elder accepted *Tender and True*, which they brought out in two volumes; they paid Spence £20 for the copyright, so when they reissued it in one volume in 1861 the new edition brought her nothing.[20] *Mr Hogarth's Will* earned £20 from the *Weekly Mail* and £35 as a half-share in the profits from its publication in three volumes by Richard Bentley & Son.[21] Bentley also published *The Author's Daughter* in three volumes, but Spence left no record of her earnings from that book, from the serialisation of *Gathered In* or from her short stories. She asked £200 for *Gathered In* when she offered it to Bentley, and the prize for which she submitted *Handfasted* was £100 but she gained neither.[22] 'Novel writing' she remarked, 'had not been to me a lucrative occupation'. Since she had initially hoped to earn a living with her fiction, her discovery that she could gain from it only 'a coolie's wage and six printed copies of the work' must have been profoundly disheartening.[23]

So small a return, and her difficulty in finding publishers for her later novels, could be seen as reflecting on the merit of her fiction. Those of the Australian literary establishment who have recognised her historical significance – as the first woman to have written an Australian novel – have usually discussed her work in those terms.

As early as 1856, Frederick Sinnett, a discerning critic writing about *Clara Morison* in the *Journal of Australia*, approved her characterisation: 'The personages are not mere wooden figures pulled about by perceptible wires, but, with few exceptions are full of life and truth.' While disliking 'the abruptness of [the hero] Mr Reginald's literary love making', he admired the women that Spence had created. 'Female writers, like the author of *Clara Morison*', he observed, 'have an advantage in not being afflicted by the necessity, under which most male writers seem to labour, of making all their agreeable feminine characters fit to be fallen in love with by anybody at a moment's notice'. He praised the novel's realism, considering that the circumstances controlling the characters' lives 'seem to follow one another like the events of real life in a natural sequence'. But his greatest accolade was reserved for the fact that, while being Australian, the novel was also 'a work of art'. *Clara Morison*, in Sinnett's view stood

> quite alone among all Australian stories yet published, in that it is free from the defect of being a book of travels in disguise … The novel is no more Australian than results from the fact that the author, having been

long resident in Australia, having a gift for novel writing, and writing about what she knew best, unavoidably wrote an Australian novel … She has merely illustrated Australian life insensibly in the process of illustrating human life.[24]

Later critics expressed approval more temperately. H. M. Green praised her realism and observed that in her portrayal of the Lindsays in *The Author's Daughter*, 'occasionally she is more than true to life; she is vital'. In a scene that forms part of that portrait – when Jessie Lindsay proposes to George Copeland and, having been rejected, rebukes him for trying to kiss her – Green thought that Spence was 'at her height. Scott himself could scarcely have improved upon those two passages'.[25] E. Morris Miller considered that the 'natural and homely' characters of *Clara Morison* 'fit in appropriately with contemporary Australian society'.[26] John Barnes maintained that Spence was 'more of a realist – and more of an artist – than any of her contemporaries'.[27]

But even Sinnett's review leaves an overriding sense that Spence's first novel gave him great, unintended, amusement. H. G. Turner and Alexander Sutherland, writing at the end of the 19th century, considered his judgement curious and noted that few people of their own generation had ever heard of that novel.[28] Green's approval was countered by his comparison of her imagination with those of Kingsley, Clarke and Boldrewood: it 'is not so vivid or illuminating as theirs; it was within its limits constructive, but it was not a creative imagination'.[29] Miller dismissed her stories as 'slow-moving and drawn-out', her style as 'somewhat ponderous' and repetitive.[30] And Paul Despasquale, after discussing something he described as her 'obsessive opposition to romance', dismissed Spence's fiction as having no literary merit whatever.[31]

Of course, Spence suffered misgivings over weaknesses in her fiction but she did not see her failure to become a bestselling author as proceeding from her own deficiencies as much as from those of her readers. In an article on 'The Unknown Public' she remarked sharply that 'even … what are considered the educated classes … cannot be called discriminating'.[32] And she, like H. M. Green later, considered that there were peculiar difficulties in being a colonial writer. In her autobiography she expressed surprise that her books had found English publishers, and observed, 'If stories are excessively Australian they lose the sympathies of the bulk of the public. If they are mildly Australian, the work is thought to lack distinctiveness'.[33] 'I felt' she recalled, 'that though Australia was to be a great country there was no market for literary work, and the handicap of distance from the reading world was great'.[34] She tried to overcome the distance by setting long sections of *Mr Hogarth's Will* and *The Author's Daughter* in Britain, and most of *Handfasted* in an imaginary hidden valley in America. She tried to woo the colonial market by extending the sphere of society she depicted to include a peer of the realm in *The Author's Daughter,* and the station hands and a pair of dissolute and murderous gentlemen in *Gathered In*. But she refused to join those novelists whose work was to become part of the legend of the 1890s by writing an 'offensively Australian' novel.[35] She thought that 'the specialism which … has invaded fiction' meant that 'In modern novels provincialism seems to have run a little mad'.[36] She considered the dominance in Australian writing of

> the 'deadbeat' – the remittance man, the gaunt shepherd with his starving flocks and herds, the free selector on an arid patch, the drink shanty where the rouseabouts and shearers knock down their cheques, the race meeting where high and low, rich and poor, are filled with the gambler's ill luck –

as 'false in the impression they make on the outside world and on ourselves'. Better she believed, 'to see Australia steadily and see it whole'.[37]

That view, expressed in 1902, suggests why Spence's novels have met treatment at the hands of Australia's men of letters as unappreciative as their treatment by her publishers. 'Provincialism' can be found as readily in relation to the separate spheres of women and men as in geographical chauvinism. It is only because, as Simone de Beauvoir observed, men describe the world from their own point of view, which they confuse with absolute truth, that such provincialism is not recognised more often.[38] Novel-writing may have been the line of least resistance to a woman trying to make her living, but writing novels that did not depict the favoured subjects brought Spence straight up against a brick wall. When seeking a publisher in Sydney, she was assured that 'the only novels worth publishing in Australia were sporting or political novels'.[39] Those to which the critics have awarded places in the Great Tradition of Australian Fiction were, likewise, those concerned with the public sphere and predominantly masculine adventures and heroics. Read by the same people in the same way, Spence's novels could only gain, at best, negative approval. It is striking that even Sinnett's enthusiasm is chiefly for what *Clara Morison* is not, rather than for what the book does. As Susan Sheridan wrote recently:

> The masculine myth-making tradition appears to have dominated the literary scene during the colonial period. Certainly it has dominated twentieth-century critics' versions of that period, and they have obscured the fact that there was also a feminine (though not feminist) tradition within which our 'lady novelists' are by no means anomalous. This tradition had been established in Australia as early as 1854, when Catherine Helen Spence published *Clara Morison*, a novel combining social satire and domestic realism with the feminine form of romance – a tale of courtship and marriage.[40]

Read with the insights gained from scholars of the women's movement of the mid- to late-20th century, Spence's fiction appears quite different from those versions of it presented by earlier critics. Like Sheridan, Drusilla Modjeska sees her as the founder of a genre of Australian realist fiction.[41] We still await a full exploration of Spence's novels guided by those insights. In the meantime, it is possible to suggest that, rather than reading her stories to assess how far short of some masculine ideal they might fall, it is more appropriate to read them for what they do show us.

Above everything else, Spence's novels depict a world with its core in the domestic sphere. In all but two, the central characters are women, and in those two the heroes are often over-shadowed by their female counterparts. The main plot in each is 'the feminine form of romance – a tale of courtship and marriage'. The environments in which the most important parts of the action take place are domestic. The heroine of *Clara Morison*, a young Scots woman who emigrates to South Australia in about 1850, spends most of the novel in kitchens, parlours and bedrooms, so that her direct experience of colonial life is mostly enclosed by the walls within which she resides. But her story is also set in a wider context of a range of imaginative experience, deftly composed from passages of dialogue, letters, and reports brought by the visitors who move in and out of the central domestic environment.

It was probably that clear focus of attention which prompted Miles Franklin to compare Spence with Jane Austen. Spence herself drew a similar comparison when she observed that Austen's 'circle was as narrow as mine, indeed narrower … She represented well-to-do grown-up people, and them alone … The life I led had more breadth and wider interests. The life of Miss Austen's heroines, though delightful to read about, would have been deadly dull to endure.'[42] Just so, agreed Franklin, noting that Spence's circle was not only wider than Austen's but could range over 'the differential calculus, all of politics including the Mexican constitution, the current sermons, housing, the prices of commodities, the scarcity of domestic helpers and the changes of vocations for young men and women. Nothing was taboo apparently except bad language'.[43] And that included money. Another comparison with Austen which can be made was Spence's treatment of money. Ellen Moers has pointed out that 'From her earliest years, Austen had the kind of mind that inquired where the money came from on which young women were to live, and exactly how much of it there was'. Spence was neither as precise nor as witty about money as Austen, though many readers echo Clara Morison's laughter at Mrs Tubbins's newly-acquired riches in the shape of a piano on which she puts the children to bed at night, but she shared the realism which led Moers to observe: 'Marriage makes money a serious business in Austen's fiction; her seriousness about money makes marriage important'.[44] Clara Morison is eventually relieved of her burdensome struggle to win an independent livelihood by her marriage to the adequately provided pastoralist Charles Reginald. But in *The Author's Daughter* such realism has to be got out of the way if Spence is to present her moral theme clearly, so she takes pains to establish that the three masculine elements competing for dominance over her orphaned heroine – her English stepbrother; the English peer who is her suitor; and her childhood suitor, the colonial son of Scottish emigrants to Australia – are all more-than-adequately endowed financially. Such a concern in Austen, Moers considered, 'may be the first obviously feminine thing about her novels, for money and its making were characteristically female rather than male subjects in English fiction'.[45] In Spence's novels it is one of the most basic considerations in domestic life.

Spence did present direct experience of the public world in three of her novels. *Mr Hogarth's Will*, the book she had completed for serialisation in the *Weekly Mail* shortly before she left on her visit to England and Scotland, has excursions to a séance in London, an electoral meeting in rural Scotland, a discussion among scheming crooks in a public hostelry in rural South Australia, and defeat of the schemers on the streets of Melbourne. *Gathered In* takes its readers through a murder beside a deserted, water-filled mine-shaft and a public trial of an innocent hero. In *Handfasted*, the hero's wish to show the heroine a world of which she knew nothing provides a rationale for trekking tourist-fashion through a variety of different public environments in the United States and Britain. There is a vividly realised moment of feminist wish-fulfilment in *Mr Hogarth's Will*, in her portrayal of Francis Hogarth's election meeting. Young Hogarth, showing a thoroughly Spenceian refusal to pledge himself to any political party, is addressing his constituents. One of them reminds him to take care of the interests of those who have no votes, at that time a large body.

> 'Yes, a very large body indeed, when you include the women and children', said Francis.
>
> 'Oh! the women and children', said the weaver, with a disappointed air, 'I was na thinking of them; they are weel enuch – the men taks care o' them'.
>
> 'Not always the best care in the world', said Francis. 'Children need protective legislation to guard them from being overworked by parents and masters. Women are supposed to be free agents, but they do not really get all the rights of free agents – they should be empowered to protect themselves; the law should support them in obtaining their just rights. A wife ought not to be treated as a chattel; her earnings should be protected if she wishes it. And women, too, should have a wider field of labour. The difficulties which are thrown in the way of the weaker sex, in their attempts to earn a livelihood, both by law and society, are very unworthy of the age we live in'.
>
> 'Weel, Maister Hogarth, though I dinna just see the needcessity for bringing in women to compete wi' men at their trades, we could do ill without them at our mills, an' maybe ye're in the richt. Ye'll find us Whigs at Ladykirk united, and in that case ye're safe to carry the day' said Sandy Pringle.[46]

(Perhaps Sandy Pringle, like Mrs Lindsay in *The Author's Daughter* and Donald the Highland shepherd in *Gathered In,* owes something not only to Spence's childhood but also to her familiarity with and esteem for Scott.) But in all the other instances where she endeavours to depict direct experience of a kind that might find greater favour with publishers and readers, Spence's writing loses immediacy. The murder in *Gathered In* is anti-climatic, indeed almost mundane; the trial is without persuasiveness. The attempted murder in *Handfasted* does introduce some action into a story which, since it is primarily an exploration of the society established in the hidden valley in America by a lost party of Scottish emigrants and the local American Indians, relies heavily on report and discussion, but it suffers from the same deficiencies.

As Miles Franklin wisely remarked, her 'attempt to conform to taste' was 'a procedure false and usually fatal to a writer's creative ability'.[47]

Spence's fiction is strongest when she remains closest to her own experience, as she did in *Clara Morison*. In the letter accompanying the manuscript of the novel to Smith, Elder she observed:

> The domestic life represented in my tale is the sort of life I have led – the people are such as I have come in contact with – the politics are what I hear talked of – the letters from the diggings are like those I have seen – the opinions I give are what are floating about among Australian society – so that it may be considered a faithful transcript of life in the Colony.[48]

She may have emphasised the novel's documentary value to make it more attractive to publishers: 'I had an idea' she recalled, 'that, as there was so much interest in Australia and its gold, I might get £100 for the novel'.[49] But she was not making an exaggerated claim; events in the novel follow events in the colony so closely as to suggest that she wrote with copies of the *Government Gazette* and a pile of daily newspapers beside her. And the public events are, more successfully than in any of her other works, integrated into the plot so that they often form part of the conditions determining what the central characters in their domestic sphere may do.

A simple 'transcript' could well have produced a chaotic story. It does not, because Spence took great care with her plots. She believed that they 'should not be merely possible, but probable', and that cost her some effort:

> With me the main difficulty was the plot … I have heard scores of people say that they have got the good plots in their heads, and when pressed to tell them they prove to be only incidents. You need much more than an incident, or even two or three, with which to make a book. But when I found my plot the story seemed to write itself, and the actors to fit in.[50]

Her view of probability was formed from the conventions of 19th-century fiction: her plots depend on coincidences. But only in *Mr Hogarth's Will*, where the succession of discoveries about the nature of Francis's birth undermines the realism of the rest of the book, are the coincidences startlingly improbable.

The main action in each of the novels centres on the conventional story-line of popular romantic fiction, a tale of courtship and marriage. Clara Morrison and

Charles Reginald; in *Tender and True* first Robert North and Mary Lancaster, then Rose Lancaster, Miles Davenant and Edward Masefield; in *Mr Hogarth's Will*, Jane Melville and Francis Hogarth; Amy Staunton, Lord Darlington and Allan Lindsay in *The Author's Daughter*; Kenneth Oswald and Edith Gray in *Gathered In*; Liliard Abercrombie and Hugh Victor Keith in *Handfasted*: all become romantically entangled, and each entanglement results in marriage. But there are some extremely unconventional features about the difficulties placed in the way of the lovers, and sometimes about the nature of the relationships that they form, which indicate that Spence did not adopt those plot conventions unthinkingly. Rather, she seems to have engaged with them, as a realistic framework within which she could depict her characters and explore the themes which concerned her.

She drew her characters, at least partly, from people she knew. In her autobiography she said that she shrank from the idea that she was capable of 'taking off' her acquaintances. But she also confessed that Reginald in *Clara Morison* was her friend John Taylor, and that Margaret Elliot in the same novel was herself.[51] Her 'shrinking' may have had more to do with consideration for the originals of such characters in that novel as Mr and Mrs Bantam, Miss Withering, Mrs Tubbins and Mr Humberstone – all of whom are most appropriately named. Jeanne Young noted that entries in her diary 'included very precise views on men, on friends, and on associates', suggesting that Spence was a close observer[52] or rather, listener. For Spence considered that both of her sisters and her sister-in-law were 'more observant of features, dress, and manners' than she was. 'I took in more by the ear. As Sir Walter Scott says, "Speak that I may know thee". To my mind, dialogue is more important for a novel than description; and if you have a firm grasp of your characters, the dialogue will be true'.[53]

Sometimes her dialogue is more than true; it is extremely funny. Here is the new-comer, Miss Withering, talking with the South Australian-born Minnie Hodges, in what Kay Daniels has likened to 'a verbal War of Independence'.[54]

> 'It would have been a great thing for you, Miss Hodges, if you had been two or three years in a good boarding-school in England. It would have made you see things in the same light in which they appear to an Englishwoman like me'.
>
> 'And I think that a very unpleasant light', said Minnie. 'We have gone with Mrs. Bantam to see five ladies today; I have been quite happy in

these visits; would it really have been better if I had been as dissatisfied as you have been?'

You would find yourself much at a loss in English society, Miss Hodges. It is not customary for young ladies there to talk about babies cutting teeth, or the wearing out of children's shoes; or to discuss the best method of ironing and clear-starching, or what shape of pinafore sits best on the shoulder, and is most easily made'.

'What is the great end of conversation, Miss Withering? Is it not to suit what you have got to say to the tastes and capacity of the person you address? I like to please those I am with, and though you may think my subjects low and commonplace, I both gave pleasure and felt it'.

'That is a sort of truckling I could not submit to', said Miss Withering. 'I was born to rule, and cannot stoop to my inferiors. A master-mind like mine was not made "to chronicle small beer" '.[55]

Later in *Clara Morison*, a minor character, Mr Humberstone, overseer of a station owned by one Escott, is on a visit to Adelaide with a salary rise and his employer's wish that he 'pick up a wife'. After a night on the booze at a public-house dance, he returns to the household of the three Elliot sisters so early in the morning that all but the eldest, Grace, are doing the washing in the kitchen.

> Here was an opportunity for Mr Humberstone – Miss Elliot was alone, and now was the time to speak, for he really admired her very much, and he could afford to marry. After a few stammering common-places, he began to describe the home-station with great minuteness; then he diverged to tell how long he had been with Escott, and how comfortable he had always been; how he had obtained a great rise in his salary since the bad times came, and at last how there was only one thing now wanting to make him perfectly happy. Then he made a long pause, and Grace wondered what could make him so communicative.
>
> 'I am in want of a companion', said he, after much hesitation, 'in fact, a wife'.
>
> 'Indeed!' answered Grace; 'then why don't you try to find one?'

'Am I not trying all I can?' asked he, in return. 'Will you have me? I am sure you are just the woman – I beg pardon, I mean the lady – for me, and I would make you a good husband'.

'I thought everybody knew I was engaged?' said Grace, scarcely less amused than astonished.

'Engaged – whom to?' asked Humberstone, eagerly.

'To Henry Martin, who is now with my brothers at the diggings. We have been engaged for two years and a half, and I never dreamed of you not knowing it'.

'Two years and a half! Henry Martin of the Burra! Why, Bless my soul! who would have thought of such a thing? And you don't think you could like me better? I am rich enough, and would cross you in nothing, and Escott is so anxious to have a lady about the place'. Grace shook her head. 'Could you speak a good word for me to your sister?' said Humberstone. 'If I cannot have you, I should like her next best. She is not engaged to anybody, I hope'.

'Which sister do you mean, for it would be awkward if I recommended you to the wrong one?' Grace answered, with comic gravity.

'I mean your tall sister, with the clear blue eyes; the one that sang with Reginald. I think she would suit me nearly as well as yourself'.

'Well!' said Grace, almost laughing outright, 'I will mention the thing to Margaret'.

'Will you beg her to come and see me now?' quoth the impatient suitor. 'Only don't let her know that I asked you for she might not like to wear your old shoes, you understand'.[56]

Clara Morison is undoubtedly the novel in which Spence's prose most nearly has, as Kay Daniels has observed, 'a Jane Austen sparkle and economy'.[57] But the dialogue in her later novels, even without the humour, is just as telling. Listen to Robert North, from *Tender and True*, asking his wife how they managed for money while he was away, and obtaining an answer which resonates well beyond this particular exchange.

> 'What have you and the servant been living upon? Air, I suppose?'

> 'I had some money over from last week, and you know it is easy keeping house when there is no gentleman in it'.⁵⁸

Spence conveyed many of her views about the injustices that surrounded women in the societies that she depicted, through dialogue. Hear the victorious suitor of Rose Lancaster, Edward Masefield, in conversation with the man to whom her former suitor had, in haste, married his mistress.

> 'You have no right to beat her, and to expose her to such weather as this'.

> 'I have', said Evans, 'when she gives me any of her infernal temper. She must keep a quiet tongue in her head if she wants to lead a quiet life with me. But I'll have none of your interference, Mr Imperdence: you have no business to come between a man and his wife'.

> 'I have business to take her to a place of safety, in the name of her mother, whose friend I am, and the law will protect me in doing so: you know you could be brought up for this'.

> 'Tut, no', said Evans; 'people are never hard on a fellow for lifting his hand to his wife. They all know that women are very provoking. I ain't afear'd of the law'.⁶⁰

Listen, again, to the Scottish-born Mrs Lindsay. Early in *The Author's Daughter*, the heroine's father is killed in an accident. The wife of his employer does not want to take responsibility for the child, but offers to pay her neighbours, the Lindsays, to do so. Mrs Lindsay's outburst against snobbery and meanness establishes one of the most vividly-drawn of Spence's minor characters.

> But the good man will not take a penny from you for the bairn ... We keep nae boarding-school; if we did, we would not need to send our ain sae far from us. We dinna want to be paid for common Christian charity. Our bairns are no owre find to associate wi' the daughter of a gentleman that ye all thought fit to give instructions to your sons. If ye hae na the

heart to offer a home to the orphan, please God she'll find one here, and
we'll look for nae compensation at your hands.[61]

And here, by way of contrast, is another Scottish settler, from *Gathered In,* in the
midst of what he called a 'splore', talking to his nephew newly arrived from Scotland.

> 'And ye'll no taste, just to our better acquaintance. You look like a gentleman, Kenneth, and all my making. Maybe ye'll keep that look longer if ye keep clear o' the drink, and it's likely ye have na the head to stand it … D'ye ken how muckle I can put past, and as ye see, as clear a clock when all's done? Look at the dead men there!' and he pointed to an array of empty bottles. 'All brandy, ten degrees over proof; good spirits though, or it might have upset me. I give the best price, and I can depend of the best article. And as ye see, I'm as right as the Bank. Oh! Lord, I'm rich, I'm rich. Where's my cheque-book – Mick has it hid somewhere, but you'll find it. Ye'll need siller. Tell me out of hand how muckle you want'.[62]

The warmth and vigour of any one of these passages would signal Spence's ability to create character through dialogue. Even so, she was not altogether happy with her characterisation. 'Queer' she reflected in her diary, 'that I who have such a distinct idea of what I approve in flesh and blood men, should only achieve in pen and ink a set of impossible people, with an absurd muddy expression of gloom, instead of sublime depth, as I had intended'.[63] This was a problem she shared with other women writing in that period. Charlotte Brontë complained that, 'In delineating male character, I labour under disadvantages; intuition and theory will not adequately supply the place of observation and experience. When I write about women I am sure of my ground – in the other case I am not so sure'.[64] And Margaret Oliphant acknowledged that

> The men of a woman's writing are always shadowy individuals, and it is only members of our own sex that we can fully bring out, bad and good. Even George Eliot is feeble in her men, and I recognize the disadvantage under which we all work in this respect. Sometimes we don't know sufficiently to make the outline sharp and clear; sometimes we know well enough, but dare not betray our knowledge one way or other: the result is that the men in a woman's book are always washed in, in secondary colours.[65]

Whether from ignorance, or self-preservatory femininity, Spence's heroes lack the distinctiveness of her heroines, and of many of her minor characters. Even Kenneth Oswald, the central character of *Gathered In,* the novel in which, Spence believed, 'I had at last achieved my ambition to create characters that stood out distinctly and real',[66] is a sadly unrealistic assemblage of virtues. He might be, as Elaine Showalter has suggested recently of other heroes, Spence's idea of how she would be if she were a man with the greater freedom and range that masculinity confers,[67] even when limited by the stigma of Oswald's illegitimate birth. But in that case, we can only be thankful that she was a woman.

Her female characters are a different matter. Every one of her heroines is a rebel, in one way or another. Miles Franklin thought Clara Morison would still be a rebel a century later, for she 'hated crochet and despised worsted work'.[68] Cast as a conventional romantic heroine, encountering situations which, in different hands, would reduce such a figure to illness, destitution or moral ruin, Clara finds work, makes friends and defends herself competently against lechery. Indeed, she does more: through her darkest hours she sustains herself not only by reading and keeping a journal, but also by composing uplifting sermons. The tremendous presumption of such a practice, even when kept secret, may be difficult for the secular 20th century to recognise. In the 1850s, responsibility for presenting and interpreting sacred doctrine was a privilege reserved to a caste held to be spiritually superior to other beings. And it was a caste composed entirely of men. Clara's sermons represent a secret appropriation to a servant girl of the most powerful discourse available in the Paradise of Dissent. In writing them she is very like the far more overtly rebellious Margaret Elliot. Perhaps H. M. Green was right when he discerned something of Spence in both characters.[69]

Mary Lancaster (*Tender and True*), Amy Staunton (*The Author's Daughter*), and Edith Gray (*Gathered In*) are more conventional romantic heroines: beautiful, tender-hearted, charming, sometimes gracious, sometimes pliable. But even Mary Lancaster, described as 'a clinging vine', is capable of revolt against the deterioration of her marriage. Amy Staunton does a midnight flit to escape the unwelcome and morally compromising attentions of her noble suitor. Edith Gray not only manages her father's household, but spends some time combating her love for Kenneth Oswald because she wants him to re-instate his mother's purity with the world by claiming what she mistakenly believes to be his legitimate birthright.

Jane Melville (*Mr Hogarth's Will*) and Liliard Abercrombie (*Handfasted*) are far less conventional at the opening of their stories. Jane has been given an education like that of a man, and then cast into the world to make a living. Her conversation with Mr Rennie, who will not give her a job because she is a woman, is an explicit statement of outrage at a gender-divided labour market.[70] She finally secures employment as a governess-cum-housekeeper in the household of some Australians visiting their homeland, and, like Margaret Elliot, seeks to influence the wider world indirectly. Margaret hopes to work with, and through, her brother; Jane works with the male cousin whom, once he has shed his inheritance, she marries. Liliard Abercrombie was bound to be unconventional since she had grown up in an Arcadian society, separated from the rest of the world for three generations. But she is unconventional in Columba, too. She aspires to a degree of learning and public usefulness reserved for a social group to which she does not belong. She is imaginative, spontaneous, and – aided by the odd garments into which she has knitted stories she has heard told – she is an emotionally powerful public speaker, an ability of distinction in an oral culture.[71] She is also independent, insisting upon the legitimacy of the bond she forms with the hero in Columba, even when they leave that hidden valley and enter a world which regards their union as wholly unsanctified. Only after suffering her apparent loss of reputation, and a disfiguring attack of smallpox, does she dwindle into a wife.

Spence's heroines may be less unconventional than they appear at first sight. Clara Morison asks Reginald, during one of their literary discussions, 'Is not Jane Eyre, who is neither handsome nor what is called good, a much more interesting and natural character than you will find in men's books?'[72] Margaret Oliphant noted as early as 1855 that *Jane Eyre* had changed the direction of the female tradition in English writing, and Elaine Showalter observed over a century later: 'The influence of *Jane Eyre* on Victorian heroines was felt to have been revolutionary. The post-Jane heroine, according to the periodicals, was plain, rebellious, and passionate; she was likely to be a governess, and she was usually the narrator of her own story'.[73] Spence's heroines are not sexually passionate, nor do they narrate their own stories. But they are often plain, often governesses, sometimes passionate about public affairs, and always – however mildly – rebellious. Moreover they inhabit worlds in which there are other remarkable women: Margaret Elliot, a blue-stocking; Rose Lancaster, an intellectual; the independent-minded Mrs Lindsay, and her daughter, Jessie, who proposes to the man she loves on her way to do the milking. All of these characters are most unconventional when compared with Thackeray's schemers or Dickens' insipid and virtuous beauties, just as Jane Eyre was unconventional. Spence was, alone in Australia, pioneering a literary tradition that was still being formed by women writing at the same time in Britain.

All of her novels are also, and perhaps primarily, moral purpose novels. One of her reasons for writing *Clara Morison* was to combat the impression that she thought Thackeray had made when he wrote about 'an emigrant vessel taking a lot of women to Australia, as if these were all to be gentleman's wives'.[74] The 'motif' of *Tender and True* 'was the jealousy which husbands are apt to feel of their wives' relations. As if' she remarked scornfully, 'the most desirable wife was an amiable orphan – if an heiress so much the better'. Her lesson was that 'the domestic virtues which make a happy home for the husband are best fostered in a centre where brothers and sisters have to give and take; and a good daughter and sister is likely to make a good wife and mother'.[75] *Mr Hogarth's Will*, she said, 'took up the woman question as it appeared to me at the time – the difficulty of a woman earning a livelihood, even when she had as much ability, industry, and perseverance as a man'.[76] Both *The Author's Daughter* and *Gathered In* are explorations of nobility as a moral quality rather than one ascribed by social convention or wealth. *Gathered In* also depicts first the pain caused to both partners and their offspring when their relationship cannot, for social and financial reasons, be recognised by society, and second, the torment following from a hasty, infatuated marriage of virtue and vice.

Handfasted carries the argument behind *Gathered In* to a logical conclusion, portraying a society in which marriage is preceded by 'handfasting', a custom which allows to people to spend a trial period of a year and a day living together to find out if they wish to be married. Offspring of that time, if the trial results in separation, and if neither mother nor father wishes to keep them, are designated 'God's bairns' and are given more education than other children, to fit them for being the public servants of Columba's communal state. Spence may have heard of the medieval Scottish practice of handfasting from her father, since it left traces in Scottish law until the mid-19th century.[77] She had certainly read about it in Scott's novel *The Monastery*,[78] and she had used 'irregular Scottish unions' as devices in two earlier novels. But the judge of the competition for which she submitted *Handfasted* rejected the novel, fearing that 'it was calculated to loosen the marriage tie – it was too socialistic, and consequently dangerous'.[79] Such a judgement may account for the comparative conventionality of the marriages that she refers to, rather than depicts, in *A Week in the Future*, and perhaps for the lesson of her curiously abrupt short story 'Afloat or

Ashore' which insists, though without much conviction, that wives should be with their husbands, even if those men spend much of their lives on board a ship. Spence may well have concurred with the wise old grandmother who says of handfasting, at the end of that novel, 'Oh no, my dear – society is not prepared for it yet'.[80] But she would not have focussed a whole novel upon the custom had she not considered it a good one. She believed that fiction exerted a powerful influence on its readers, and that a good writer expressed 'good and noble thought'.[81]

Exploring the themes of Spence's novels, in a thesis written in 1962, Kay Daniels writes with discerning appreciation of Spence's 'clear, easy prose style which has aged little in a hundred years', of the lack of pretension in the novels, and of the values that Spence approves or satirises in her portrayal of the impact of a new way of life on the manner and ideas of groups and individuals.[82] In her first two novels, those values reflect her continuing concern with the qualities most desirable in a colonial population. In the next three, where she has expanded her characters' environments, they portray the qualities most desirable in a human being: expounding those values shows Spence at her funniest (with Miss Withering in *Clara Morison*); at her cruellest (in the introductory portrait of Mrs Oswald in *Gathered In*); and at her most earnest (in Kenneth's spiritual tribulations and Henderson's unworldly faith, again in *Gathered In*). And those values do, initially, as Daniels point out, derive directly from the protestant virtues in which she had been schooled.[83] However, when Daniels goes on to argue that, in *Handfasted* and *A Week in the Future*, the values that Spence approves align her clearly with American progressivism and the impetus that it derived from an urgent evangelicalism, she overlooks the importance of the ideas of the Enlightenment in the doctrines of the church Spence had joined, and the distance she had moved, by the late 1880s, from the Presbyterianism of her youth.[84] Similarly, Daniels argues that Spence's identity with the 'grey middle-class conformity – intelligent, Christian, progressivist' of late 19th-century South Australia, left her only one point of creative tension ('the question of the role of women'), so that her fiction shows 'no creative conflict and no deep radicalism'. But in doing so, she ignores the way in which precisely that one point of creative tension saturates Spence's fiction with a very marked radicalism[85] – though less of class than of gender.

Simply by writing novels characterised by domestic realism, Spence challenged the patriarchal dominance of Australian culture. By the privileged place she continually accorded to Scots within a predominantly English, or English-colonial, society, she fostered a nationalist subculture which can be seen as a parallel to the 'female subculture' which Elaine Sowalter discusses. In the women she portrayed, and in their struggles for self-realisation in a constraining society, she protested at their fetters. Even where she showed those women reduced – like Margaret Elliot, to living for and through her brother; like Jane Melville, to living for and through her cousin/husband; and like Liliard Abercrombie, cowed by social disapproval and disease – the discomfort and discontent that we experience in reading about their compromise reflect the subversive care with which Spence presented her juxtaposition of a conventional realistic plot with female characters who would, in a different world, not have had to compromise so grimly. In her two visionary works, *Handfasted* and *A Week in the Future*, she experimented with a literary genre which, a century later in the science fiction/future vision novels of Ursula Le Guin, Marge Piercy, Joanna Russ and Sally Gearhart, traces its descent from Charlotte Perkins Gilman's *Herland*.[86] *A Week in the Future*, a story which bears traces of the influence of Edward Bellamy's *Looking Backward* published in the same year, is a testimony to the distance Spence was setting between herself and the ideas and interest of South Australia's rulers. And *Handfasted*, for all its inchoate structure, is an inventive exploration of gender relations, written nearly 30 years earlier than Gilman's.

Had she done nothing else besides writing novels, Catherine Spence would deserve careful, appreciative attention from those students of literature who have transcended the androcentric assumptions of earlier, parochial, criticism. That she not only produced all these novels, but later moved on to tackle lines of far greater resistance in a patriarchal society, signals the calibre and intransigence of her independent mind. But her quest for self-fulfilment took a long time to overcome her submission to patriarchal convention. At the same time of the publication of *Clara Morison*, her first major achievement, she had still to resolve her struggle with her childhood's religion.

3
Faith and enlightenment

The faith in which young Catherine Spence had been nurtured was a harsh one. In the religious allegory which she wrote in the 1880s, she depicted it as a doctrine of fear.[1] She had learned that the creator 'hath foreordained whatever comes to pass', that 'our first parents being left to the freedom of their own will, fell from the estate wherein they were created, by sinning against God, and that all people, being descended from Adam, sinned in him, and fell with him in his first transgression'.[2] This crude and narrow version of Calvinism, drawn up in the 17th century expressly 'for the more rude and ignorant', puzzled and appalled her.[3] She found the deity who exacted retribution for Adam's sin, from all his posterity for all time, unjust. 'Why oh! why!' she exclaimed 'had not the sentence of death been carried out at once, and a new start made with more prudent people?' God's injustice made him 'unlovely', but 'it was wicked not to love God', so she saw in her question and judgement her own condemnation. Furthermore, if she, an outwardly virtuous person, was already damned, so too must be almost everyone in the world. Even children could not be saved. One book that had profoundly influenced her childhood told of three child pilgrims following the path of Bunyan's Christian. But the children had the added burden of an imp called 'Inbred Sin' which never left them, not even at the point where Christian's burdens had fallen away. Spence was tormented by this doctrine which, she remembered, 'made me doubt of my own salvation and despair of the salvation of any but a very small proportion of the people in the world'.[4] Yet the same doctrine which, she said, had made her 'shrink from bringing children into the world with so little chance of salvation',[5] also taught that the deity's chosen could be known by their good works, and this undoubtedly fostered the ambitions she had formed even before she reached South Australia.

The dark night of her soul lightened as she adapted to colonial life and began to feel more self-sufficient. The Spences had immigrated to a colony which held religious liberty as one of its founding principles. During the early years of settlement, as Douglas Pike observed in the study he entitled *Paradise of Dissent*, the 'presence ... of so many ministers and preachers and so varied a swarm of sects, most of them with places of worship, created a record surpassing that of New England's first decade'.[6] Debate over government funding for church or chapel building, for salaries for ministers, and for religious instruction in schools, resounded in the columns of the South Australian press during the 1840s and 1850s.[7] And the 1840s saw South Australian Presbyterians cautiously arguing the issues which in Scotland led the Free Church to break away from the Establishment.[8] Yet, despite sectarian squabbling, rival claimants for the colonists' souls were often able to co-operate. The Anglican minister could offer his church to the Scottish Reverend Robert Haining for the colony's first service for adherents to the Established Church of Scotland.[9] In such an environment, the teachings of any one faith could seem more a question of individual choice than of divine truth. Spence began to doubt herself less and the faith of her childhood more. In 1850, when she was 25, she told Haining that she would not take communion any longer because she was not 'a converted Christian'. Her announcement surprised the minister less than her continued attendance at church after making it. She had probably not lost her faith completely, and she may have needed the social security of belonging to a congregation. But with her faith suspended, her ambition triumphed over her doubts of her worthiness. In August 1854, John Taylor brought her £30 and the assurance that her first novel was to be published.[10]

Soon afterwards, at a ball, Caroline Emily Clark sought an introduction to Miss Spence because an uncle in England had written to her 'that "Clara Morison", the new novel, was a capital story of South Australian life'. She was the first stranger to acknowledge Spence's achievement; she won her lasting gratitude – for that, and for the community into which she introduced her. Spence admired Emily Clark and her literary brother, Howard, and warmed to their mother who was, she thought, like her own 'in her sound judgment, accurate observations, and kind heart'.[11]

Caroline Clark was sister to the five Hill brothers who won renown in England as social and educational reformers. Rowland Hill was already known as the founder of penny postage; Matthew Davenport Hill had been a member of the House of Commons and was Recorder of Birmingham.[12] Caroline, with her husband Francis, their five sons and three daughters, had left the English winters for South Australia in 1850.[13] Francis Clark established himself and his sons as a mercantile and accounting firm in Adelaide,[14] and in 1853 bought a house and property which he called Hazelwood Park near the foot of the Adelaide hills.[15] After his death in the same year, his sons continued the firm; Emily, the eldest daughter, remained at Hazelwood with her mother. In 1858 Howard took his first bride to live in Hazelwood Cottage, within sight of his mother's house.[16] Howard was rapidly becoming known as a literary critic and composer of occasional verse. Hazelwood became a centre of cultured and entertaining hospitality for the large family circle and their friends, Spence among them. Spence enjoyed the Clarks' company: they all had, she considered, 'great ability and intelligence'.[17]

At about the same time Spence probably saw much of another man of 'fine literary tastes'. William John Wren was courting her younger sister Mary. When they were married in 1855, he confirmed Spence's opinion of him by making his first present to his new bride, copies of the poems of Elizabeth and Robert Browning.[18]

Both Wren and the Clarks were Unitarians. Spence's admiration for the intellectual cultivation of her new friends, coupled with the doubt and unhappiness over the faith in which she had been taught, made her curious about the new Unitarian congregation in Adelaide and their beliefs. The Clarks, and Howard Clark's future father-in-law, E. M. Martin, all members of a Unitarian congregation in Birmingham before immigrating to South Australia,[19] had founded the Unitarian Christian Church in Adelaide at a meeting at the offices of Francis Clark & Sons in 1854. By September 1855 they had secured a minister, an Irishman called John Crawford Woods, who conducted their first publicly advertised service in Green's Land Exchange on 7 October 1855. It was attended by 'a respectable and deeply attentive congregation of 200 persons', some undoubtedly concerned to find out about a doctrine which many contemporaries considered close to heresy.[20] Unitarianism, which had developed out of the work of the Enlightenment scholars on the early texts of the scriptures, maintained that there was no biblical authority for the concept of the trinity. Throughout the 19th century Unitarians debated claims for and against the divinity of Jesus. In Britain, such beliefs were so ungodly that Unitarians did not gain freedom of worship, legally, until 1813, and effectively until 1844, when they were granted the right to 'hold chapels'.[21] But even state sanction did not prevent worshippers in other communions regarding Unitarians as heretical. Spence was led to hear what the Reverend Woods had to say for the faith, and instead of being deterred, she was impressed. She told Haining that for three months she would listen to him preach each Sunday morning, to Woods each Sunday evening, and read nothing but the bible as a guide.[22]

From May to December 1856, Woods devoted one Sunday evening a month to a discourse on the fundamental tenets of Unitarian teaching.[23] He was, among Unitarians, doctrinally conservative: he lectured on 'Jesus Christ, the Son of God, not God the Son', but not – as some of his more radical contemporaries in Britain and the United States might have done – on Christ as no more than a man.[24] That undoubtedly suited his congregation; they had voted against a motion that the word 'Christian' be dropped from the name of their church.[25] More important, to Spence, was all that Unitarianism had derived from the rationalism and faith in scientific discovery of the Enlightenment. Its deity was not the interruptive and oppressive providence of the Church of Scotland's shorter catechism, but rather an embodiment of justice and benevolence. Christians believe, said Woods, 'that God is not like a man with a liability to change his mind and repent of what He had done, with personal favourites and personal foes … but that He is infinitely wise and infinitely good, a God of love'. For Unitarians, merit consisted in striving to live in accordance with the creator's laws, and they were, Woods explained, the laws of nature. People should follow the laws of health in the same way as the laws of morality. Intelligence should seek fuller understanding of those laws, unhampered by restricted reading and unrestrained by deference to any authority – even the bible. The chief guides to salvation were reason and knowledge.[26] It is not difficult to understand the appeal of such teaching to a mind tormented by the vengeful, irrational, authoritarian deity with which Catherine Spence had grown up.

At the end of the three months that she had allotted herself, she decided: 'I became a convinced Unitarian, and the cloud was lifted from the universe'.[27] The doctrine that Woods preached brought her to her 'first clear vision' of a benevolent deity and a perfectible humanity. Many years later, she told Woods's third wife:

> No one owes more to your dear husband than I do. The dark pall which enveloped heaven and earth was lifted; the confused conscience was made

clear and straight; the rebellious heart was made submissive and contented under his ministrations. I have been a very cheerful person ever since, more comfortable to my friends, and more serviceable to the world.[28]

Spence's conversion, a decision which she probably reached in 1856,[29] in her 31st year, ranks second in her formation only to her decision not to marry. From Unitarianism she learned to regard the Calvinist doctrine of innate depravity as 'one of the most paralysing dogmas that human fear invented or priestcraft encouraged'.[30] In its place, her new faith offered her a deity that was an omniscient creator of marvels that were slowly unfolding to the inquiring human intellect, a benevolent teacher whose lessons the rationalist scientific expansion of knowledge was beginning to reveal.

> When we think of thirty millions of suns with worlds revolving round them which is far as modern astronomy has reached – when the six days of creation are infinitely extended – and when we think of all things *becoming* rather than existing – when we turn from the infinitely great to the infinitely small and distinguish and divide and subdivide the infinitesimal atom into even more infinitesimal atoms, the most recent discovery – and when we see that one great spirit is in all, and through all, as well as above all, we stagger at the greatness of the thought of God.[31]

By the time she wrote that, Spence had been a mainstay of the Unitarian congregation for about 20 years. The joy and wonderment that she expressed, even after so long, shows how liberating she had found Unitarian doctrine, and how important it had been to her own development. Adelaide's Unitarian Christian Church introduced her not only to the rationalism of the Enlightenment, but also to, as she noted, 'a number of interesting and clever people'[32] whose company and conversation could not but have confirmed and encouraged her own hunger for learning.

Woods also taught that Unitarians 'think there is something better for a man to be, than in the condition of concern merely for his own personal salvation'. Better he argued, to 'catch … the spirit which has been called the Enthusiasm of Humanity … which is no less a spirit of unselfish loyalty to God'.[33] Such teaching in Britain in the 19th century inspired a host of philanthropic and social intervention activities designed to combat Old Corruption, address immediate disruptions, and regulate the whole social order. Mary Carpenter's campaign for reformatory schools for children convicted of crime in the 1850s and 1860s, Rosamond Davenport Hill's work on the

Catherine Helen Spence.
With kind permission of Mrs Marjorie Caw, 1970.

Faith and enlightenment

London School Board in the 1880s and 1890s, Octavia Hill's rent-collecting and Beatrice Webb's work for Booth's survey of the London poor, furnish only four of many possible examples.[34] But in South Australia, a colony founded with the express intention of implementing social and political measures thought unachievable in Britain, the Unitarians' collective zeal for change was less marked. As Spence observed in 1897, 'In my long membership with this church I do not recall any effort outside of itself'.[35] Nevertheless, as members of a minority faith – Unitarians were never more than 1 per cent of South Australia's population during the 19th century – the Adelaide congregation was concerned with the spread of religious toleration. They aimed at 'the removal of prejudices and the creation of a spirit of enquiry which … must in the end be beneficial to the cause of liberal Christianity'.[36] The readiest means available to them was that expressly urged upon them from their pulpit – education.

Unitarian Christian Church, Wakefield Street, Adelaide.
Image courtesy of the State Library of South Australia SLSA: B27777.

Many of them belonged to the few large families which, by intermarrying extensively, bound the congregation together with ties of kinship and established a common culture among them. Family gatherings at Hazelwood to perform home-made burlesques set the pattern for social gatherings in the Unitarian Church Hall.[37] And several members of the congregation were also engaged, according to their lights, in a variety of educational enterprises outside their own community.

John Baker, one of the church's 12 founders, and an elected member of South Australia's first and second partly elected Legislative Councils, would probably have liked to make education universally compulsory. In debates on the Constitution for South Australia, to come into force with self-government in 1857, he sought to disenfranchise the uneducated. In his speech after laying the foundation stone of the Unitarian Christian Church in Wakefield Street in 1857, he berated parents who put their children to work instead of sending them to school, ignoring the financial necessities of labouring families and asserting that 'In this colony, where every man can educate his children, there can be no excuse for the prevalence of ignorance'.[38]

Arthur Hardy, another of the church's founders, erected and presided over a mechanics institute in the village next to his house and property at Glen Osmond, aiming to keep his quarry workers out of the public house in the evenings and to enhance their education.[39] Three other Unitarians were closely associated with the South Australian Institute which for many years sustained the reputation of being one of the principal education factors in the colony.[40] The most active of them, John Howard Clark, also taught and examined students at J.L. Young's Adelaide Educational Institution, wrote book reviews, literary articles and comic verses for the *Register*, and from 1870 to 1878 was its editor. He joined the South Australian Society of Arts, and he chaired the meeting which formed the Adelaide Philosophical Society (later the Royal Society of South Australia), becoming the first secretary of that would-be august body.[41] His activities offered a Unitarian example to South Australian society.

However, the Unitarians were educators and disseminators of culture not only because they were themselves well educated, and not only because such activity conformed to their church's teaching; they also had the time and financial resources to devote to such aims. A few of the congregation were leading colonists. The Bakers, the Everards, the Hardys and the Martins conformed to Wakefield's ideal of the gentleman immigrant who invested in land. They were early colonists, a source of prestige in Adelaide.[42] Arthur Hardy and John Baker were not merely members, but office-bearers, in the exclusive Adelaide Club. Furthermore, as David Hilliard has pointed out, some of the more prominent politicians among them (John Baker, for instance, and Sir William Morgan) also established close links with Anglican churches.[43] Most of the church members were engaged in businesses – ranging from hairdressing and photographic artistry, through wholesale grocery and ironmongery, to the management of mining companies from city offices.[44] And they prospered: the Simpson family's rapid rise from a small safe and bedstead manufacturing business to wealth and social prominence offered a Wakefieldian example to their fellow worshippers.[45] These men may not have been members of the Adelaide Racing Club, the Adelaide Hunt Club or the tennis, yachting and cricketing clubs which the more muscular wealthy established for their diversion, but they were office-holders in such bodies as the Municipal Corporation of Adelaide, the Chamber of Commerce and the South Australian Horticultural and Floricultural Society.[46] These organisations contributed quite as much, if more formally, to the solidity with which bourgeois hegemony was established in South Australia. Members of a minority sect they might have been, but they had vested interests in maintaining the freedom, not only of worship, but also of financial enterprise which they had gained in a new society. Woods's 'Enthusiasm of Humanity' could be exercised very comfortably in Adelaide.

For the women of the congregation, Woods's teaching could simply have blended into the dominant conventions determining what women might and might not do, held by church and dissenting communions alike. As Margaretta Grieg reflected in England in the mid-19th century: 'A lady, to be such, must be a mere lady, and nothing else. She must not work for profit, or engage in any occupation that money can command …'. And Sarah Ellis, exhorting the Daughters of England in 1842, announced that, 'As women, then, the first thing of importance is to be content to be inferior to men – inferior in mental power, in the same proportion as you are inferior in bodily strength.'[47] Unitarian women in Adelaide often did conform to such a view. They taught in their church's Sunday School, supported the Female Refuge, and raised funds for the Adelaide Children's Hospital.[48] Emily Clark and Catherine Spence gave 20 years of voluntary work to a scheme designed to benefit destitute children. But some women from this congregation also did more, denying the patriarchal conventions with which such exponents as Ellis threatened their claim to bourgeois respectability. In the later decades of the 19th century, Annie Martin established and ran a school which gained a reputation for enlightened and progressive teaching.[49] The Misses Kay also founded a school,[50] and Edith Cook (later Hübbe) became headmistress of South Australia's government-funded Advanced School for Girls.[51] Enlightenment thought depicted differences between women and men as the product of social circumstance, not of innate or 'natural' constitution;[52] the elements of Enlightenment rationalism in the 19th-century Unitarian congregation in Adelaide, for all its respectability, offered to women a less constrained social environment than they were likely to have encountered in any other community.

Spence was able to proclaim: 'I did not enter into my human responsibility to God and man until my eyes were opened by the preaching of Unitarian faith by Mr Woods – and instead of feeling it was a burden it was a light a peace a joy'.[53] She saw no conflict between her 'human responsibility' and her personal ambition. She argued that well-balanced people made a 'sort of instinctive compromise' between altruism, and 'egoism' – which she defined as a 'reasonable regard for our own control'.[54] In her religious allegory she depicted a pilgrimage like Bunyan's. She allowed her pilgrim a respite in the halls of learning, to be taught the importance of specialist knowledge in combating superstition and ignorance. But she made him move on, too, because his mission was 'to teach and work in the world … not to study in schools'.[55] It was a statement of her own spiritual change, and one to which, 20 years after she first went to listen to Woods, the Unitarians contributed a second inspiration.

This was a woman preacher. From 1873 to 1875, while Woods and his wife were on holiday in England, the services in the Unitarian Christian Church in Wakefield Street were taken by C. L. Whitham, later an inspector in the South Australian Education Department.[56] During that time Whitham arranged to exchange pulpits with the Melbourne Unitarian Church for three weeks. The preacher who appeared in his place was Melbourne's new Unitarian pastor, Martha Turner. Born in 1839 and educated at a secondary school in Dijon in France, Martha Turner came to Australia in 1870 to visit her brother, Henry Gyles Turner, by then a prominent figure in Melbourne banking and commerce, and a founding member of the Melbourne Unitarian Church. When the previous pastor died in 1870, the congregation was unable to secure another minister, so it resorted to a system of regular lay preachers, one of whom was H. G. Turner. The sermons he read were often composed by his sister, so, on occasions when he was indisposed, she read her own compositions. Thus, through what she called 'the mere force of circumstances', Martha Turner became the recognised pastor of the church, the first woman to become minister of a church in Australia. She was licensed to solemnise marriages and to consecrate children. She had, her brother noted, a 'special aversion, to the ordinary pastoral supervision of a flock'. But in the pulpit, Emily Clark's cousins observed:

> Miss Turner's quiet and deeply reverent demeanor, her sweet voice and her excellent delivery are favourable to the satisfactory discharge of her solemn office while she seemed also to possess the intellectual and spiritual gifts still more essential to success.[57]

It is not difficult to imagine her impact upon the novelist, who, 20 years earlier, had depicted her heroine drawing solace against the difficulties and powerlessness of her position by composing sermons in her journal.

Spence was electrified. She was, she recalled, 'thrilled by her exquisite voice, by her earnestness, and by her reverence'. She was not shocked. She said that George Eliot's description of Dinah Morris preaching in *Adam Bede* had prepared her. But, she exclaimed:

> When I heard a highly intelligent and exceptionally able woman conducting the services all through, and especially reading the Scriptures of the Old and New Testaments with so much intelligence that they seemed to take on new meaning, I felt how much the world had been losing for so many centuries.[58]

She was able to hear Martha Turner again, when Woods exchanged pulpits with Melbourne. But in 1878, Turner married a banker called John Webster and tendered her resignation to the church. As Dorothy Scott noted, 'In Victorian society it was unusual for a single woman of the middle class to pursue a career, except that of a governess. For a married middle-class woman to be paid a salary for working was extremely rare'. Nevertheless, her congregation unanimously urged her to continue her work until they could find a replacement, so she did this until 1883. Perhaps her position disturbed her less than it did her extremely conservative brother; the *Woman Voter* described her, in an obituary early in the 20th century, as 'reserved, and simple, conceding little to fashion and conventions of the time. She like "quiet loafing" … was a good conversationalist, decidedly humorous and sarcastic yet withal kindly'.[59] Spence must have relished opportunities to listen to her, both in Adelaide and more often later in her life when she went to Melbourne herself. By then she, too, had become and eloquent preacher.

Spence did not seek this distinction but she did seize the opportunity when it was presented to her. One day in 1878, Woods was ill, and there was no layman available to take the service. Spence had, some seven years earlier, given two lectures to the South Australian Institute, so the congregation knew that she was capable of speaking in at least a semi-public forum. Some of its members suggested that Miss Spence might step into the breach by reading one of James Martineau's sermons. She complied, and followed that up by offering to preach a sermon of her own. On 24 November 1878 she preached an original sermon in the Wakefield Street pulpit for the first time. A dream fulfilled? Spence's own account would suggest a happy circumstance rather than an aspiration realised. But it is difficult to forget Clara Morison scribbling in her journal. Spence knew the power attached to the pulpit in her society; she could not have been unaware of the symbolic power, both for herself and for that society, of her presence – a woman's – in it. Once started she never looked back. In her autobiography she reported, 'I suppose I have preached more than a hundred times in my life, mostly in the Wakefield Street pulpit; but in Melbourne and Sydney I am always asked for help; and when I went to America in 1893-94 I was offered seven pulpits'.[60]

Preaching gave her great pleasure. She recalled, 'The preparation of my sermons ... has always been a joy and a delight to me, for I prefer that my subjects as well as their treatment shall be as humanly helpful as it is possible to make them'. They enabled her to make use of the wide knowledge of scripture which Miss Phinn had commended. She could express in them the ideas she drew from her wide reading. She preached on the parallels between different branches of Buddhism and the congregational and hierarchical Christian churches, on Luther, on Milton's unjust concept of God in *Paradise Lost*, and on Tolstoy as a prophet. She could exhort the congregation to pursue each new reform that caught her attention. She preached on the merits of the work of William Booth and the Salvation Army, and on child welfare in Britain. She could expound her own views on the best attitudes and virtues to be developed: she preached recognition that Jews – who were, she announced with unquestioning prejudice, all capitalists – were also a pro-liberal influence in politics because they had always been oppressed; she preached that 'Experience is an education and not a snare'; she preached that 'meliorism', rather than optimism or pessimism, was the attitude that would assist human progress most. Moreover, in Unitarian congregations, she could expect a sympathetic hearing when she protested against traditions that repressed individuality, and argued that 'acquiescent and submissive mediocrity is too often the attitude of good women'.[61]

Spence may have learned a more secular approach to her faith from Martha Turner, for although she was critical of the new humanist depiction of Jesus arising in Unitarian discussions, Turner was maintaining that 'God speaks by the voice of science today as he spoke by the prophets of old, and it has given us the gospel of natural law, of cause and consequence, of evolution … and upon these foundations we have to build the temple of the spirit'.[62] Apart from her excursion into astronomy and atomic physics, Spence did not follow Turner into a terrain still throbbing from the impact of Darwin and his followers upon the churches. But, unlike Turner, she did come to believe that 'Jesus Christ was not to us an incarnate God, but a more or less godlike man',[63] doctrine which showed how far her views had slowly diverged from those of Woods. When she wrote expressing her sympathy to Woods's widow on his death in 1906, she observed, 'my faith has undergone some modifications – for we cannot stand still'.[64] In the early 1880s she had written a religious allegory which simultaneously marked the conclusion of her spiritual journey away from the infant pilgrims burdened with 'Inbred Sin' which had terrified her childhood, and demonstrated her seizure of the independence of mind so strongly endorsed by the church she had joined. She said she wrote *An Agnostic's Progress from the Known to the Unknown*

> to satisfy myself that reverent agnostics were by no means materialists; that man's nature might or might not be consciously immortal, but it was spiritual; that in the duties which lay before each of us towards ourselves and towards our fellow-creatures, there was scope for spiritual energy and spiritual emotion.[65]

Such a spiritual exploration carried her far beyond the teachers of her youth, into an arena in which most men trod warily.[66] Writing it was an act of great courage; finding a public for it, an even greater one.

Towards the end of her life, the church's founding fathers may well have regarded Spence's preaching with some qualms. Certainly, she could draw a large congregation to the Wakefield Street church to hear her deliver a stinging tirade against monopolisers and 'greedy men' who appropriate 'the victory and the spoils of political life', or to expound the 'great wave of socialism which has invaded all the churches'.[67] A journalist from the weekly paper of opinion and satire, *Quiz and the Lantern*, went one Sunday evening in 1895 to hear her preach on 'The Democratic Ideal'. The church was well filled, he observed, and the congregation included 'men who belong to no religious party or sect, but men who have been actively associated with Democratic movements, and who were anxious to hear what Miss Spence had to say'. They impressed him: 'Earnest faces they were too; faces which had grown lined puzzling over the problem of existence. And throughout the entire service there was manifest a rapt attention'. With them, he watched Spence climb the steps to the high pulpit, giving a glimpse 'of a somewhat stout, rather bent form, the movements of which were indicative of suppressed energy': a grey head 'crowned by a black bonnet, which was fastened under the chin by black ribbons', and 'a dress with no pretensions to fashionable cut'. When she stood up to announce the opening hymn, he observed a 'rounded face, somewhat white of complexion and little marked by the usual disastrous effects of age', and blue eyes, he said, which 'flashed through the spectacles'. He liked the slight Scots accent of her clear, firm voice, and her unselfconsciousness: 'the whole tone is that of a cultured woman'. He even felt slightly shamed by her 'vigorous incisive' attack on the growth of monopoly and luxury in the United States, and her appeal against any social organization which left some people in poverty. 'Truly', he concluded, 'all who were present must have gone away impressed with the idea that Miss Spence is one of the most remarkable women of the day'.[68] But none of the regular congregation publicly identified themselves with the causes which, by then, she represented. The founding fathers may well have agreed with Woods when he grumbled: 'The discourse was more political than I like in a place of worship and I object more because I think her politics bad'.[69] Nevertheless, their daughters were still rallying to the Girls' Literary Association over which she presided,[70] and learning a great deal of independence of mind from the example of Miss Spence.

4
Edging out of the domestic sphere

If the Unitarians of South Australia were not generally active in promoting social change, those in England were.[1] Catherine Spence met a number of them during her year in Britain in 1865-66. Furnished with introductions from Emily Clark, and preceded by her reputation as the author of *Clara Morison* and a political pamphlet, she was welcomed into the circles of Emily Clark's cousins, Florence and Rosamund Davenport Hill, and those of her uncles Rowland Hill and Matthew Davenport Hill.

Matthew Davenport Hill joined Mary Carpenter in the campaign for changes in the punishment of juvenile delinquents and the establishment of reformatories in the 1850s.[2] The Davenport Hill sisters were at work on a book about ways of caring for destitute children: Florence was to read a paper about boarding out children from workhouses at a meeting of the National Association for the Promotion of Social Science in 1869, and Rosamund was to become a member of the London School Board ten years later.[3] They introduced Spence to the gentlemanly Frances Power Cobbe who, having subjected her generous Anglo-Irish warmth to a chilling stint as a teacher in Mary Carpenter's reformatory for girls in the 1850s, had moved on to philanthropic action over the care and education of pauper children, and to struggle in the campaign for female suffrage. Her *Essays on the Pursuits of Women* had appeared in 1864.[4] At Rowland Hill's house, Spence met the golden-haired philanthropist, feminist and artist Barbara Leigh Smith, on whom George Eliot modelled the character of Romola. She was already justly famous for *A Brief Summary in Plain Language of the Most Important Laws concerning Women*, a pamphlet which had drawn attention to injustices so startling that it engendered the campaigns which finally bore fruit in the *Married Women's Property Acts* of the 1870s and 1880s. Her wide-ranging philanthropic activities included the sanitarian measure, as she told Spence, of introducing thick plantations of the Australian eucalypt into malaria-ridden Algeria, where she spent the winters with her husband Eugene Bodichon.[5]

Philanthropy was clearly offering women a gateway out of the domestic sphere and into the edges, at least, of the public world by the middle of the 19th century in Britain.[6] Spence was impressed, perhaps envious. She wished that Adelaide could offer some equivalent of Madame Bodichon's salon and its 'very clever men and women'. It may be, she observed, that 'society girls and society gentlemen … despise … active philanthropists as being ill-dressed, strong-minded, and most fatiguing'. But 'if anything could tempt me to remain in England, it is that I, too, might aid a little in [their] work'. On her way back to Australia she wrote a sonnet which is almost indecipherable, rejoicing in the friendships she had formed with 'that band of thoughtful men and women who would raise the level of life – the wise the brave and the true'.[7] How glad she must have been to find the cause which brought Emily Clark hastening to meet her ship when it docked: boarding out the destitute children of South Australia.

Attitudes to the pre-history of western welfare states have varied considerably during the later decades of the 20th century. Some historians have accepted the view held by the philanthropic groups, voluntary welfare workers and paid government officials of the 19th century: that theirs was a period of extensive social reform. Such historians depict an accumulation of haphazard humanitarian responses to deprivation, immorality or godlessness slowly engendering a regulated, state-funded provision of social services. Spence's book, *State Children in Adelaide: a History of Boarding Out and its Development*, written towards the end of her life, in 1907, is one such account, understandably, as she had participated in some of the work it describes. Revisionist examination of the practices and efforts which did not conform to the reformers' claims have added detail and complexity to such accounts, but they have not questioned the point of view from which the first stories were told.

Some other historians, however, have considered the same developments from the point of view of the people who were the objects of the philanthropists' and government officials' concern. They have presented quite different accounts: of 'reform' as the extension of class domination and state regulation of private lives. Elizabeth Windschuttle, for instance, has argued that the philanthropic activities of the women of Sydney's ruling-class circles during the first half of the 19th century constituted an attack on the culture of the people they sheltered.[8] Margaret Barbalet, in an absorbing study of some of the children to whom Emily Clark and Catherine Spence directed attention in South Australia in the 1870s and 1880s, has contended that Clark and Spence spoke with 'the voice of an elite; the correctional voice of a small group who wanted to rid their society of a threatening growth' – pauperism.[9] Kay Daniels, too, in an article which anticipated Barbalet's argument, has maintained that in the boarding out system which Clark and Spence endeavoured to establish, 'the emphasis was placed on getting rid of poverty by *consolidating a viable family unit* among the respectable poor and *dispersing the family* in the residuum'.[10] It was a means of dividing the working class and getting rid of its disreputable elements. Daniels has pressed this point further. Assuming that women stood at the centre of domestic groups in all classes, she argues that a system which involved judgments about the respectability of the households of the poor provided a means of imposing 'middle class discipline particularly on the women of the lower classes'. Accordingly, Spence was participating not only in the extension of bourgeois state regulation of the domestic lives of the proletariat, but also, Daniels contends in creating new patriarchal structures in colonial society'. It is a convincing argument. And there can be no quarrel with the position in which Barbalet and Daniels locate Clark and Spence in the class structure of South Australian society.

Yet perhaps both kinds of attitude to the pre-history of welfare states are too simple. Both present a reductionist view of the state as either alleviating the condition of the poor or contributing to their oppression, whereas it can be shown to embody both as contradictory tendencies interacting with each other.[11] Why else do welfare recipients of the 1980s complain at having to undergo degrading procedures to obtain welfare allowances? Why else do the same welfare recipients take to the streets in protest against reductions in those allowances? Both views also assume that welfare states operate in similar ways in relation to women and to men, or as in Daniels's argument, that particular kinds of class discipline supplement patriarchal discipline to increase the oppression specifically of working-class women. But recent analysis of 20th-century welfare states have shown not only instances in which certain measures have done this, but also instances in which particular welfare provisions have assisted women's independence of men. Child endowment furnishes only one example.[12] Further, views such as Daniels's derive from analyses of welfare states that were more developed than the state was in South Australia in the 1870s and 1880s. It is probably more fruitful, and more accurate, to consider the state in that period of the colony's history as a site of struggle – responsive, within the limitations imposed by a capitalist economy and a patriarchal gender order, to pressure. Besides, there are discrepancies between the events in which Clark and Spence were involved and the account which Spence gave of them in her book *State Children in Adelaide*.[13] This should prompt us to ask questions about Spence's perception of the constraints and opportunities which Emily Clark's project offered, and what she did with them. Spence's introduction to philanthropic work coincided with her introduction to women deliberately trespassing into the world of men, along a line of rather more resistance than novel writing. If we consider the work that she did in this field, and the ways in which she wrote about it, we may find that there are more than two ways to tell this story.

Paradoxically, the systematic colonisers' attempts to found a society in which the economy, religion, education, even poor relief, would operate freely, unhampered and unassisted by government, engendered instead a society in which primary responsibility for poor relief became centralised in a department of the colonial government. No doubt this irony owed something to the high degree of centralisation of South Australia's financially and politically powerful in Adelaide. Clearly it owed much to traditions established in the early days of settlement, when colonists clung so fiercely to the foundations of the fortunes they were making from land speculation, that Gawler was unable to raise the subscriptions necessary to build an infirmary. His successor, Grey, found it necessary to allocate funds from the general revenue for minimal provision for the destitute, lest they starve. And Grey's successor Robe, felt compelled to make grants-in-aid to religion and education.[14] The government agencies established to administer such funds – the Destitute Board, for instance, and the Education Board – were, in accordance with the founders' voluntaryist principles, voluntary bodies, even though they were appointed by government. Their members gave their services gratuitously so they were not open to the charges of indifference, place-seeking or corruption that voluntaryists might level at paid government officers.[15] Further, those boards were administering funds from the general revenue. Until late in the 19th century, that came largely from indirect taxation and land-sales, so the major profit-makers undoubtedly considered that they were contributing quite enough to general welfare without endowing large charities or schools for the poor.[16]

Provision for the destitute was not a question which attracted widespread discussion in respectable Adelaide. Concern to mitigate the plight of the impoverished in Britain had played a part in the systematic colonisers' plans, but their theories designed a society in which emigrant paupers would become self-sufficient.[17] When Spence wrote *State Children in Adelaide*, her story assumed a government commitment to poor-relief in the early days of settlement. She was mistaken; government action had been nothing more than a grudging response to desperation. She also confused two government bodies.[18] Official decision to provide systematically for the destitute had to wait until 1849, when Young's administration gazetted a board for the relief of the Destitute Poor to administer what aid the government was prepared to provide. The Board appointed a salaried relieving officer to inquire into cases of distress and act as its secretary.[19] Subsequently, it persuaded Young to allocate funds to build an asylum for the destitute poor.[20] That was erected on Kintore Avenue – gruesomely, next to the Morgue – with an orphan free school attached. In 1873, Emily Clark's visiting English cousins, the Davenport Hill sisters, described it as 'cheerful … though not ornate in style … handsome and somewhat too inviting in aspect, giving to the beholder an impression that a very comfortable life may be led inside.'[21] Their view encapsulated the attitude held widely and firmly among the aspiring urban gentry of Britain, that poverty was the result of individual moral turpitude rather than any deficiencies in the operation of a capitalist economy; destitution should be treated punitively, to discourage such moral failure. It is a view not unfamiliar to many Australians in the 1980s; it was the view held by most members of successive governments of South Australia in the 19th century. In 1863, the government passed an Act to regulate the asylum, leaving most of the regulations to be drawn up by the Destitute Board. They were gazetted in April 1864, and they compelled cleanliness, industry, sobriety and Godliness, and prohibited visitors and jaunts out of the asylum.[22] Governments seem, then, to have left the Asylum to look after itself.

In February 1866, a parliamentarian told the House of Assembly that he had received accounts of brutal treatment of inmates of the Destitute Asylum by the resident relieving officer who 'was reported to be very addicted to intemperance'. Arthur Blyth raised a laugh by declaring that any government officer found 'disguised in drink' would be dismissed, but he also promised to make inquiries about the Destitute Asylum.[23] These showed that almost half the inmates were children, and that their numbers were increasing. Blyth's government resolved to build an extension to the Asylum to house the children.[24] That resolution provided Emily Clark with an opportunity for action.

Clark had just read Frances Power Cobbe's *The Philosophy of the Poor-Laws*. It was a fierce attack on the report of a parliamentary committee of inquiry into poor relief in Britain, made in 1861. The two points which impressed Clark most strongly were about pauper children, and they formed the policy and program of her campaign in South Australia. The first was the assertion that:

> As a matter of right, no child ought to bear the stigma of pauperism; as a matter of public interest for the future of the community, every dependent child ought to be separated and removed as far as by any means may be possible from pauper moral influences and pauper physical and social degradation.

The second was the suggestion about one way of effecting such a removal:

> to send the children out first to be nursed, and then boarded, by respectable poor families, under proper inspection. As they reach the age of going to school, the persons who have charge of the children being obliged to send them to one in the neighbourhood chosen by the inspector, and to produce certificates from the teacher of the child's attendance.[25]

Boarding out pauper children, usually with an allowance paid to families taking them, was a practice favoured by an increasing number of boards of poor-law guardians in England during the 1860s. Cobbe's article in 1864, like the Davenport Hills' book in 1868, belonged to a rising tide of publications advocating the boarding-out system.[26] Emily Clark introduced their ideas to Australia.

In March 1866 she wrote to both the *Register* and the *Observer*, referring to Cobbe's article and arguing that the money for extensions to the Destitute Asylum would be better spent on boarding the children 'among our healthy and industrious population instead of fostering them in the hot bed of their own moral disease'. In March she was primarily concerned that the children be removed from the Asylum: if they could not be boarded out, they should at least be taken to live in the country 'removed from sight and sound of evil among their elders'. By September she had decided that this was not enough. Her friend Annie Martin had accidentally discovered that none of the children in the Asylum could even dress themselves; the nurses found it less trouble to do it for them than to teach them how to look after themselves. Clark remarked, 'when we remember that these children were to be sent out as little servants to help others when they could not help themselves, it may be imagined how useless they would be'. Clearly, Clark had taken over, wholesale, the ideology informing the philanthropic groups pressing for boarding out in Britain: pauperism threatened the social order; paupers must be transformed into docile and industrious workers, in this case into domestic servants. She formed a Boarding-Out Society and headed a deputation, which included Catherine Spence, to persuade the government to supply allowances for the children whom the Society would board out.[27]

She achieved only half her aim in 1866. Blyth's government agreed with her that the children should be separated from the adult destitute; it acknowledged that boarding out was an excellent system, but refused the Boarding-Out Society's request and proceeded to pass legislation almost identical to Victoria's *Neglected and Criminal Children's Act* of 1864. This, following precedents in Britain, provided for building government industrial schools and reformatories, but not for boarding the children with members of the community.[28] She had to wait six more years, until 1872, to achieve the rest of her aim. Faced with overcrowding in the new industrial school, and recognising the precedent established in 1870 by the English Poor Law Board, the South Australian Parliament passed the *Destitute Persons' Relief and Industrial and Reformatory Schools Act, 1872*: it was a piece of portmanteau legislation demonstrating how similar poverty and crime, or at least juvenile crime, were thought to be. This Act permitted boarding out.[29]

However, the legislation was less a triumph for the Boarding-Out Society than a recognition that after six years of disastrous maladministration, action of some kind was urgent. Indeed, action had been urgent for most of those years. In November 1866 the children in the Destitute Asylum had been removed, to provide barracks for two companies of the Fourteenth Regiment returning from the war against the Maoris.[30] Over 100 children were lodged in the Exhibition Building for several months, so 'seriously deficient in the most ordinary appliances of cleanliness and decency; that their health rapidly declined … very many of the children presenting a squalid and emaciated appearance'. They were moved to a house called the Grace Darling at Brighton. It was large enough for only a third of their number; it needed repairs; the matron was harassed not only by lack of space and assistance, but also by difficulties in getting her requisitions attended to by the new Destitute Board, and by its chairman's interference in the Orphan School.[31] In July 1867, a parliamentarian told the House of Assembly that the children at Brighton were 'dying like rotten sheep'. The Destitute Board supplied a report showing that of the 102 children at Brighton, 53 were sick. Twelve had died, four from gangrene following measles.[32] This appalling information brought, at last, immediate action. Temporary relief followed by the opening of the government industrial school at Magill, by January 1869, improved the children's condition. But the water supply at Magill was inadequate, and there were no proper lavatories; a 'nuisance' in the east parklands in October 1869 was accused of coming from Magill. By 1872 the building was overcrowded. The chairman of the Destitute Board began boarding out the children who could not be fitted into the industrial school.[33] He paid allowances to their guardians, but made no arrangements for supervising or inspecting them. Only the ages of the children boarded out distinguished his practice from baby-farming. The legislation of 1872 was making a virtue of necessity when it legalised his actions.

When Emily Clark discovered what was going on in 1872, she sprang into action again. She re-formed the Boarding-Out Society, its original members constituting a committee with Clark as secretary and Catherine Spence as treasurer. They then offered the Destitute Board their services for superintending the boarded-out children. The Board accepted, and laid down conditions for the Society's work. They were to visit the children and their guardians once every three months, at irregular intervals, and report each visit to the Board within three days of making it. Most of the Board's conditions were designed to compel the Society to fulfil the task it had undertaken, or relinquish it, and to preserve the guardians and children from undue interference. The Society added one condition of its own: 'Should ill-treatment be suspected, the Visitor shall immediately investigate the case, and if necessary report upon it to the Destitute Board and to the Hon. Secretary of the Society'.[34]

The Boarding-Out Society was a small body with a continually changing membership. Any subscriber of five shillings, and anyone appointed as a visitor, became a member: the largest number of subscribers recorded was 26, and the largest number of visitors 123, and as many as 23 visitors resigned in one year.[35] But the core of the society, its committee, remained much the same. It met on the first Tuesday of every month to consider duplicates of the visitor's reports to the Destitute Board and appoint a visitor for each area in which children were boarded out. The committee was well-suited to its task: its patroness, the governor's wife, Lady Musgrave, was a north American and was the Society's source of information about measures introduced in the United States for dealing with children deemed delinquent; its members included Lady Ayers, Mrs Colton, and Mrs Davenport, all wives of wealthy public figures in the colony. Their acquaintance was wide, and their social prominence might have attracted social climbers as well as the genuinely philanthropic to the ranks of the visitors.[36]

Spence's office as treasurer was not arduous: the Society's funds came from subscriptions, seldom amounted to more than £10 a year, and were spent on stationery. For several years, she combined that office with Emily Clark's as secretary: in l877-79 when Clark was abroad, and from 1883 to 1886, when Clark's health compelled her to resign. Spence also visited the industrial school and the girls' reformatory quite frequently. In the mid-1880s, she remarked that she 'would visit it oftener if it were not so far away, making a fatiguing day'.[37] It is possible that she walked the five or so miles from her house in College Park to Magill. She undertook, too, a good deal of visiting for the Society.

The children to be visited were divided into three groups. The first were children under the age of 12, attending school, living with people who received an allowance for them from the Destitute Board. These were the children who were, in Spence's and Clark's view, properly 'boarded out'. The second were children under 12 and at school, who were referred to as 'licensed for adoption', because they were taken without the Destitute Board's allowance. The chairman of the Destitute Board, Thomas Sadler Reed, preferred placing children with families to whom he did not need to pay an allowance. Between the beginning of 1873 and June 1883, he arranged for a total of 2239 children to be adopted. During the same period only 591 children were boarded out under subsidy.[38] Emily Clark found Reed's procedures most annoying. 'Unfortunately', she commented, 'he afterwards made a great mistake in trying to substitute adoption in place of boarding out, and we were extremely vexed to find him taking them for nothing'. Spence, too, considered Reed's parsimony with government funds obstructive; she held that it was directly responsible for there still being 103 children in the industrial school in 1885, suffering an epidemic of ophthalmia.[39] The third group were adolescents between the ages of 12 and 16 who were apprenticed to their guardians and received wages, most of which were put in the bank for them. This practice dated from 1848, long before the formation of the Boarding-Out Society.[40] The Society visited children in all three groups, but since the government subsidy was paid for only those in the first group, it had little power to affect the conditions of life of those in the second and third.

Visitors' reports described the conditions of the children as 'good', 'tolerable', and 'unsatisfactory'. Spence explained that 'The reports marked "tolerable" and "unsatisfactory" are for the most part so designated on account of the behaviour of the children, indifferent health, or irregular attendance at church or school. Very few of them are so marked on account of the badness of the home'.[41] Perhaps she disliked the thought of passing judgment on anyone else's domestic arrangements.

This was, as Margaret Barbalet has pointed out, a period in which there was no old-age pension, no widow's pension, no deserted wives' pension, no child endowment, no supporting parent's allowance.[42] That consideration makes the processes by which children arrived in the Industrial School appear less a policy directed towards breaking up those families whose poverty might be thought to constitute a drain and a danger to the state, than a piecemeal practice of preserving life and health. Emily Clark's alarmist rhetoric derived from publications in England where the disreputable poor could more seriously be regarded as a threat to the stability of a social order prized by the middle class. It found little echo in public opinion in South Australia. In any case, the Boarding-Out Society was not concerned with the prosecutions which committed children to the Industrial School. Rather, it wished to rescue those children from institutional living and secure for them satisfactory family homes. Certainly the members of the Boarding-Out Society considered that only in domestic environments could those children learn to become docile and competent domestic servants, but their practice was also designed to augment the families of the respectable working class.

Yet the very possibility of judging a household respectable or not, and the criteria used in making the judgment, offer support to Daniels's argument: that Spence's work with the Boarding- Out Society was an aspect of the extension of middle-class domination of the domestic lives of the poor, and, since the quality of 'the home' was held to be a woman's responsibility, simultaneously the formation of a patriarchal state apparatus for regulating the lives of at least some working-class women.

However, two other possibilities may complicate the story a little. One springs from the Society's vexation with Reed for disrupting the lives of households and children in order to save government funding for the boarding-out subsidies. Their annoyance undoubtedly expressed their frustration at the way such interference removed their power as supervisors. But it may also have reflected a recognition that the subsidies offered a real, if small, financial advantage to some households, so that

Reed's policy inhibited even the tiny measure of re-distributing the colony's wealth which the government allowances for boarding-out children could have constituted. It is possible, too, that they saw the boarding-out subsidy as financial assistance given specifically to the women responsible for those households. I have not found any evidence to support such a suggestion, but both possibilities are at least consistent with Spence's eagerness to claim that the Society's supervision seldom led to reports that were derogatory about the households where children were boarded out.

The other possible complication arises from the same source. Clark's and Spence's annoyance with Reed clearly reflected indignation at bureaucratic action denigrating the importance of the society's work: at a man undervaluing a group of women working on his own patch of the public sphere. Clark and Spence wanted acknowledgment of the kind that they saw Clark's cousins, Frances Power Cobbe, Louisa Twining, Mrs Nassau Senior, Octavia Hill – to name only a few – gaining for similar work in England.[43] In this they were successful.

The Society's work achieved for it, eventually, inclusion among the government's instrumentalities. A parliamentary commission, appointed to examine the operation of legislation concerning the destitute, passed in 1881, and to investigate allegations of mistreatment and proselytising in the state's reformatories, found the evidence that Emily Clark and Catherine Spence submitted to it impressive. The Commission's report, made in 1885, recommended that a council be appointed to take over those functions of the Destitute Board that were concerned with children, and the functions of the Boarding-Out Society. It also recommended specifically that members of the council include Miss Clark and Miss Spence. If such recognition was a goal in the sub-script of Clark's and Spence's endeavours, then their appointments were a triumph. The State Children's Council, gazetted in December 1887, had 11 members, seven of them women, among them Miss Spence and Miss Clark.[44] Its first president was Edward Charles Stirling, a young man Spence had known well during his boyhood in South Australia, recently returned to the colony with a string of degrees from Cambridge, and by then teaching physiology at the new University of Adelaide.[45] But Stirling did not remain on the Council for long: throughout 1888 the voluntary Council quarrelled with the government's chief secretary; it resigned in a body in January 1889; and, when after Spence recalled, 'great searchings of heart', its members resumed their voluntary offices, Stirling and one other member, refused reappointment.[46] The Council met monthly to direct the work of its small government-appointed paid staff, whom Spence considered grossly underpaid.

A Ladies' Committee, which took over much of the work previously done by the Boarding-Out Society, met fortnightly.[47] The function of both expanded as their members found new arenas into which their regulatory practices could move, and persuaded the legislature to sanction their enterprise' The South Australian government introduced licenses for foster-mothers in 1881 and for lying-in homes in 1895, and established a separate court for hearing charges against juveniles, unofficially in 1890, legally in 1895.[48]

Spence's chief work for the Council was as a publicist of its work and of the measures it introduced. She extended her earlier campaign for more widespread adoption of the boarding-out system, carrying it as far as the United States in 1893 when she volunteered to speak to the International Congress of Charities, Correction and Philanthropy held in Chicago. She addressed the first Australian Charity Conference in 1890 on the advantages of South Australia's centralised administration for the provision of welfare services, preached in Melbourne on South Australia's efforts to reduce infant mortality (which ranged from the introduction of deep drainage to supervision of licensed foster-mothers and inspection of lying-in homes). She wrote and spoke enthusiastically about South Australia's establishment of a children's court. And in 1907, at the State Children's Council's request, she wrote *State Children in Adelaide*, a history of the work of the Council and the Boarding-Out Society.[49] This book is a triumphalist account in which she mistakenly assumes government commitment to poor relief in the early years of settlement, she omits details indicating some of the difficulties and poignancies that the Society encountered, and she makes exaggerated claims for South Australia's leadership in implementing the boarding-out system.[50] Such discrepancies between the events she participated in and her account of them arise from her unstated purpose in writing it – to commemorate Caroline Emily Clark, her good friend and colleague, and also a woman whose activities in the world of men should be acknowledged.

Her concern with poverty expanded when, in January 1897, she was appointed to the Destitute Board. There, besides pressing for more flexible, less oppressive conditions within the Destitute Asylum, she devoted considerable attention to ideas designed to prevent destitution occurring.[51] In 1884 she had spoken to the Parliamentary Commission on the Destitute about a scheme devised by a clergyman, W. L. Blackley, for compelling wage-earners to save their earnings, rather than spend them. This scheme, called 'compulsory providence', proposed to take a portion of each person's wages from them each week and lodge it in bank accounts where they

Caroline Emily Clark.
Image courtesy of the State Library
of South Australia SLSA: B47543

could not touch it until they retired. Spence reiterated approval for such a scheme when she addressed the second Australasian Conference on Charity in 1892.[52] She considered, too, Sidney Webb's neo-Malthusian observations about the necessity of altering 'the economic incidence of child bearing', by 'deliberate volition in the regulation of the married state' as a means of reducing the number of the destitute, though her fragmentary note did not say whether she considered such a proposal either possible or desirable.[53] In 1906, she wrote a pamphlet on *The Elberfeld System on Charity* which she endorsed because its 'measures for the destitute are preventive rather than curative'.[54] This system, implemented in a textile town in Germany and copied by such philanthropic interventionists as Octavia Hill in London, recruited a number of middle-class men in a municipality or housing settlement to be 'fathers' to some four families whom seasonal casual employment had reduced to appealing for poor relief. The 'father' was supposed, through intimate and personal supervision, to exert a morally uplifting influence on each family, and to provide practical help in the search for employment for those family members willing to work. He also had thoroughly paternalist punitive powers; it needed only his report to condemn the idle, the gambler or the drunkard to a term of imprisonment with hard labour. Octavia Hill translated the 'fathers' into Lady rent collectors; Spence turned them into gender-neutral 'Helpers'.[55] It was her support for the idea of the Elberfeld system which provided Daniels with the key point in her analysis of Spence's voluntary welfare work as assisting the extension of middle-class interference in the lives of the working class.[56]

Yet the other main point in Daniels's argument maintains that the attitudes which Spence expressed in such work derived from her identification with Adelaide's urban intelligentsia. This is less easily sustained. Her later refusal to align herself, as Daniels notes, with the political parties of either capital or labour, and her advocacy of political rights for minorities, certainly may have taken colouring from her membership of the educated Unitarian congregation. Unitarians were well represented in her initial venture into welfare work: four of the eleven members of the first Boarding-Out Society committee were members of that church, and ten of the Society's first 18 subscribers were connected with it.[57] But by the 1880s and 1890s, Spence's views had already moved away from those of at least some of the members of her church. It seems quite as likely, if not more so, that Spence's concern with minority interests was, during the last decades of her life, an expression of her identification with a minority interest to which she had belonged all her days. Her concern with compulsory providence can be seen as a response to the needs of aged married women who had spent their lives being economically dependent on wage-earning husbands. Her endorsement of the Elberfeld system focused not so much on its interventionary aspects as on the criticism for which her account of Elberfeld serves as introduction: of the South Australian government's meanness with the rations provided as out-relief, of its policy of refusing rations to the families of men out of work, and of the problems that women in paid work faced in supporting families. Her work with the Boarding-Out Society and the State Children's Council was intended to provide strong cohesive bonds, as she explained, between 'the unfortunate members of the working-class' and 'the comparatively prosperous of that class'.[58] She was hostile to the idea of boarding out children from Magill with wealthy families, and she considered it worthy of not only notice, but approval, that in the boarding out 'movement', 'the rich and the great of the colony have taken a very subordinate place'. In both cases it was the solidarity, cohesiveness and mutual responsibility of sections of the working class that she saw at stake.[59]

Edging out of the domestic sphere

In 1905, Spence told the National Council of Women that:

> My work on the State Children's Council I look on not as benevolence, but as justice … Sympathy transfers this keen sense of your own personal rights to the rights of other people. Without sympathy says Herbert Spencer there can be no justice.[60]

Spence's sense of personal rights was predominantly bound up with her life-long struggle, as a woman, to earn a living and win recognition in a world that was the almost-exclusive preserve of men. Such a struggle may not have led her to identify with the impoverished, or even the prosperous of the working class. But it did not lead her to identify with their oppressors either. In 1907 she told a 'State Children' Convention held in Adelaide that 'above all things… [the visitors] must love the children. There was a terrible objection nowadays to kissing, on the ground that it was unsanitary. Every child she visited, except the big boys, she kissed, because she wanted them to feel that they were of the same flesh and blood, and that she loved them'.[61]

5
Learning for the future

Spence was in her mid-50s when she composed *A Week in the Future*, her vision of a co-operative society in 1988, a century from the year in which she wrote. Her dream of its educational practices owed something both to discussions she had listened to in England in the 1860s, and to developments in education in South Australia, but she had carried those ideas much further than many of her contemporaries would have considered possible, or even desirable. In a period when South Australians were still arguing about whether or not parents who could afford to educate their children should be allowed to send them to government-funded schools, and had just established, as a separate institution, the government-funded Advanced School for Girls,[1] Spence's vision depicted an organisation of learning which sought to eliminate intractable hierarchies of class, gender and authority from education.

> In the schoolrooms … the children … received instruction in reading, writing and simple calculation, and above all in knowledge of things as distinguished from knowledge of words. The nursery teaching was thoroughly natural and delightful in the manner in which each lesson in knowledge and in skill was felt to be learned as much by the learner's own intellectual or artistic effort as by the teacher's guidance. I could see how early the lesson of bearing and forbearing, of respect for the rights of others, was inculcated without needing any severe punishment or risking any serious shock to the delicate organization of a young infant or little child.

This was her dream of pre-school education in 1988. The older children, those between the ages of eight and fourteen would go to 'State schools' where there would be far fewer differences between 'the professional classes and the manual workers' than there were in 1888. There would be 'the most perfect equality' between girls and boys, who would be taught together, a practice, said Spence, that 'I had always approved of as it makes them quicker and brighter and more courteous'. It would take several generations' experience of co-education to prompt feminists to ask, almost a century after Spence was writing, whether girls benefited as much as boys from such a practice. Her dream included notions about discipline derived from the Enlightenment but still rare in her time: 'When pupils did wrong, the teachers assumed that it arose from ignorance of what was right or from weakness of self-control, and every encouragement was given that might strengthen the conscience and rightly direct the will'. Schools would be places where students would practise the self-regulation that such principles encouraged. 'In the school playground, I noticed that the pupils themselves elected their monitors and prefects, who kept order. The teacher was the last resort, but was seldom called in'. The same principle would operate in universities where 'students elected conduct committees from their number'; even Spence could not envisage universities of the 1980s where students can consider 'conduct' largely irrelevant.[2]

This vision marks not only a considerable distance between Spence and her fellow colonists, but also the transformation in her views about education that had taken place since 1846 when she abandoned her attempt to run a school, and 1850 when she gave up teaching altogether. In those years, like many other colonists, she was primarily concerned with the place of religion in publicly funded education. Just as the colony's early governors had decided that state provision for the destitute was a necessity, so too they had felt compelled to provide government grants to schools. The conditions which Robe imposed on such grants in 1847 ensured that, in practice, those schools which received government funds were either run by clerics or controlled by 'religious communities by which they were more or less exclusively supported'.[3] The systematic colonisers' plans may have had to undergo considerable modification among the vicissitudes of establishing a viable white settlement in South Australia, but a measure that was effectively state aid to selected religions was more than the powerful in the Paradise of Dissent could stomach. When the first partly-elected Legislative Council took their seats in 1851, they abolished Robe's measure and passed an Education Act which severed the interconnections between state and education, and state and religion. No minister of religion could be a member of the central Board of Education which was appointed to administer government grants to schools; schools receiving funds 'must provide good secular instruction, based on the Christian religion, but apart from all theological and controversial differences of discipline and doctrine'; teachers should read a chapter from the old and new testaments every day.[4] This legislation remained in force until 1875, and after that year bible readings were given only on request and then, out of school hours. Denominational religious instruction did not appear in South Australian state schools until 1939.[5]

Nevertheless, questions about the place of religion in education continued to provoke frequent and fervent debate. In 1850, Spence considered religious instruction integral to any education, and her difficulties with her own religious beliefs mean that she was profoundly troubled at the prospect of teaching. Mrs X 'must keep the moral responsibility of her children to herself', she wrote in her diary, when she was about to go to a live-in post as 'nursery governess': 'I shall not have it. I will do them as much good and as little harm as I can, but I hope I may not have their souls to answer for. It is a dark subject'.[6] By 1856, her despair and anxiety dispelled by her conversion, she had translated dogma into general morality. When she added a youthful voice to the general clamour in the press, she argued not for religious instruction, but that

> teachers endowed by public money … should be bound to teach morality, not upon utilitarian principles, not because honesty is the best policy, but because goodness, truth, honesty, courage, patience, temperance and obedience to law are eternally and immutably right, noble, and beautiful and in conformity with the will of our Heavenly Father.

She was prompted to the expression of such worthy sentiments by precisely the kind of interventionary motives that Kay Daniels has ascribed to her. She considered that religious and moral principles were better taught by parents, but went on to observe:

> when I look at a shipload of female immigrants, and consider that these are the future mothers of South Australia; when I recollect how much the education of principles and feeling has been neglected in the mother country, I maintain that we ought not to trust implicitly to parental guidance.[7]

Almost 20 years were to pass before Spence again expressed close interest in the colony's publicly funded educational system. But by then, her attitudes to its social function had changed as markedly as her religious views had begun diverging from those of her church's minister. By 1880, she argued for state responsibility for education, not because she considered that a government could provide a better education than anyone else, but rather because she considered – like J. S. Mill – that democratic societies should ensure that their citizens had access to the means necessary for them to exercise their democratic rights.[8] Further, she had come to believe that education was a basic civil right. In 1882 she countered the voluntaryist objections to parents in economically secure circumstances sending their children to state schools. Every child, she asserted, had a right to education 'at the expense of the State'.[9] Toward the end of her life she considered public education a 'socialist movement', and expressed approval at the cost being distributed evenly throughout the community – a view which should have led her to advocate taxing the wealthy more heavily. She did not do that, but she did condemn denominational schools as unnecessary extravagance.[10]

It was probably her visit to Britain in 1865-66 which wrought much of the change in her approach to the social function of public education. Like many other colonists, not only in South Australia, and not only in the 19th century, Spence often looked to Britain for ideas. She had already found political inspiration in the work of Thomas Hare and J. S. Mill, and the visits she paid them confirmed her enthusiasm. In London, at the feminist Barbara Leigh Smith's salon she listened to discussions about the higher education of women, discussions which eventually bore fruit in the establishment of Girton College. These did not immediately propel Spence into similar plans for South Australia: the colony did not have any institutions for tertiary education in 1865, and such plans may have seemed premature to a colonist appalled at the state of elementary education in England. But they undoubtedly contributed to her later enthusiasm for better education for women; and they certainly conveyed clearly the concept of education as a right.[11] At Edwin Hill's house, Spence met William Ellis, founder of the Birkbeck schools. These were institutions which in the early 1850s had been providing schooling for working-class girls and boys in London, Manchester, Edinburgh and Glasgow. Their primary concern was to teach a form of social science and political economy, to prepare the children for adult wage-earning. Such education was also, incidentally, intended to prevent strikes.[12] Spence found Ellis a 'predominant talker', but his talk convinced her that he himself was 'noteworthy', and that his schools, which were secular, were 'good for something' because they taught 'things that make for human happiness and intellectual freedom', 'lessons on the right relations of human beings to each other'.[13] From that conversation Spence derived an increased concern that education should explain ordinary, every-day practicalities.

Later, back in South Australia, she was provoked to public statement by the question of the content of elementary education. In Britain, a liberal government passed a first measure for universal elementary schooling in 1870. In South Australia, dispute over education raged from 1872 until a royal commission on education reported in 1882. In 1873, discontent among the colonists sharpened in response to reports of the implementation of the 1872 *Education Act* in the neighbouring colony, Victoria, which provided generally free, compulsory and secular schooling.[14] When the South Australian parliament met in July 1873, the government promised to bring in a bill which would make use of 'the experience gained from the working of the new *Education Act* in Victoria'. But the South Australian bill was first amended beyond recognition in the House of Assembly, then in December, thrown out by the Legislative Council.[15] Dispute centred on continued bible reading and government provision of fees for all, or only destitute, children. Divided opinion inside the parliament was a pale reflection of that outside. In the advertisements, articles and letters in the press, at the meetings held in local schoolrooms and the Adelaide Town Hall, practical determination of the content of the education to be imparted was lost from sight.[16] Despite defeat in parliament, the government probably retained some hope for improvements within the existing system. At the beginning of 1874 its negotiations with the old Education Board, initially appointed in 1851, resulted in the Board's resignation. The government appointed a new board, and made John Anderson Hartley its chairman. Hartley, the headmaster of the private, denominational boys' school, Prince Alfred College, had been a member of the old Board since 1871, but his attempts to increase professionalism throughout the education system had been unsuccessful. As chairman of the new board he won his colleagues' support for a policy of sweeping change.[17] One of his first moves was to draw up new examinations for teachers requesting certificates which entitled them to government grants. Then, in July 1874, he published the first results from the new examinations. The account which appeared in the daily press presented the teachers for general mockery and derision.[18]

Spence was furious. In the first place, she protested, the teachers were 'inadequately prepared': 'The promised list of books recommended for teachers to prepare from was not published until *after* the examination'. The examination was divided into three standards, but no-one knew what was expected in each. Enraged by pretentious laughter at the published blunders, she took a swipe at the members of precisely that elite to which Hartley was appealing: 'even ladies and gentlemen who have had much culture in books, newspapers and society' she declared, would have failed the second class paper. Who could have passed the first? The grants made to the state-funded schools were far from extravagant. The Education Board must 'bid considerably higher' if it wanted 'higher attainments'. Inspection of a teacher engaged in teaching pupils 'to read, write and calculate in the best manner in the shortest possible time', would reveal capabilities for the work; asking for answers as recherché as the date of the Licinian Rogations would not. Besides, she demanded, what use was such learning to a teacher educating children, who, in most cases, would spend no more than six years in school? What South Australia needed was sound basic education.

Spence spelt her indignation out, at length, in a letter to the *Register*.[19] Her fierce defence may have cowed the mockers: there were no more derogatory remarks about the examination results published. She may also have shamed Hartley into making sure that teachers at least had fair warning of the books they should prepare from: a far higher proportion of teachers passed the Board's next examination in 1875.[20] She also offered a sensible and well-timed reminder of educational priorities in an agricultural economy where seasonal changes created urgent demands for child labour on farms, and generated cries of 'useless' whenever clauses to make primary schooling compulsory were included in proposed legislation. Her intervention in 1874 signalled clearly the nature of her concern and involvement with education for the rest of her life. And that represents an intervention against the assumptions of an intellectual elite, rather than, as Kay Daniels has maintained, an attempt to regulate the working class in accordance with the attitudes of such an elite.

Her objections to specialist knowledge for teachers were not, as Hannah More's, founded in the belief that the labouring person's education should be restricted to what was good for them to know. On the contrary, Spence seems to have had a thoroughly realistic grasp both of the qualities necessary in teachers, and of the most effective ways of providing children with the means to pursue their own education for the rest of their lives. She did not think it important for elementary teachers to have taken university degrees because, she said, 'for our elementary teachers we want breadth rather than depth'.[21] That breadth should be applied first, she maintained, to 'teaching a child to read intelligently, fluently'; that 'is of more consequence to his development than all of the rest of his school education together. It is giving him the key to the universe'. Second in importance, she thought, 'comes writing, not of copies only, but the thoughts of other, as in dictation and his own recollection of lessons in his own words', and third came 'arithmetic by which he may learn to buy and sell and manage his own affairs'. She considered that these basics could be supplemented with 'grammar, intelligently taught, because it is the only mental training that children under 12 are capable of receiving, and to be able to perceive differences and make distinctions between different classes of words helps a child understand better anything he reads'. Basic education could also include 'such scientific instruction as deals with the objects that come into the child's daily life'. Even though she thought that teachers should also 'keep order and discipline and enforce cleanliness and good manners', her view of teaching and learning was very far from 'the drill education system, which like the bed of Procrustes, stretches or cramped [sic] varied intelligence to suit one mediocre standard'. Rather, it was, as she claimed, a 'scheme by which the poor child's time may be economized so … that he shall be put in possession of the tools for self-cultivation as easily, as cheaply and as quickly as possible'.[22] So far from designing ways to keep working-class children docile and uninformed was her idea of education, that she urged making familiarity and curiosity an incentive to learn, and advocated the cultivation of initiative and independence. She was to tell the Criminological Society, in 1897:

> It used to be a maxim that the first thing to be done in education was to *break a child's will*, so as to produce instant and unreasoning obedience … [but] if the *ipse dixit* of the parent is made the only law of life, the child has no guiding rules for his conduct in the world. The will should be trained and strengthened, for it is indeed the real 'ego'.[23]

Such views suggest commitment to enlarging the mental worlds and practical opportunities of 'poor children', not to preserving disciplined subordination.

With those views, Spence watched the changes in public education in South Australia during the 1870s and 1880s with approval. Despite her initial indignation at Hartley, she sympathised with his aims. Hartley's power had increased. In 1875 the South Australian parliament passed an *Education Act* which dissolved the new Education Board, appointed a Council of Education, and left most of the details of reorganising the education system to be drawn up as regulations by the Council.

Hartley was made the Council's permanent, salaried president, so that the regulations were very largely his work. In 1878 parliament passed another *Education Act* which, while it reorganised the central administration and its relations with the government, did not materially alter the provisions of the 1875 Act.[24] Hartley, with the new title of Inspector-General, remained in executive control of the colony's public education. As chairman of the Board in 1874, he drew criticism for his attempts to make the education system more efficient. As president of the Council, which controlled courses of instruction and standards of education within schools, appointments, removals, examinations, certification and salaries of teachers, he was widely and emphatically criticised as authoritarian and centralist.[25] After reading a particularly violent attack on him in the press, Spence was so distressed that she could not sleep. She did not, then, know him personally, but that did not stop her: at one o'clock in the morning she got out of bed and wrote to him offering her sympathy and support.[26] Hartley responded, and their subsequent friendship led to Spence's active involvement in South Australia's public education. It led, too, to her first official appointment to a public office, to a recognised place in the public world of men.

The *Education Act* of 1875 made elementary education compulsory, and provided for appointment of local boards of advice to supervise school attendances and to inform the Council of local requirements.[27] Implementation was slow, but in November 1877, Spence wrote triumphantly to C. H. Pearson, a professor of history who had emigrated from London to South Australia, and had then gone on to Melbourne to lecture at the university and, as headmaster, to rule over the Presbyterian Ladies College.[28] 'I am a member of the Board of Advice for the School District of East Torrens', she boasted, 'and I hope in time to have a seat on the Council of Education itself'.[29] She had every reason to be proud. She was the first woman in South Australia to gain such a public appointment.[30] However, while she announced this at the beginning of a chapter in her autobiography, she made less, there, of this achievement than of her work with the Boarding-Out Society and, subsequently, with the *Register*. Perhaps she saw her work for a local school board, rightly, as less central to the development of a state instrumentality than the work she was engaged in with Emily Clark. Perhaps she was to see it, again rightly, as making far less of an inroad into the public sphere than her work for the *Register* would carve. But it is most likely that she learned to dislike the work that her membership of the East Torrens School Board involved.

The Board's principal task was to interview parents who said that they could not afford school fees, and those whose children had not been at school for the prescribed number of days. Spence told one story about an interview which clearly afforded her a great deal of amusement. She was, together with the chairman of the Board, visiting a household which included a grown-up daughter who had that morning left her job as a domestic servant with the chairman's mother. He had enlarged on this fact to Miss Spence during their morning's drive. When they arrived his first question to the mother of the household was 'why is your eldest daughter out of a place? … She might be earning good wages, and be able to help you pay the fees'. 'Oh!' came the unexpected reply, 'she had to leave old Mrs. – this morning; she was that mean there was no living in the house with her!' Miss Spence could not, of course, afford to laugh aloud, but she still remembered the exchange more than 30 years later. 'Knowing her interlocutor only as the man in authority', she recalled, 'the unfortunate woman scarcely advanced her cause by her plain speaking, and I was probably the only member of the trio who appreciated the situation'. Despite her amusement, Spence considered that such encounters inflicted indignity upon those being interviewed, and she considered school fees a burden to the poor. She rejoiced, accordingly, when they were abolished,[31] but that had to wait some time; compulsory schooling was not made free in South Australia until 1891.[32]

The Education Council was replaced by a government department of salaried public servants, so Spence did not achieve the second official appointment that she had hoped for. However when one of the successive ministers of education suggested to Hartley that senior students at the state schools should have a text about the laws and institutions of the colony, Hartley asked Spence to write it. It was, she recalled, 'to lead from the known to the unknown – it might include the elements of political economy and sociology – it might make use of familiar illustrations from the experience of a new country – but it must not be too long'. She set about writing what was the 'first economics text for Australian secondary [sic] schools'.[33]

The South Australian education department published *The Laws We Live Under* in 1880. It is short – 120 pages; divided into 17 chapters; with headings and summary statements in heavy type, conforming to Hartley's requirements. It ranges widely from the necessity for the rule of law to the functions of government; from a justification for government-funded education to an explanation of wealth. Spence steered a careful course between the arguments – topical at the time – for and against protective duties, but she gave to free trade the extra clout of being practised by

England, and sanctioned by the laws of the creator. While she devoted one chapter to trades unions and strikes, she was prepared to argue that workers in such essential services as the post, telegraph, gas supply and the railway should not be allowed to strike, and – taking a leaf from William Ellis's book – she maintained that 'As a general rule, strikes, when they are successful, are a loss'.[34] Such views probably sounded less conservative in 1880 than they do now; unionism was still a new growth in Australia at that time, and Spence did make clear her approval for craft unionism. She was criticised for covering too much ground: 'political economy, trades unions, insurance companies, and newspapers', her detractors objected, 'were outside the scope of the laws we live under', but Spence considered that 'in a new State where the optional duties of Government are so numerous, it was of great importance for the young citizen to understand economic principles'. She was proud of the book, and towards the end of her life, hoped that it had influenced the citizens of the day.[35] Jeanne Young remembered children wishing that Miss Spence could be left in the cupboard.[36] Nevertheless, Spence's book may have stirred some of the young women who read it. In its first chapter she announced that

> The progress of the world … depends on the character and conduct of its women as much as on that of its men; and there can be no greater mistake for girls to make than to suppose they have nothing to do with good citizenship and good government.[37]

By this time she was supporting, with active promotion, the advanced education of girls.

Secondary education for boys had been available in South Australia, to those who could afford it, since 1847 when wealthy Anglicans formed a proprietary school that was to become St Peter's School Collegiate. Other denominational and private schools for boys followed. But while there were countless attempts to found private secondary schools for girls, none had survived that offered an education comparable with that provided at Melbourne's Presbyterian Ladies' College.[38] The question of government-funded advanced education for girls gained considerable attention during the 1870s, when the whole education system was under debate. Howard Clark asked Spence to write some articles on the subject for the *Register*. Spence complied, arguing first that changes in population growth and movement were forcing unprecedented numbers of women into the paid labour force, and second, that industrialisation of domestic produce was leaving housewives idle and frustrated. Both should be enabled to find rewarding work, but to do so, they must have access to a more useful education that 'the pretentious programme of the young ladies' seminary'.[39] The University of Adelaide, established in 1874, was to assist the struggle when, in 1880, it announced that it would admit women to courses for degrees.[40] By then Morgan's government had already capitulated: the state Advanced School for Girls was opened in October 1879.[41]

Advanced School for Girls.
Image courtesy of the State Library of South Australia SLSA: B25677/42.

The Advanced School for Girls was an academic high school which, while supported by the state, was able to charge fees, so that it was expected to pay its own way. Indeed, Alison Mackinnon has argued recently, it was at least as much the contention that it would support itself, as any arguments for social justice for young women, that achieved assent for the project in the House of Assembly.[42] An education inspector considered that the most important effect of making such education available to young women was that they would ensure that their sons and daughters were educated, a view that can still be encountered, however encrusted with antediluvianism, today. But within a year of the School's opening, education minister J. Langdon Parsons arranged for the academically distinguished, though under-aged, acting headmistress to replace the two preceding appointees, who had resigned. This young prodigy was Edith Cook, and she was determined to sustain the school's commitment to academic achievement for its students, and to teach 'the higher branches of learning'. The school taught English, French, German and Drawing, and, to the senior classes, Latin, Algebra and Euclid. Edith Cook also gave lessons in Physiology, and arranged for some of the advanced students to attend classes in Physiology at the University – a daring move in an era which still contested women's access to schools of medicine. The Royal Commission on Education in 1882 asked her, apparently without irony, about teaching cookery. A subject which would do nothing to gain admission for young women to the university, but one which the commissioners probably considered vital for future wives and mothers, was and still is, widely considered to be a soft option appropriate only for girls. In 1882 it was not offered at the Advanced School for Girls, not because it was considered inappropriate, but because there were not facilities. It is not difficult to imagine satisfaction and amusement in Edith Cook's mind as she offered that response to the commissioners.

A month before it opened, Spence had, in the press, been defending the state Advanced School for Girls against charges of expense.[43] She probably regarded it as a more important achievement than the admission of women to university degrees. She complained that, since she regarded 'special knowledge and special culture as a means for advancing the culture of all', except for women who graduated in medicine, she found university women deficient in those 'altruistic ideas' which 'complete [the] development of the human being'.[44]

She was, no doubt, highly delighted at the appointment of Edith Cook, a sister Unitarian and family friend, to the post of the school's headmistress, which she held until 1885.[45] Although she had given up teaching in 1850, Spence continued to enjoy the change of giving a lesson. *The Laws We Live Under* was used in the Advanced School for Girls as well as in the elementary schools, and Edith Cook occasionally invited her to take a lesson on the subjects it treated. Spence's capacity for entertaining children probably made her a thoroughly engaging teacher. One of her students recalled a day which created an awe and excitement among the students that was quite disproportionate to the shrivelled tissue of the written account. In talking about local manufacturing, Miss Spence referred to the tweed factory at Lobethal. 'One girl said, "My dress is made of Lobethal tweed". Miss Spence replied, "Take your fingers out of your mouth, Miss Lobethal tweed. We bow to you", and she did'.

6
Round woman in her round hole

'You may try, but you can never imagine, what it is to have a man's force of genius in you, and yet to suffer the slavery of being a girl'. This cry of anguish blazes from the pages of George Eliot's novel, *Daniel Deronda*. Spence quoted it in an article on Eliot's life and works; she paused at several points which suggest parallels with her own life, observing that the sentiment best expressed the condition Mary Ann Evans experienced in her youth. Since Spence considered 'the province of genius' to be not so much superlative creativeness, but rather 'to call forth a responsive spark from the souls with which it is in communion', Deronda's mother's outburst could stand as her own.[1] For 30 years, Spence defied social convention to work as a journalist, but she did so without acknowledgement, recognition, or even much in the way of financial return.

The patriarchal social order which so constrained her attempt to maintain her independence – to become her own breadwinner, while retaining freedom from the double subjection of women of the working class – made a 'lady journalist' a contradiction in terms. Margaret Stevenson, wife of one of the *Register*'s earlier directors, might have contributed not only poems but also political articles to that paper; Spence might have had occasional pieces printed in her brother-in-law's *South Australian*; but both sheltered behind initials and pen-names.[2] The daily and bi-weekly press required news-hounds, and that was deemed an occupation unsuited to a lady.

As a young woman, Spence came close to quarrelling with her friend John Taylor, because he had been boasting about her contributions to the press. When she went to a subscription ball, with her sister Mary and her brother John, Mary found that she had been pointed out and talked of 'as the lady who wrote for the newspapers'. Mary was indignant and Catherine injured: 'I did not like it even to be supposed of myself'.[3] Much later in the century and coming from a society more fluid and flexible than South Australia, Henry James was to repel ladies from such an occupation with his portrait of Henrietta Stackpole. There were not even discouraging examples in Australia to whom Spence could look for precedence, and on the newspapers and journals produced in the colonies, there were certainly no equivalents of Martha Webster in the church, to offer her inspiration. Spence sheltered her work in anonymity for decades, but she refused to allow patriarchal convention to prohibit her working altogether.

Some of the circles she moved in undoubtedly helped her develop the clear, usually economical, persuasive immediacy of style which characterised much of her journalism. With both her brother and brother-in-law she had opportunity to discuss the qualities desirable in articles in the press. Murray developed the *South Australian* into a significant voice for conservatism in the debates of the 1840s, and he was undoubtedly proud of the quality of reports of events in Britain and the up-to-date book reviews with which he filled its back page.[4] He would not have accepted Spence's contributions if he had considered them likely to detract from his paper's reputation. Similarly, it seems most unlikely that even fraternal loyalty and affection would have compelled John Spence to put his name to the articles that he and Spence sent off to the *Argus* each week if he had not approved of them. When Murray went to his job on the *Argus* in 1852, he left the *South Australian* in the hands of John Spence and W.W. Whitridge, with instructions that Catherine Spence should write any articles that might be needed on state aid to the churches. The paper did not last more than three months longer.[5] However Spence's acquaintance with Whitridge may have led to her introduction to Andrew Garran, and she could only have benefited from paying attention to the journalism of both men. Whitridge and Garran produced a weekly paper called the *Australian Examiner* in South Australia for nine months of 1851, displaying in it the talents which later earned Whitridge the reputation of being 'one of the most virile writers on *The Register*', and made Garran the highly-regarded editor of the *Sydney Morning Herald*. Through Murray, Spence encountered another journalist who offered her encouragement, too. When she was nursing her sister Jessie and looking after her children in Melbourne during 1854, she was invited to a ball given to celebrate the opening of the *Argus*'s new offices in Collins Street. There she met the paper's editor, Edward Wilson, and probably argued with him the relative merits of the different forms of land settlement in South Australia and Victoria.[7] However, Wilson's later encouragement was very far from inclining Spence to claim public recognition for her own journalism. None of the men associated with the press did as much to help her overcome either their complicity in, or her deference to, patriarchal convention, as she did for herself by establishing a firm reputation as a woman of letters.

Her reputation was first unequivocally founded in 1864. Critics had speculated about the identity of the author of her first two novels. In 1864, their questions were answered by one of their number who knew her, perhaps through Andrew Murray, but most probably through Howard Clark. Frederick Sinnett had immigrated to Adelaide in 1849, gone on to Melbourne to work on the *Argus*, but had returned to Adelaide where, in the early 1860s, he was editing an evening paper called the *Telegraph*. He was among Howard Clark's most intimate and valued friends, and, like Clark's sister Emily, he thought very highly of Spence's first novel.[8] In 1864 Spence was at work on her third, and Sinnett told her that it would help his paper to serialise her story in the pages of its weekly publication, the *Weekly Mail*. The work was announced as a 'New and Original Tale, by Miss Spence, Author of "Clara Morrison" [sic], "Tender and True", &c'.[9] However, the revelation seems scarcely to have rippled the cultural air of the colony, perhaps because it was a novel rather than an article. The foundation of Spence's reputation had to wait through more than another ten years of her anonymous and unrecognised writing for anything to build upon it, but Spence's work during the interval did much to prepare for its unveiling.

While she was in London in 1865, she called on the reader for Elder, Smith & Company, to see if she would earn anything from the second edition of *Tender and True*. She would not, it appeared. But perhaps the reader felt impelled to offer her something: after talking with her about her perceptions of life in the heart of the British Empire, he told her that if she could 'put these ideas into shape' he would have them printed in the *Cornhill Magazine*. Her article, 'An Australian's Impressions of England', appeared in January 1866.[10] The same month saw her in print in another English periodical too. Edward Wilson had retired from the *Argus* and gone to live in London where the doctors treating his failing eyesight had forbidden him even to dictate material for publication. He was restive under such a prohibition.

Discussions pre-figuring the second *Franchise Reform Act* of 1867 in England were being rehearsed. He was eager to write an article on the representation of classes, based on the ideas that he had formulated in Victoria. He heard that Spence was in Scotland, staying with her aunts, so he sent her a message, asking if she would write the article for him 'from some letters reprinted from The Argus and a few hints from himself'. Anonymity had long since ensured that Spence would not be too proud to accept such a notion; she 'gladly undertook the work'. 'Principles of Representation' appeared in the *Fortnightly Review*. Spence's article in the *Cornhill Magazine* was printed anonymously. Her article in the *Fortnightly Review* was published as Wilson's, appearing under his name, for which favour he paid her £10.[11]

However, Spence was able to make something of both, back in South Australia. In 1866 the committee of the South Australian Institute, on which Howard Clark was so active, invited her to write a lecture for them on her impressions of England. It seems not to have occurred to anyone, not even Spence, that she might deliver it herself. In Europe, Britain and the United States, women had been delivering lectures, to mixed audiences, for some decades by the 1860s, but their appearances often encountered opposition, and were still rare.[12] Howard Clark read the lecture for her. But he had such difficulty with her handwriting that he could only fumble his way through it. Nevertheless, the lecture did, at least, let his audience know that Spence had appeared in two substantial English periodicals. It also told them that she had met George Eliot. That encounter, based on a mistake, had been brief and unrewarding. Spence felt as though 'I had been looked on as an inquisitive Australian desiring an interview upon any pretext'. Her account could not have led anyone to suppose that she claimed even acquaintance with her idol,[13] but it did draw attention to her familiarity with the work of this writer: something which probably attracted attention in literary circles, not only in Adelaide. Five years later, in 1871, the Institute's committee asked her for 'two literary lectures'. Spence not only offered to read these herself, but chose to lecture on Elizabeth and Robert Browning.[14] Robert Browning was considered an obscure and difficult poet, so her lecture must have enhanced her reputation as a literary authority. But it was another lecture, on George Eliot, which led – finally – to her appearance in the Australian periodical press without the protection of anonymity.

In about 1875, she spoke to the Unitarian Church's Mutual Improvement Society on George Eliot. This led, she recalled, to her introduction to Martha Webster's brother, Henry Turner. A leading figure in Melbourne's world of banking and commerce, Turner was also a leading light in Melbourne's intellectual circles. Together with Arthur Patchett Martin and Alexander Sutherland (who was the head of Carlton College, acting professor of English Literature at Melbourne University, and acting-registrar of the University at the time of his death in 1902), Turner was planning to establish a new periodical. They held that earlier attempts to 'acclimatize periodical literature' had been too lightweight and parochial to compete successfully with the imported English monthlies and the local weekly papers. But this venture, the *Melbourne Review*, would devote its pages to 'subjects of more solid character and more permanent interest' than those of its predecessors; 'articles on Philosophy, Theology, Science, Art and Politics', they declared, would form its leading features. Turner asked Spence for the manuscript of her lecture to include in his new undertaking. Her article appeared in the second number of the *Melbourne Review*, in 1876, and this one appeared over her name.[15]

That signalled the end of her anonymity. Two years later, the *Register*'s editors offered her regular employment on it literary pages. Spence was jubilant. 'What a glorious opening' she exclaimed, 'for my ambition and my literary proclivities came to me in July 1878 …!'[16] She was to take the place of Howard Clark. He had become a part-proprietor of the *Register* in 1865 and its editor in 1870. He did not, a later editor judged, have 'a news nose', but as a writer he was held to have possessed 'abilities of the highest order'; 'the versatility of his talents found full play in the humorous column', in theatrical criticism, and in entertaining literary articles and book reviews. His death in 1878 left a noticeable gap in the paper. His successor as editor, John Harvey Finlayson, wanted to maintain and, if possible, improve the standard of its literary pages, and hoped that Spence's appointment might make up for the loss of Clark. Given Clark's reputation, that was already both a tall order and a measure of the esteem she had won.[17] However, she was not restricted to literary articles. In 1877 both the *Melbourne Review* and the English journal, *Fraser's Magazine*, had printed articles she had written on land legislation and imperial union. The *Register* had noted the first, remarking that it was 'characterized by the clearness of thought and argument and attention to detail displayed in all Miss Spence's writings'.

John Howard Clark.
Image courtesy of the State Library of South Australia SLSA: B3902

Her appointment to the paper invited her to contribute not only literary but also 'social' articles. 'Leading articles', she remembered, 'were to be written at my own risk. If they suited the policy of the paper they would be accepted, otherwise not'.[18]

Spence 'felt as if the round woman had got at last into the round hole which fitted her'.[19] She was employed in the public sphere, in a world occupied exclusively by men. She was at last earning her own living. Her articles for the *Register* were not the first to bring her payment – she had earned £12 from the *Cornhill Magazine*, £10 from Wilson, and £8.15s. from *Fraser's Magazine* – but now, for the first time in her life, she was her own independent breadwinner. By the 1880s she considered that she was bringing in 'a very decent income' with her pen. 'I don't think the said income was ever more than £300 a year', observed Lucy Morice, 'and generally less'. But it meant independence. And she had access to an established public forum – the colony's oldest newspaper. She rejoiced in 'the breadth of the canvas' on which she could draw her 'sketches of books and life'.[20] She had had to wait a long time for such a break in the solidity of the patriarchal order of her society; she was in her 53rd year. It was possible, undoubtedly, only because her appointment did not require her presence among the men in the offices and around the press in Grenfell Street. Spence's appointment was as a regular 'outside' contributor. That meant that she worked at home, but it meant, as well, that while she was working in her 'little study' with her books, pigeon holes, and her mother knitting in the rocking chair by the low window, she was reaching out into the world beyond the domestic sphere that she inhabited.[21] She had made a real breach in the barrier dividing the domestic and public spheres.

Spence did more, too with her journalism. Her articles ranged widely, treating matters such as land legislation, wages, agricultural machinery, quite as much as questions about marriage, domestic labour and forms of hospitality. Simply by writing about them, she was asserting women's right to hold views about the concerns of the public sphere, and to have those views heard. Likewise, she was claiming, in the public sphere, the propriety of attention to the concerns of the domestic. Just as her decision not to marry evinces a resolution to encounter the whole world directly, not only part of it, so her journalism shows her regarding the whole world with two eyes, not

Bay window in the house in Trinity Street, College Park, where Catherine Helen Spence lived and wrote.
Photograph by Susan Magarey.

merely one. By expressing that vision in the daily press, she issued a tacit invitation to other colonists to follow suit. Spence's journalism, by transcending the separation of the separate spheres, worked to subvert it. One reader, at least, assumed she was a man; he wrote to Finlayson from Wallaroo: 'When we come again to Adelaide and … collect a few choice spirits, be sure to invite the writer of this article to join us'.[22] Spence must have chuckled at the thought of his reaction to learning that the writer he proposed to take off to one of those heartlands of Australian misogyny – the pub or the club – was a woman. Towards the end of her life, she was able to despise the work of an American journalist as 'essentially woman's work, dress, fashions, functions, with educational and social outlooks from the feminine point of view'. She was not attempting to deny her own gender; rather, she was asserting the far wider range of activities and views that women could embrace. Her own work, she maintained, 'might show the bias of sex, but it dealt with the larger questions that were common to humanity'.[23]

Spence's 'sketches' included some ventures that were simply fun. She wrote at least two short stories for children, called 'The Hen's Language' and 'The Story of Three Pigs', and she contributed to such characters as 'Mr Dryasdust, R.R.S., M.P, … Captain Fribble, Sophy Lounger, Mrs Martinet, [and] Fanny Smart', to the *Register*'s weekly, the *Observer*.[24] But most of her journalism was serious, lively, literary and social criticism.

She often combined the two. Her article on Balzac in the *Melbourne Review*, for instance, contained more biography and discussion of social values than literary criticism.[25] Most of her literary discussions evinced the same concern with moral and social values as her own fiction did, and her judgments clearly followed that concern. She admired George Eliot not only for her artistry and range but also for the high moral purpose that she discerned in her work, and in her life; she had no compunction about turning discussion of such values into comment upon those which she encountered directly in her own environment. In her first article on George Eliot, in the *Melbourne Review*, she concluded with a sharp observation upon pretension and snobbery:

> It is the easier and the cheaper kind of wit to sneer at ignorance of things conventionally deemed indispensable, but some little mistakes in grammar or pronunciation, and ignorance of etiquette, do not prevent me from thinking many of the mothers in our colonial society more intrinsi-

cally gentlewomen than the daughters who make themselves odious by looking down on them.[26]

In a later article, on Eliot's life as well as her work, she offered her readers a double-edged defence against any moralizing condemnation of Eliot's unconventional domestic arrangements. She pronounced:

> With regard to the marriage question, it is the point where the highest and the lowest natures meet, for to act in opposition to custom may be due to the loftiest motives, or it may be the result of a selfish craving for personal gratification. And perhaps the marriage law of the future will owe more to the rebels of the first class than it will suffer from the influence of the last. It appears to me that the experience of George Eliot should serve rather as a plea for greater liberty of divorce than a weakening of any true marriage bond.[27]

Thus, in the guise of a defence of the sanctity of the marriage of true minds and hearts, she argued for a greater freedom for divorce. Spence's literary articles did not use literature simply as a springboard for sermonizing. She distinguished artistic from social or moral value: she praised Eliot for balance and artistic completeness, as well as for her ethical purpose; she observed of Olive Schreiner's *Story of an African Farm*: 'As a novel the book in nowhere, as an expression of revolt it is everywhere', went on to remark not only that it was 'a strange book to come from such a nest of missionaries', but also to credit its originality; and she commented on Mona Caird's *The Wing of Azrael* that its author 'has ability, but she wants balance and proportion, and often sins against good taste'.[28] Readers of Spence's account of George Eliot's works encountered occasional illuminating insight, and discerning judgment, but her prevailing concern was with social and moral values. Her review of a book by 'Mrs Alick MacLeod' (Catherine Mackay/Martin), *The Silent Sea*, a novel set in a gold-reefing district of South Australia, conveys little information about the story, but a good deal about its humour, and about Spence's view of humour, and descriptions of nature, as refuges in the face of 'mental suffering'.[29]

It was, however, with her social and political articles that she really began to hit her straps. Of course, Spence used her access to the daily press to advance each of the causes that she was involved with: education, particularly advanced education for girls; the welfare of destitute children; and, endlessly, electoral reform. She also found fresh opportunity to express many of the concerns that she dealt with in her fiction, but she addressed other issues, too, that did not become so wholly absorbing to her. In her discussions of land legislation, the relations of labour and capital, industrialization and its effects not only on paid work, but also on domestic labour, she found expression for the political convictions that she had been forming, at least since the time of her religious conversion.

Fundamental to these was her argument for greater economic equity. Among her impressions of England was 'a strange feeling of awe' at the 'contrast between the wealth and the poverty', at the painful juxtaposition of 'the splendid equipages, the liveried servants, the perfectly appointed equestrians, the idle gentlemen, and the handsome and elegantly dresses ladies in Hyde Park', with 'the ragged beggars … at every street corner'. In America in 1893 she argued that wealth encouraged vulgar materialism, spiritual and artistic decay, and the formation of monopolies which destroy the social and political rights of individuals. She labelled the wealthy American a 'plutocrat', accused him of reverting to 'barbarism', and of sinning against the true spirit of democracy. 'The plutocrat', she announced, '… loves to monopolize what is pleasant and beautiful and luxurious; the true democrat wishes for nothing which his fellows cannot share with him, or possess as absolutely as he does'. She castigated Americans 'from Boston, from New York, from Philadelphia, from Chicago, from San Francisco' for their 'exclusiveness, monopoly [and] vulgar display'.[30]

She proposed several specific measures to counteract such injustice and decadence. She foreshadowed the first when, in England in 1866, she remarked: 'Although I am not so much of a Radical as to suggest a division of property, I must say that I think every facility should be given to the transfer of land, and that some step should be taken to prevent the inheritance of colossal fortunes'. There was no need to urge greater facility in land transference in the colony which had introduced the *Torrens Land Act,* but Spence continued to be troubled by the moral debilitation of people who could inherit wealth accumulated by their fathers, and by the permanence of economic inequality fostered by such inheritances. Early in the 1870s she devised a scheme for countering both, but when she submitted it in a letter to the *Register* it roused only passing interest.[31] However in 1877, debate over land taxation in Victoria furnished her with a fresh opportunity.

In Victoria, conflict between pastoralists and selectors had continued despite legislation in 1858, 1862, 1865 and 1870. By 1877 the failure of successive governments to balance their budgets had made a new land tax seem imperative. The nature of taxation to be introduced, and its effect upon pastoralists and selectors, became a leading issue at the elections of May 1877. Among the advocates of a tax with wide ramifications was C. H. Pearson who, as part of his electoral campaign, gave the *Melbourne Review* an article called 'On Property in Land'. Pearson argued for a land tax which would increase in proportion to the size and value of a single estate, and rise so sharply for holdings greater than a specified size as to become prohibitive.[32]

Spence considered his analysis of Australian conditions alarmist, and his remedy oppressive and unjust. She joined issue with him with her own article in the *Melbourne Review*. First, she argued, all previous attempts to restrict large estates and promote the yeomanry 'had failed to call out the yeoman spirit'. When a small proprietor sold his land, he did so freely and because it was more profitable than working it. Legislation to prevent a larger proprietor buying from him would simply lead to evasion of the law. Secondly, she asked whether it was 'just to force enormous sales of land bought in perpetuity by a law of limitations made afterwards, and to make a heavy differential tax on such property act as a deterrent from the investment of capital in this, the most conservative of investments?' She feared that such a measure would only 'set class against class, and one house of the Legislature against the other', and recommended a 'milder method' of achieving the same result: this was a graduated tax imposed not on bequests, but on inheritance of land. She observed that in the United States, where there was no law of entail and no custom or law of primogeniture, there was a tendency for great fortunes to be dispersed in a generation or two, and she proposed that a similar tendency be ensured in Australia by legislation. This might be a slow cure for overgrown estates, but, she asserted, it was a surer and safer one than Pearson's.[33]

In this essay Spence allowed her concern for justice and the retention of Wakefieldian incentives to enterprise, industry and thrift, to cloud her eagerness for the distribution of property. She was annoyed when the *Argus* quoted passages from her article and labeled her argument that of an 'aristocrat'.[34] She learned from the experience. Almost immediately afterwards she argued in the *Register* that 'although a rise to a higher class is a wonderful stimulus to energy and thrift, it is perhaps of more consequence that the material and moral condition of the hewers of wood and drawers of water should be tolerably comfortable'.[35]

Four years later she had abandoned both her own and Pearson's remedies for economic inequality to argue for the introduction of a single tax. She was cautiously enthusiastic about Henry George's proposal. It 'first takes the startling shape of confiscation of land' she wrote, 'then softens down to confiscation of rent; and finally settles down to the drawing of all taxation from the land, and the land alone'. She did not 'anticipate such glorious results' from this measure as George did, but she did 'anticipate a greater amount of benefit than from any other reform in the world'.[36] Spence was to claim that she had pioneered the single tax movement in Australia in the *Victorian Review* in 1881, but her claim does not hold. *Progress and Poverty* had been serialized two years earlier in a Sydney newspaper, and George did not tour Australia until 1890. The vociferous single tax movement in South Australia, which developed out of the Anti-Poverty Society in the wake of George's tour, had not noticed her article, printed nine years earlier, in another colony.[37]

By the time Spence visited the United States in 1893, her argument for greater economic equity was broader, vaguer, and far more sweeping. Against the competition and monopolies of a society dominated by the 'plutocrat' she asserted the spirit of 'the true Democrat'. She considered her attack, itself, the first step towards reform. 'The diagnosis of the disease' she argued 'is … an important part of the physician's work, and for the ailments of society it is necessary first to see how we stand and then to endeavour to discover in what direction we should move'. The direction she proposed was co-operation. In 'social intercourse' this meant 'welcoming a friend to such a dinner as we eat everyday, and as he eats everyday', instead of collecting 'a number of people to whom we owe dinners, for something which is the daily set-out of people three or four times richer than we are but which costs time, money, and fatigue for us'. It substituted 'evening receptions' where husbands and wives might meet each others' friends, and where young men and women might become acquainted, in place of the 'one-sided … one-sexed' social intercourse of clubs and afternoon calls, and 'courting … done no one knows exactly where'. In industry, co-operation meant joint labour and enterprise for mutual benefit, instead of competition. In politics it meant equitable representation and co-operation of 'the party of order and the party of progress' for the benefit of the whole people. Such recognition of mutual dependence and service should engender a sense of security and create genuine democracy. The 'true democratic spirit', she contended,

> is that of activity, yet also of repose. Not eager to rise, not fearful lest it fall, it plants its foot firmly on the daily task. This sense of security is what

ought to be the habitual frame of mind of the true Democrat in a really Democratic Society.[38]

Just as arguing for greater economic equity could lead Spence to consider modes of hospitality, so her discussion of the development of machinery led her through George Howell's arguments about unemployment, J. C. Morison's nostalgic advocacy of the abolition of machinery, and Alfred Marshall's defence of increasing production, to a stinging attack on funds 'squandered on armaments' and a wholesale condemnation of war.[39] It also led her to expect greater value, and higher pay, to be accorded to domestic servants as their numbers dwindled under the impact of 'the good pay and the comparative independence of factory life'.[40] However she did not depict industrialization as a wholly unmixed blessing: 'this steady wave of advance had ebbs and flows. Things which should move simultaneously precede or lag behind each other'. The object of her criticism was the sewing-machine, 'born of the urgent needs of the American housewife', but 'invented before the middle-class woman was prepared for the leisure she might gain from it for better and wiser ends'. Sounding a note which reverberated in the rational dress campaign, Spence observed:

> when watching the yards, we may say miles, of flouncing, kilting, ruching, puffing, and piping – the cutting up of stuff into smaller portions in order to stick it on again … the covering of costly stuff with more costly trimming – one feels for the moment really sorry that the irresponsible machine should lend itself so fatally to the vagaries of fashion.[41]

Her argument was clear: it was not technology itself which was at fault, but the purposes to which technology might be harnessed.

Commercialisation of production for household consumption, running parallel with industrialization, had led, she considered, to 'English society … getting filled up with idle gentlewomen for whom there is no work and no room'. That was destructive. 'Life all amusement is more intolerable than life all labour'. However, she did not use such an argument to urge a return to any romanticised golden age; rather, it was an explanation for 'the widespread movement which is going on all over the world for the admission of women to new fields of labour'. Even in South Australia, she observed, 'we see this band turning in the direction of education – for one male teacher that offers there are three or four females'. Spence saw that movement as having a greater variety of causes than technology and commerce, and she regarded it as inexorable. That did not stop her arguing for it, however. Women in the paid workforce would not threaten the conditions and wages of men, she contended. Besides, 'to tie the hands of half the human race in order that there should be more work for the other half to do can scarcely be wise economy'. Women did not wish to push men out of their jobs, or to find an easy way into the professions: 'all they ask is a fair field and no favour'. Girls were desiring, and would get, a proper education that would enable them to earn a living. Then, 'Men and women will have more common ground; if there will be less outward defence on one side and less softness on the other there will be more mutual respect and more thorough understanding'. The double standard of sexual morality would fade. A woman in the future would be able to choose 'not between destitution and marriage but between the modest competence she can earn and the modest competence her lover offers'.[42]

She had no scruples about raising the threat of revolt in the face of economic injustice and oppression. Considering the effects of mechanisation on Britain's trade and industry, she did not exclude the possibility of 'social and economic revolution',[43] but this was a rhetorical device. She was not a revolutionary. She promoted all the changes she favoured within the social structure she knew; she did not seriously question the justice of the structure itself. Despite her strenuous arguments for greater economic equity, she did not advocate uniform distribution of wealth throughout society. She thought it both impossible and unnatural:

> Socialists have wild ideas as to a reconstruction of society in which a miracle will transform the egoist into the altruist, and when each man will love his neighbour better than himself, and yet will have no sacrifice to make through that principle of action.

She considered that 'the nationalizing of things, as in the Utopias of Bellamy and Grönlund and William Moris, is not desirable even if it were practicable'.[44] She had, earlier, considered seriously the advantages of life in a society somewhat like that depicted in Edward Bellamy's *Looking Backward*, when she wrote her short story *A Week in the Future*.[45] She approved warmly of the village settlements established on the River Murray by the unemployed in the 1890s which, she said, three-fourths of her friends condemned as unnatural and communistic.[46] She considered state control proper for those services she called 'natural monopolies' such as railroads and telegraphs.[47] Late in her life she even favoured some increase in state responsibility: she lectured the Women's League on the nationalisation of health.[48] However she considered total state control akin to monopolies – unjust and oppressive.⁴⁹ She found co-operation preferable to socialism because, while both aimed at increasing general welfare, co-operation's methods required voluntary effort, not compulsion. The difference between Bellamy's militarist state socialism and the co-operative social organization portrayed in *A Week in the Future* was the compulsion of the individual in the first, and the preservation of freedom and initiative in the second. She told the Americans: 'It must needs be that individualism should be allowed to do its best'.⁵⁰

Spence's preoccupation with individual freedom formed the core of the liberalism which pervaded her journalism. She opposed Pearson's land tax, Bellamy's socialism, and social conventions rendering middle-class wives idle, alike, as the imposition of restrictive authority upon individual liberties and achievements. It was a preoccupation arising directly from her own experience. And just as her experience had, finally, enabled her to break through patriarchal convention into a field in which she felt that she expressed her own talents and ambitions freely, so she used that freedom to argue for greater freedom for every individual. She might not have considered a revolution made by the working class either desirable or possible, but she did hold that the huge social changes that would follow upon women's entry into the public sphere – into paid employment, education, even the legislature – were not only desirable but imperative. She also believed them inevitable. 'These things may be called utopian or premature', she wrote,

> but no one can thoughtfully watch the stream of tendency all over the world without being convinced that they are at our gates, and the sooner our community is prepared for them the more wisely they will be met, and the less mischief will accompany the benefits they may be expected to bring.⁵¹

Spence's journalism won her accolades which she treasured. She sent a copy of her article on George Eliot to the author in an effort to excuse herself for the impression that she thought she had created at their interview in 1865. Eliot replied, an unusual thing for her to do by 1876, as she pointed out, and told Spence that while she made it a rule not to read writing about herself, Lewes thought highly of Spence's essay. He had said:

> This is an excellently written article, which would do credit to any English periodical, adding the very uncommon testimony, 'I shall keep this'. Then [wrote George Eliot] he told me of some passages in it which grati-

fied me by that comprehension of my meaning – that laying of the finger on the right spot – which is more precious than praise, and forthwith he went to lay *The Melbourne Review* in the drawer he assigns to any writing that gives him pleasure.[52]

A series of four articles that Spence wrote for the *Register* so impressed Finlayson that he had them reprinted as a pamphlet called *Some Social Aspects of South Australian Life*. H. G. Turner reviewed it in the *Melbourne Review*, praising 'its clear simplicity of statement, its picturesque homeliness, and its direct applicability to ourselves and our surroundings', and proclaiming it an 'excellent contribution to the social history of colonial life'.[53] Those articles contained many assertions of the desirability of greater equality of the sexes, and a suggestion that women might be given the vote, so that praise from the man who wrote a verse dialogue mocking women's suffrage[54] suggests that her contemporaries found her pen persuasive.

Spence considered newspapers and journals to be the principal means available, in her time, of expressing public opinion, commenting on public affairs, and urging new measures upon the community. 'The newspaper' she told South Australian school children, '*partly leads* and *partly follows* public opinion', a responsibility properly fulfilled only by 'the wisest and best people whom the common folk can understand'.[55] She was not merely making a recommendation. Her admiration for Howard Clark must have reinforced her view; she considered that Andrew Garran had enriched Australia's intellectual life with his work for the Adelaide and Sydney press;[56] and she prized her own access to the columns of the *Register* as a means of influencing the community. In her religious allegory she presented her pilgrim as the 'commander-in-chief' of the reformers in the City of Vanity Fair, because he could urge not one but a variety of reforms upon the whole city, in the articles he wrote for 'the broadsheets that come out day by day in thousands'.[57] In her autobiography she remarked, 'When I recall the causes I furthered, and which in some instances I started, I feel inclined to magnify the office of the anonymous contributor to the daily press'.[58]

Her experience largely justified her claim. Her major concerns, electoral reform, destitute children, education and the position of women, were all assisted by the influence she exerted as a contributor to the press. Her later fame and prominence were advanced by the press, and her social and literary articles probably contributed to the climate of opinion in which she won that fame. A memorialist was even prepared to assert that she was 'so influential in forming public opinion that no calculus can integrate the innumerable little pulses of knowledge that she made to vibrate in the minds of her generation'.[59] That is probably an overstatement. Spence's journalism may have introduced her readers to her extraordinarily extensive and wide-ranging reading. There seems little doubt that they enjoyed her clear, direct exposition, telling illustration and occasional barbed reflections. But for all the proliferation of newspapers and periodicals in 19th-century South Australia, the fourth estate did not wield a fraction of the power in that century that it has acquired in our own. Spence did not have a regular column in either the *Register* or the *Observer*. If those papers did amount to a formative influence in the life of the colony, then it was probably through their leading articles and general political line. In that context, Spence's journalism undoubtedly offered occasional illuminating comment, provocative argument, or humorous insight, but the paper would not have continued publishing her work if it had not, at least broadly, conformed with its editors' views. A number of leading articles that she submitted were rejected, though, she noted, not one social or literary one.[60]

Nevertheless, for Spence herself, gaining access to such a forum was a hard-won confirmation of the abilities that she had exercised anonymously until she was fifty-three. And while, even towards the end of her life, she did not always put her name to her articles, her pen-name, 'A Colonist of 1839' was by then so well known that it no longer meant anonymity. Further, her achievement of a place in the daily and weekly press, a place that was acknowledged to be hers, made a substantial breach in the constraints of patriarchal convention which operated to exclude women from the public sphere.

7
Prophet of the effective vote

By the 1890s, Spence's voice already had an established place in South Australia's public affairs. She could, on occasion, be heard by anyone worshipping in the Unitarian Christian Church in Wakefield Street. A member of a district school board, and of the State Children's Council, she could ask questions and proffer advice in committee meeting rooms. As a regular contributor to one of the colony's daily newspapers, the *Register*, her ideas could reach far more people than she was likely to encounter face-to-face. Yet, at that time, most South Australians heard her voice indirectly, through her articles in the press, or muffled by the sheltering walls of the church and committee room. She was still susceptible to descriptions like Geoffrey Blainey's, delivered from a vantage point in the public sphere, as 'the veiled maid of Adelaide'.

To have made even as much of an inroad as Spence had by that time into the world of men, might well have seemed enough to anyone in their sixties, but it was far from enough for Catherine Spence. Her voice was to be heard on platforms, in meeting halls throughout South Australia – indeed across south-eastern Australia, and the United States. She was to speak where people could hear her directly, where she risked the immediate impact of interjections, scoffing and jeering, but where, instead, she would win love and acclaim for her persuasiveness and her power as a public speaker.

She knew well how deeply embedded in custom and lore were the conventions she flouted. As she reflected, at the end of her life:

> law and custom have put a bridle on the tongue of women, and of the innumerable proverbs relating to the sex, the most cynical are those relating to her use of language. Her only qualification for public speaking in old days was that she could scold, and our ancestors imposed a salutary check on this by the ducking stool in public, and sticks no thicker than the thumb for marital correction in private. The writer of Proverbs alludes to the perpetual dropping of a woman's tongue as an intolerable nuisance, and declares that it is better to live on the house-top than with a brawling woman in a wide house.

Against such an armory, we might marvel that she, or any other woman in that period, dared open her mouth, even within her own household. However Spence went on to note:

> A later writer, describing the virtuous woman, said that on her lips is the law of kindness, and after all this is the real feminine characteristic. As daughter, sister, wife, and mother – what does the world not owe to the gracious words, the loving counsels, the ready sympathy which she expresses? Until recent years, however, these feminine gifts have been strictly kept for home consumption ...[1]

By the early 1890s she had resolved that those gifts, the product of a specifically feminine education, should be taken into the heartland of public life – the electoral platform. For however much Spence may have believed that women had a specifically woman's contribution to make to public life, she had also believed for most of her life that women could speak on behalf of all people quite as well as men could.

The cause which propelled her into the glare of the public sphere was, characteristically, not one automatically associated with anything particularly feminine or feminist. At her 80th birthday party, she proclaimed: 'Injustice in England is not rectified by injustice in South Australia, nor does injustice in Alexandria rectify injustice in Torrens. Injustice rectifies nothing. It is an evil everywhere and always'. She was not talking about votes for women. She went on: 'I who speak here tell you that Proportional Representation is the hope of the world'.[2] In that powerful, but peculiar assertion she expressed her life's major conviction and mission. Reform of electoral injustice had been, she wrote later, 'the foremost object of my life'.³ Spence was 66 when she first mounted a platform to explain to South Australians why they should demand the introduction of proportional representation. She was 67 when she set out for the United States to teach North Americans how to vote, but 'this subject is not with me one of to-day or of yesterday' she told a meeting in London in 1894.⁴

She dated her interest in electoral methods from her childhood in Scotland, where her mother urged the benefits of the *Reform Act* of 1832 in the local press.⁵ That concern had developed during her early years in South Australia, when the municipal council which employed her father was elected by quota representation. The provision had been introduced into the legislation by Rowland Hill, copying the system that his father had devised for electing committees in his school in Tottenham,⁶ so Spence's acquaintance first with Emily Clark, subsequently with Clark's uncles and cousins in England, undoubtedly reinforced her interest. The Adelaide Municipal Council did not use Hill's electoral system again; the *South Australian* declared it a 'novel but very absurd principle',⁷ and, for once, most of the colonists must have agreed with the paper's judgment. When Spence sustained a thoroughly anti-labour, anti-urban argument in favour of the principle throughout those and subsequent early electoral campaigns, her arguments found no favour anywhere.⁸ She may have shifted her allegiances a little after she had joined the Unitarians and encountered doctrines less elitist than those of the Shorter Catechism, but the chief factor in changing the way in which she regarded manhood suffrage came from her wide reading. In 1859, she read J. S. Mill's review, 'Recent Writers on Reform', in *Fraser's Magazine*, and that gave her, she wrote later, her 'strongest political inspiration'.⁹

Mill was considering three books about parliamentary reform in England. The third was Thomas Hare's *A Treatise on the Election of Representatives, Parliamentary and Municipal,* which Mill acclaimed as 'the most important work ever written on the practical part of the Subject'. By developing 'what is commonly called the Representation of Minorities', wrote Mill, Hare showed opponents of 'purely democratic suffrage' how they could accord to 'the most numerous class, that of the manual labourers', the majority representation which justice to their numbers demanded, without conceding total representation. Hare's electoral scheme ensured that minorities would retain a representative voice in the legislature. It would also, Mill considered, 'prodigiously improve the personnel of the national representative': 'An assembly thus chosen would contain the *elite* of the nation'.¹⁰

Mill's article showed Spence, she said, 'how democratic government could be made real, and safe, and progressive'. She saw in his account of Hare's electoral system a way of at once safeguarding the right of minorities like the religious minority she had recently joined, and of preventing such bodies as the South Australian Political Association (which, earlier called the 'Working Man's Association', had campaigned against continued immigration at public expense during the 1860 elections) from returning a parliament like that in Victoria, which Spence considered to be a bunch of incompetent demagogues.[11] Her perception electrified her:

> I read Mill's article one Monday night, and wrote what was meant for a leader on Tuesday morning, and went to read it to my brother at breakfast time, and posted it forthwith.[12]

She sent it, as with so many other articles she had written under her brother's name, to the *Argus*, but the *Argus*, which had kept up an abusive editorial commentary on the results of the 1859 elections in Victoria throughout August and September of that year, nevertheless rejected her argument. They were, they told her, committed to the representation of majorities.[13] Rebuffed, Spence fell silent on the issue for a year or so.

In 1861, the South Australian press and parliament debated yet another electoral act amendment bill, the fourth since the first Act was passed. During those debates, Lavington Glyde MP offered the legislature a muddled exposition of Thomas Hare's scheme, without any success.[14] The *Register* discussed his proposals in a sub-leader, acknowledging the justice of the scheme, but objecting to its effects.[15] The following day, the paper printed a letter in which Spence supported the scheme, and a few days later it carried another letter she had written refuting objections to Glyde's proposals.[16] Once again, her arguments, and Glyde's, encountered only rejection. The bill to reorganise electoral districts and their numbers of representatives, a response to population shifts and the small turn-out at the 1860 elections, did only what it was designed to do.[17] However this time, Spence did not give up as easily as she had before. At her brother John's suggestion, she wrote a pamphlet urging the adoption of Hare's electoral system in South Australia. In preparing it she read Hare's book, probably for the first time.

Hare's *Treatise on the Election of Representatives* was an expanded, reshaped version of a pamphlet called *The Machinery of Representation* which he had published after the 1857 general election in Britain.[18] It contained the detailed provisions of the electoral system still known as the Hare system of proportional representation. These were formulated as 33 clauses of an Act, to make the proposals more precise and show its practicability, and embedded in 300 pages of verbose argument. The principle features of his system were voluntary combination of interests – intellectual, professional, religious, economic, regional, or otherwise – to form constituencies, and preferential voting with a single transferable vote. These measures, he claimed, would remove the iniquities of the existing system of representation in Britain, and resolve the difficulties in schemes proposed for reform. Further, voluntary combination into electorates would stimulate candidates appealing to a nation-wide constituency to deserve nation-wide esteem, and would create strong bonds between men of different ranks and stations. Preferential voting, ensuring that every man's vote contributed to the election of some candidates, would rouse electors to a greater awareness of individual and communal responsibility; it would nourish 'the habit of scrutinizing with attention the conduct of public men, and of forming an estimate of their relative merits'. Thus, as Mill observed, proportional representation would raise 'the tone of the whole political morality of the country'.[19] Hare went so far as to assert that it would so elevate politics, that election day should be celebrated by a special religious service.[20]

Spence's pamphlet lacked the conservative emphasis of her letters to the press.

> I made a mistake in introducing this subject in the *Register*, under the title of 'Representation of Minorities', instead of 'Equality of Representation'. I felt the democratic strength of the position as I had not felt it in reading Hare's own book.[21]

This was hardly surprising, as Hare initially opposed manhood suffrage, the ballot, and votes for women. However her 'democratic strength' was grounded in Hare's contention that proportional representation would educate electors. She echoed him when she proclaimed 'I want every man to have a vote and to use it, for it is the most valuable element of education that every man should feel his weight in the state'.[22] *A Plea for Pure Democracy Mr Hare's Reform Bill applied to South Australia*, signed 'C.H.S.', was printed in late 1861. A rambling and ill-organized essay, it represented a new stage in the development of her reasons for her enthusiastic support of proportional representation. She appealed to conservative and popular interests alike for acceptance and implementation of Mill's definition of 'pure democracy': 'the government of the whole people by the whole people equally represented'.[23]

The pamphlet 'did not set the Torrens on fire'.[24] It might have attracted more attention had she lived further east: the *Argus* discussed Mill and Hare on the representation of minorities in 1861, and in 1862 a proportional representation bill was passed by both houses of parliament in New South Wales, but was not implemented because the government resigned.[25] However colonists in South Australia saw no need to seek moral and intellectual elevation by changing the electoral law. With the ballot inhibiting electoral bribery they may not have considered such elevation wanting. Nor did they find it necessary to take special measures to secure electoral equality. Districts based, more or less, on population, and multiple electorates, already provided a semblance of equality. Moreover, they seemed safe from any tyranny by a majority. Even in the Assembly returned after the Political Association's efforts, there was no consistent majority.[26]

Emily Clark sent copies of Spence's pamphlet to the English relatives and to Henry Parkes asking him to give it to J. S. Mill. The English relatives and their friends responded: Spence received compliments from Hare, Mill, Rowland Hill and Professor Craik, and they welcomed her when she visited London in 1865. Describing her visit to England she boasted, 'It was the little pamphlet rather than the novels that procured me introductions into the best society, or what I call the best, the most intelligent in London'.[27] That included both Thomas Hare and John Stuart Mill. The friendship extended to her by Hare and his family added personal loyalty to her enthusiasm for proportional representation. Hare's concurrence with her insistence that proportional representation made manhood suffrage both safe and desirable allowed her to boast: 'I took this reform more boldly that Mr Mill … I was prepared to trust the people'.[28] Mill's courteous interest in what she could tell him about South Australia, and his earnest advocacy of women's suffrage, in their one conversation, suggests that he was impressed with Spence more for her potential value in the struggle for the rights of women than with her urgency for proportional representation.[29] Spence was not, she maintained, to be distracted. Perhaps she was more so than she was prepared to acknowledge later in her life; she did little more for her cause for over a quarter of a century.

She did not lack occasion. In 1871, Glyde, as a member of a select committee on electoral districts, again raised the question of proportional representation of minorities. In 1872 a bill proposing proportional representation with the single transferable vote was introduced in the House of Commons. In 1880 one of the members for Burra made a plea for the Hare system of representation during debates on another

Prophet of the effective vote

electoral districts bill. In the same year, debate over an electoral bill in New South Wales prompted the *Sydney Morning Herald* to pronounce the Hare system the only one capable of achieving really proportionate representation. In 1882 Spence's brother John, in debate in the Legislative Council on another electoral districts bill, argued for making Adelaide a single electorate and asserted that interests attached to people not places. In 1884 the British Proportional Representation Society was formed to agitate for the introduction of proportional representation in the *Representation of the People Act*.[30] Spence allowed these opportunities to pass, probably because her work for the press and the Boarding Out Society kept her extremely busy, and perhaps because she hoped that her brother, elected to the Legislative Council in 1881, would achieve more than she could, and possibly because she thought the current state of politics in South Australia made the task either needless or fruitless. The Acts amending electoral divisions revealed the power of entrenched interests: men occupying the treasury benches were able, despite or perhaps because of, unequal electoral divisions, to retain the constituencies that had elected them.[31]

John Brodie Spence.
Image courtesy of the State Library of South Australia SLSA:B22103/80.

Spence's concern for electoral justice took fire in 1891 from personal and political circumstances markedly different from those of the 1870s and 1880s. Her contributions to the press had dwindled. Her work with the Boarding Out Society had lost its urgency with the establishment of the State Children's Council in 1886. Her niece and nephew had grown up and left home, and in December 1887 her mother died. The following year she was summoned to Gippsland to attend the deathbed of her sister Jessie. In 1889 her nephew married and took over the house she had lived in with her mother. Spence, with Ellen Gregory and the young Hoods, moved her papers to another house and lived quietly, recuperating from her exhaustion and grief.[32] However she did not live so quietly as to ignore political developments in the colony, and these fanned her enthusiasm for electoral justice into a flame. The political situation which prompted her to take to the platform paralleled that in which she had her 'political inspiration'. In 1894 she told an English audience, 'I was led to abandon my position as an obscure, anonymous writer for that of a public speaker on any platform open to me, by the democratic developments in my own country of Australia'. Personal politics and rapidly changing ministries in South Australia had yielded place to 'something like real organization of parties, these being capital and labour', and this convinced Spence that 'now was the time to speak'.[33]

Labour was the first to organise. In 1890, the introduction of payment for members of parliament and the Maritime Strike prodded the United Trades and Labour Council (UTLC), the metropolitan unions, working men's clubs and democratic associations into organising for representation in parliament. Their joint committee set up in January 1891 became the administrative centre of the United Labour Party (ULP). By 1895 there were ten ULP candidates in the South Australian parliament and internal organisation was stable. In 1904 the party's first annual conference created a ULP Council, separating the party from the UTLC. In 1905 it was strong enough to form a coalition government headed by its leader Tom Price.[34]

Capital marshalled its forces in defence against organised labour, creating a pressure group rather than a party. The National Defence League, formed in July 1891, converted into a branch of the Australian National League (ANL) in 1896, endorsed candidates it favoured, but did not bind them to its program. Nevertheless its influence dominated the Legislative Council during the 1890s, and in 1906 it combined with the Farmer's and Producer's Political Union (FPPU) for joint support and selection of candidates.[35]

However, political opinion in South Australia did not align itself exclusively with the two major organisations. From 1893 to 1899 the government came from neither, though it had strong support from the ULP. Conservative discontent with the ANL's extremism spawned a number of liberal and independent groups, prototypes for the FPPU formed in 1903, and A. H. Peake's Independent Country Party. The latter, renamed the Liberal and Democratic Union (LDU) in 1906, formed one half of the 'Lib-Lab' coalition government of 1905-10.[36] Radical discontent with the moderation of the ULP, the product of late industrialisation and moderate unions, found expression in many small, often short-lived groups which for a short time exerted considerable influence. In the early 1890s the ANL feared them as much as, if not more than, it feared organised labour.[37]

These groups were the source of the South Australian labour movement's Utopianism, and its search for visions, programs and strategies that could counter exploitation and ideological domination. The District Democratic Clubs and Associations, the Land Reform Leagues, the Single Tax League, the Society for the Study of Christian Sociology, the Allegemeiner Deutscher Verein, the Working Men's Patriotic Association, the South Australian Fabian Society, and the district Sociological Classes[38] – all were collectively 'the Forward Movement' or the 'Reform Movement'. In the early 1890s, they were all working strenuously for 'A Distinct forward movement, lifting up instead of levelling down society'.[39] Their major fundamental link was their faith in the new social and moral order which they believed particular reforms would bring. Their faith gave their demands – for the single tax, nationalisation of land, distribution of wealth, and justice to labour – the ring of a sacred creed.[40] This proceeded partly from their fervour, and partly from their connections with the churches. The movement was extremely Christian. J. Medway Day, vociferous agitator for land reform and instigator of the Reform Convention, held in September 1893, had been a minister in the Baptist Church. The Reverend Dr Jeffries gave a series of discourses in the North Adelaide Congregational Church on 'The Socialism of Christianity'. The Wesleyan minister, G. E. Wheatley, addressed the Reform Convention on 'The Churches and Reform'. D. M. Charleston, speaking on 'The Ethics of Socialism' shared the platform with the Primitive Methodist minister, J. Day Thompson, lecturing on 'The Simple Gospel'.[41] The new moral and social order was co-operative. One speaker referred to Bellamy's Utopian state socialism and asserted that 'of the many plans set in operation for the benefit of humanity none had a nobler aim or more extensive field than co-operation'. Another proposed to establish a co-operative settlement at Mount Remarkable. The movement as a whole applauded the village settlements on the Murray, and greeted William Lane and his vision of 'New Australia' with wild enthusiasm;[42] their second, and scarcely less important link was their opposition to capital – the appropriators of land, the accumulators of stock, the exploiters of labour. They depicted all capitalists' ideas as part of a conspiracy against them. Medway Day scoffed: 'Bimetallism, protection, and all other artificial nostrums remind me of the little boy who expressed his wonder that his father should first of all wear braces to keep his trousers up and also straps to keep them down. With well-developed hips, neither the one expedient nor the other is required'. A. T. Saunders, lecturing on 'Bimetallism, a scheme to reduce wages', asserted that 'if he had no other reason for concluding that bimetallism was not proposed in the interests of the workers the names of the promoters in this colony would be sufficient, including, as they did, several of the most prominent opponents of Trades Unionism'.[43] Federation, likewise, was a capitalist plot. Charleston claimed that 'The subject … had not come from the people, but from their rulers', and Medway Day proclaimed 'The old cry of patriotism is now little more than cant – a sing-song phrase; for how can we grow enthusiastic over the rule of money-bags and the sacrifice of humanity'.[44] Both their vision of a new society and their hatred of capital was fed by their reading. A ballot of books on reform showed the overwhelming influence of Henry George, whose various works were first, second, fourth, sixth and seventh on the poll. (George had spent some days in Adelaide on his visit to Australia in 1890). Davidson's *The Old Order and the New* came third; *Looking Backward*, fifth; Grönlund's *Co-operative Commonwealth* eleventh; and Donnelly's *Caesar's Column*, twelfth. Marx had a place among 'Other authors given', together with Carlyle, Spencer, Mill and Longfellow.[45]

The Reform Movement did not achieve parliamentary representation. Some reformers condemned existing forms of government so that to seek election would have compromised their principles. Two single-taxers, J. N. Birks, a chemist, and Cornelius Proud, a sharebroker and chairman of the first meeting of the Reform Convention, stood as ULP candidates in 1894. Their lack of success combined with protests from the unions in 1895 to exclude all but wage-earners from ULP selection.[46] But in the early 1890s, the meetings and lectures of these groups, and their paper *Voice*, spread a spirit of idealism, a receptivity to new ideas, and a readiness for change which must have contributed to the liberal Kingston's unprecedentedly long term in office. It certainly contributed greatly to Catherine Spence's initial success.

Spence did not simply spring fully-fledged on to public platforms to urge the preoccupations of her youth the moment opportunity offered. Her preparedness to risk taking a stand on the hustings had developed, like the cause that she took with her, over several decades. It began 25 years earlier; after Howard Clark had so bungled his delivery of the lecture she had written for the South Australian Institute, Spence said, 'I mentally resolved that if I was again asked I should offer to read my own MS'.[47] That opportunity arose five years later with the Institute's request for two lectures on the Brownings. As the occasion approached, Spence was clearly very nervous. She arranged for a young lawyer friend to raise his hand if he could not hear, and, as she took her place to read the first lecture, she felt, she recalled, 'as if my knees were giving way'.[48] As might have been expected, nobody guessed that she was nervous, and her lawyer friend (later Chief Justice Samuel Way) had no occasion to indicate that he could not hear her. Spence undertook to read her own lecture, she told the Institute's audience, because she wanted 'to make [it] easier henceforward for any woman who felt she had something to say to stand up and say it'.[49]

It was undoubtedly her success with the Institute which generated the Unitarians' willingness to hear her preach her own sermons. That experience, and her participation in Adelaide's governmental committee rooms, led her to the platform at the Australasian Charities Conference in Melbourne in 1891. She read her own paper to that conference. Women had been reading their own papers to such gatherings as the annual congresses of the National Association for the Promotion of Social Science in Britain since the early 1860s, but women in similar circles in Australia had been slow to follow suit. At the Melbourne Charities Conference, Vida Goldstein's father read the paper that his wife had written.[50] The charitable in Melbourne seem to have been impressed with Spence: Dr Charles Strong, a former Presbyterian minister, founder of the 'Australian Church', invited her to speak to his Workingmen's Club.[51] She cannot have had much time for preparation, but for the purpose she resorted to her life-long preoccupation. She spoke to the workers that Strong assembled about proportional representation, building on the demand, current in the Victorian working-class, for 'one man, one vote', her own demand for 'one vote, one value'.[52] Spence was launched: she had spoken on the thoroughly unwomanly subject of electoral methods, in the equally unfeminine environment of a workingmen's club where she could expect far less protection than in the South Australian Institute or the Unitarian pulpit. She must have gone home to Adelaide feeling not only jubilant, but restless. The political temper there, no less than in Melbourne, offered her cause unparalleled opportunity.

Joanna and Robert Barr Smith.
Image courtesy of the State Library of South Australia
SLSA: B49700.

Fortunately for Spence, her friends, the Barr Smiths, agreed with her and offered to finance a public campaign.[53] Spence did not hesitate. She had ballot papers printed for mock elections to illustrate her arguments. Then, on 17 February 1892, she took to the public platforms of South Australia. A year later she had delivered 'about forty public addresses to audiences in various places and of various political standpoints', campaigning not only in Adelaide but also in the country, to the southeast and then to the north of the city.[54] She had made proportional representation the talk of the colony. One large mock-election which she conducted, progressively, at several of the gatherings that she addressed, and through the columns of the *Register* as well, elicited nearly 4,000 votes.[55]

She remodelled the cause with which she took to the hustings. Her brother John had found it a name: 'effective voting', which was easier to say repeatedly than 'proportional representation', and more likely to appeal to the temper of the Reform Movement.[56] Moreover, at least at this time in her life, Spence's reasons for seeing 'effective voting' as a mission aligned her directly with the Utopianism of the Reform Movement. She could still sound a note that reverberated back to the late 1850s: 'The feud between labour and capital will become more and more bitter', she told the Adelaide Democratic Club in 1892, 'if by your political machinery you exclude all those large bodies of independent thinkers who might bring moderation into your national Councils'. She had told the colony's school children, in *The Laws We Live Under*, that capital and labour should co-operate, to their mutual benefit, rather than struggle against each other. In 1893 she told the *Advertiser*: 'it is borne in upon my soul that in the co-operative spirit and the co-operative method applied to politics instead of the competitive, we may find deliverance from many evils that are eating into the heart and lessening the happiness of humanity'.[57]

Yet for all its appearance of moderation and eclecticism, effective voting would ensure to each of the major political opponents accurate representation of its relative strength. That meant, automatically, greater representation for labour. Co-operation was a cry likely to win her support from all but out-and-out reactionaries. One of her first invitations to speak publicly in Adelaide came from the Adelaide Co-operative Society, a body of share-holders in a non-political, moderately profitable venture in co-operative farming.[58] Spence insisted on her independence from any political group or party, but her appeal for co-operation was made, not on behalf of moderate conservatives, but in the spirit of the Reform Movement. She had already demonstrated her support for Henry George's single tax, and her readiness at least to domesticate ideas like Bellamy's. Her belief in the elevated social and moral order which effective voting would bring was identical with the Utopianism of the reformers. The Reform Movement made her cause part of their own, supplied her most vocal supporters, and publicised her activities. In June 1893, papers on 'Effective Voting' and 'New Australia' were read from the same platform.[59] As late as April 1896, Elsie Birks was writing to a friend about ' "Professor" Gilmour' and his lecture on effective voting in Renmark. 'Does not Miss Spence speak well and clearly', she exclaimed, 'she is indeed a wonderful woman'.[60]

Spence made no original contribution to ways of calculating the quota for proportional representation, that is the smallest number of votes necessary to elect a candidate. In 1861 she described only Hare's quota, calculated by dividing the number of formal votes to be cast by the number of seats to be filled. But by 1892 she had adopted 'Sir John Lubbock's mathematical quota', devised in 1868 by H. R. Droop and adopted by Lubbock, a leading member of the British Proportional Representation Society.[61] The Droop quota, calculated by dividing the total formal votes cast by the number of seats to be filled plus one, and adding one to the quotient, was supposed to prevent parties achieving majority returns, where the Hare quota only hampered such a result.[62] In 1893, Spence decided, mistakenly, that the Droop quota left even more of the votes unused, and returned to the simple Hare quota. It was, in any case, easier to understand: 'popular audiences prefer the simple quota of Thomas Hare's', she noted a year later.[63]

She did make a contribution to the method of distributing preferences, however. When the surplus votes, cast for a candidate who was already elected, were distributed at full value, the results might be different if in counting, the preferences were being taken from the top or the bottom of the pile to be distributed. Spence's first solution sounded like a recipe for plum pudding: 'Let all voting papers from all polling-places be well mixed together, and then take the votes as they come to hand'.[64] By 1894, she had decided, as have later generations of Australians voting in elections for the Australian Senate, that such random distribution in a large election stood little chance of unjustly affecting the results. However in 1894 she adopted a suggestion made by her friend Annie Martin, to give fractional values to all preferences but the first, unknowingly echoing the system devised by J. B. Gregory in 1882, and anticipating its implementation in Tasmania in the 20th century.[65] This then formed the Hare-Spence system of proportional representation, embodied in a bill submitted to the South Australian parliament almost every year from 1902 until 1910.[66]

Such technical difficulties clearly indicate why Spence's campaigns never achieved their goals. Proportional representation might be the 'fairest' electoral system that a democracy can devise. However as recently as 1980, an Australian Senator observed, 'It is an unfortunate fact, but still a fact, that the fairness of electoral systems has a direct relationship to their complexity'.[67] A political scientist noted, earlier, that 'Without compulsion, it is possible that the numbers voting would have fallen heavily in protest at difficult and complicated voting methods: e.g. Proportional Representation in Senate elections'.[68] A different analysis, sharing some of the concerns expressed by the Reform Movement in South Australia in the early 1890s, might contend that elections, fair or otherwise, are only one of several ways in which states and their policies can be shaped in capitalist economies. However for Spence, electoral reform became a creed: it was the necessary condition for the elevation, educational and spiritual, as well as economic, of all humanity. That conviction dominated the last 20 years of her life, becoming so familiar that it was like a habit, so strong that it threatened to make her a bore, but it was also the means by which she realised her childhood's ambition for greatness. On the platform, Spence achieved an even more important independence from the constraints of a patriarchal social order than she had as a journalist. Moreover, on the platform, she was there to hear when people applauded and cheered.

This they did, throughout her campaign of 1892-93. The Reform Movement offered support: its paper *Voice* reported meetings she addressed; Medway Day asserted that if he were standing for election the first plank on his platform would be Miss Spence's effective voting system.⁶⁹ The *Register*'s rival, the *Advertiser*, paid her warm tribute:

> Persons who take only a superficial view of things, very likely regard the whole affair as a fad which this excellent lady had taken into her head, and the advocacy of which furnishes congenial employment for her somewhat rare gifts of speech and intellect. But those who understand Miss Spence best will be the last to imagine her likely to allow herself to be dominated by a mere fad, and will have no difficulty in discovering a truer explanation of the arduous task she has imposed upon herself in the endeavour to arouse public interest in the proposed method of voting. Her enthusiasm in this springs from the same root as her enthusiasm in the cause of State Children and of all philanthropies – the love she has for humanity.⁷⁰

Within a month of conducting the scrutiny of the votes lodged in her largest mock-election, Spence left for the United States. She was to represent the South Australian State Children's Council at the International Conference on Charities and Correction to be held in conjunction with the World Fair being mounted in Chicago. She was to report to the Single Tax League on similar bodies in the States, to Hartley on the North Americans' education, and to the campaigners for female suffrage on the progress of the American women's suffrage movement. She carried letters of introduction to the son of the revered anti-slavery campaigner, William Lloyd Garrison, himself a single-taxer and supporter of woman's suffrage, and to the anti-poverty hero, Henry George. Lectures and drawing room meetings were arranged for her as she passed through Melbourne and Sydney.⁷¹ But her prime purpose in going was to teach the Americans how to vote. She went at the invitation of Alfred Cridge, a San Francisco journalist who was also an ardent advocate of the Hare system of proportional representation.⁷² At the age of 67, Spence departed alone, unchaperoned and unprotected, to give public lectures in a strange land. Characteristically, she left without her purse.⁷³

Miss C.H. Spence.
From *Adelaide Observer*,
8 April 1893.

She spent almost a year in the United States, and her reception there eclipsed her success at home.[74] She cast a wide net, speaking on a host of topics in a variety of places. Her chief object was to persuade America to adopt proportional representation, but the Americans elicited from her a much greater range of performances, not least in Unitarian pulpits. She complained to her brother, 'One drawback to these pulpit ministrations with regard to the Cause is that people are more interested in the Children of the State than in Effective Voting which would benefit the reformers of old abuses'.[75] She lectured on effective voting all over the country, and to enough paying audiences to begin supporting herself on the proceeds.[76] By the time she left in 1894 she had a gratifying list of achievements. In San Francisco she claimed that she helped Cridge persuade the Pacific Coast Council of the Trades and Labour Federation 'to become actively interested in political questions', and she induced the Council to pass a resolution in favour of effective voting. The Proportional Representation Congress she addressed founded the American Proportional Representation League which agitated for several forms of the system. The League issued a quarterly *Review* for three years after it was founded, then again from 1901-13. During its last 12 years it was edited by Robert Tyson, a Canadian. Spence claimed to have converted Tyson to the cause when she paid a visit to Toronto, so she could regard the regular issues of the *Review* as the result of her influence. She made a considerable, if delayed, impact on Toronto. Seven years later the Women's Canadian Historical Society opened a campaign for proportional representation with a lecture on 'Effective Voting: Its History as Developed by an Australian Woman'. She could also claim to have influenced the growing female suffrage movement in the United States. In Chicago, she said, she converted Susan B. Anthony, veteran of the suffrage movement, to her cause.[77]

However her principal achievement was her personal success as a speaker. This gave her great satisfaction. She boasted to her brother, 'I posted for Australia a number of copies of the Boston Transcript with an Editorial on Miss Spence's Crusade – written after … the Editor had heard me speak extempore to the Nationalist Club at Charlesgate the most swell hotel in Boston'. Later she added 'I am really a *Personage* in America out of New York at least'.[78]

In April 1894, she left by steamer for Glasgow. In Britain she spoke only to the converted, and their more sceptical friends, at a special meeting called by Hare's daughter and members of the inactive Proportional Representation Society. In London, when avoiding being run over by a bus, she fell over and dislocated her right shoulder. It was not quite healed by the time she reached South Australia again, so the rest of her journey must have been very uncomfortable. This did not prevent her visiting Zurich in search of English-speaking supporters of her cause, nor from discussing electoral systems with Ernest Navelle in Geneva. As Alfred Cridge had remarked, 'She was almost constantly at work'.[79] In London, and on her journey home, she laid the foundation for the correspondence which enabled her to belabour South Australia with examples of electoral reform all over the world.[80] She reached South Australia in December 1894, in the eyes of many colonists, an international celebrity.[81]

By that time the Reform Movement had already passed its peak. Groups like the Single Tax League and the Adelaide Democratic Club remained active and influential, but the fervour of 1890-94 had evaporated and many smaller groups had died. Attempts to continue campaigning for effective voting while Spence was away faded out two months after she left. The movement's paper, *Voice,* was absorbed in the *Weekly Herald*, the ULP paper. Medway Day went to live in Sydney. E. J. Hickock, secretary and driving force of the Single Tax League, died. The village settlements on the Murray were suffering from internal squabbles, and there were reports of dissension and secession from Paraguay. The hopes of the fragmenting Reform Movement, like those of the ULP and the Liberals, focussed for a time on the Liberal Kingston ministry. But as the decade wore on, and the bills passed through the House of Assembly but rejected by the Legislative Council mounted, disillusion set in. The fall of the Kingston government in November 1899 did nothing to revive the Utopianism of the early 1890s. It appeared that different kinds of action were needed.[82]

Spence redirected her efforts to the movement that was forming a federation of the British colonies in Australia into the Australian Commonwealth. She badgered Kingston, at the Premiers' Conference in Hobart early in 1895, with letters and telegrams exhorting the use of effective voting for elections to the federal Convention. When Kingston, with George Turner, drew up a bill intended to ensure equitable representation for each colony by adopting a list-system for elections, Spence decided that he was spineless and campaigned against the system. 'Federation would have been more acceptable to Australia', she stormed, 'if the large numbers and large interest of wage-earners had been adequately represented'.[83]

Her efforts did not stop at meetings, deputations, handbills and letters to the press. Urged by her new friend and colleague, Jeanne Young, and undoubtedly encouraged by the applause she had won in the press, she took an unprecedented step: she herself stood for election to the federal Convention. Her friends delayed her nomination until the last minute, to avoid investigation and possible rejection by the returning officer. Even then, there was time for speculation about whether she would be allowed to sit if she were elected. Such speculation may have discouraged support, but one of the small liberal organisations explicitly sought support for her, including her name on a ticket headed '10 best men', and awarding her an accolade only possible in a patriarchal society: 'she's the best man of the lot'. In the elections she scored 7,383 votes, coming 22nd out of 33 candidates. She regretted 'losing a great opportunity of directly urging on the Convention the wisdom and justice of effective voting', but on the whole she was pleased. She told the *Weekly Herald*, 'As my own candidature was mainly undertaken as a plea for electoral equity; as I stood or fell on a question which both parties thought it expedient to ignore … I look on my position on the poll as very satisfactory'.[84] Had she not, by then, been so single-mindedly absorbed in her cause, or if her own writing of her autobiography had extended into those years, there might be some more personal glee recorded, for the nomination made Catherine Spence the first female political candidate in Australia's history. That was more than a break with patriarchal convention. It was a confident expression of defiance.

In 1897, Spence was in her 72nd year. She devoted much energy during the last 12 years of her life to her campaign for effective voting, returning to local politics when the federation-makers ignored her, but accepting invitations to speak about her cause in Sydney as well as in the remoter regions of her own state. Her commitment and determination continued to win her personal applause for the rest of her life. The nearest her cause came to success in her own society was in 1900 when, after two years of strenuous lobbying, South Australia's Legislative Council passed a motion urging the adoption of effective voting by eleven votes to five. The Council then saw a different motion for effective voting defeated in the House of Assembly, by the speaker's casting vote. The division showed that it had been supported by eight members of the ULP and one ex-labour vote. As one parliamentarian, T. H. Brooker, observed, it cut straight across established party-affiliations. 'In democratic quarters it was urged … that it would give to labour the representation it was entitled to,' he said 'while in other quarters different reasons were assigned for its adoption'.[85]

Spence had formed an Effective Voting League in 1895, with just such mixed support; in 1900 its executive included Tom Price, leader of the Labour Party, P. M.

Glynn, a liberal conservative, Elizabeth Nicholls, president of the local Women's Christian Temperance Union and former suffragist, and T. H. Webb, president of the Free-Trade and Liberal Association.[86] However while effective voting enjoyed support from the whole range of the party-political spectrum, it found committed support from nowhere. When yet another bill for proportional representation was brought into the South Australian parliament in 1905, by a Labour man, even Tom Price slid out from under. He was, by then, leading the first Lib-Lab coalition to have achieved government in South Australia; members of his own party opposed the measure: his Liberal-Country Party deputy disliked it so much that he had written a pamphlet against it. A Labour member repeated an argument he had been using for at least five years: 'The method proposed was too philosophic for the everyday requirements of ordinary people'.[87] It *is* difficult to understand. Nevertheless, Spence was probably right when she observed at her 80th birthday party: 'If the measure promised any decided advantage to any party, that party would take it up and work for it, but it has the advantage of being perfectly equitable. "Too damned fair," I have heard it called by the profane'.[88] Moreover, her claim that it would enable labour and capital to co-operate was, by then, easy to counter. The uneasy coalition government of 1905-10 in South Australia was achieving that co-operation without it.

Catherine Spence's campaign for effective voting may not have won committed support from South Australian political parties, forming and jostling for parliamentary representation, in the decades on either side of the turn of the century. However she made for it a distinct place in the Reform Movement of the 1890s, contributing importantly to the Utopian visions which linked those disparate groups into a social movement, inviting belief in a radically different future, and offering inspiration to the labour movement. Moreover, Spence's appearance on public platforms to plead her cause, face to face with anyone who came to hear her, must have done more than any argument she could present to convince people that the social order was really changing.

Catherine Helen Spence, the Grand Old Woman of Australia. Image courtesy of the State Library of South Australia (1985).

8
The New Woman of South Australia: Grand Old Woman of Australia

The populism flourishing in South Australia in the early 1890s when Catherine Spence first took to the colony's platforms was but a brief and distant echo of the populism that she encountered in the United States in 1893.[1] In this period there were close and extensive links between populism and the multifarious activities and organisations of the Women's Movement that mushroomed throughout the capitalist industrial, and industrialising, world in the late 19th century.[2] Spence encountered a number of prominent representatives of the North American Women's Movement during that year.

In San Francisco she met 'that celebrated journalist, poetess and economic writer, Charlotte Perkins Stetson'. In 1893, the feminist thinker we now know as Charlotte Perkins Gilman was not so much celebrated as struggling against unwanted notoriety, because she had left her husband.[3] Jeanne Young, writing the last section of Spence's autobiography for her, accorded to Gilman a recognition which she acquired somewhat later, but Gilman was already active in feminist circles. To her, Spence owed 'one of the best women's meetings I ever addressed'.[4] In Chicago, Spence was in the heartland of the North American women's labour movement. In 1893, a time of severe economic depression in Chicago and elsewhere, members of the Working Women's Union, the Ladies' Federal Union and the Illinois Women's Alliance all helped in organising and supporting a strike of 3,000 garment workers.[5]

Much of that activity emanated from Hull House which Jane Addams and Ellen Starr had founded in 1889 on the model of Toynbee Hall in the east end of London. It was intended to provide occupation for the earliest generation of female college graduates in the United States by inviting them to live among the poor and labouring classes, participating in their daily lives and industrial struggles. Through her work at Hull House, Jane Addams became known as the founder of modern American settlement work, and the centre of the people who would come to be labelled 'the social feminists'; women who were also active in labour and socialist struggles referred to them as 'the allies'.[6] Spence visited Hull House and developed considerable admiration for Jane Addams's work.[7] At the World Fair in Chicago, she may not have been aware of the links being forged between Hull House and the garment workers' struggle, but there she met Susan B. Anthony, five years older than she was, and by that time president of the National American Women's Suffrage Association.[8] I have not found any evidence to support Spence's claim that she converted Susan B. Anthony to effective voting.[9] Anthony was an extremely single-minded campaigner for women's suffrage.[10] As had John Stuart Mill nearly 30 years earlier, she may well have considered that Spence's energies would be more fruitfully focussed in the suffrage struggle, a struggle which was increasingly preoccupying all of the groups and individuals of the Women's Movement.

Further east, Spence met Harriet Tubman, who was, wrote Jeanne Young, 'called the "Moses of her people" – an old black woman who could neither read nor write, but who had escaped from slavery when young, and had made 19 journeys south and had been instrumental in the escape of 300 slaves'.[11] Those journeys and escapes, 'the Underground Railroad', together with her stand on the rights and dignities of black women, made Tubman the heroine of a convention assembled in Washington three years later to form the National Association of Coloured Women.[12] North America clearly challenged some of Spence's assumptions about race. In Boston she spent three weeks staying with the family of William Lloyd Garrison, son of the famous crusader for the abolition of slavery, and there she began 'to be a little ashamed of being so narrow in my views of the coloured question'. She admired Tubman, whose 'shanty was a refuge for the sick, blind and maimed of her own people',[13] but she seems not to have thought of bringing her broadened views to any consideration of racial dispossession and exploitation at home in South Australia.

In New England, Spence spent time with a woman factory inspector, with a woman pastor in the Unitarian Church (Anna Garlin Spencer),[14] with the president of the New England Women's Club, and with a number of women writers.[15] Even if she had not been sympathetic to its concerns, she could not have avoided being impressed with the strength and variety of the Women's Movement in North America.

Catherine Spence was, though, far from unsympathetic. She had, like Charlotte Perkins Gilman (who was more than a generation younger), deliberately chosen to try to make her living independently, and was therefore familiar with anxieties about where the next week's housekeeping expenses were to come from. She had responded to such worries with a passionate and carefully reasoned outburst against a gender-divided labour market in her third novel, *Mr Hogarth's Will*. She had lived at the centre of a predominantly female household, bringing up children and forming strong views – views to be found more widely spread in the kindergarten movement towards the end of the 19th century than among the shapers of educational policy in South Australia in the 1870s – about ways of cultivating independence of mind and self-reliance in children. She had, like Barbara Leigh Smith and her friends in England, argued for and given warm support to the development of advanced education for young women. For some years, by 1893, she had been trespassing out of the domestic sphere of hearth and home, not only into the realm of voluntary welfare work, like that of the South Australian Boarding-Out Society or like Rosamond Davenport Hill's with the London School Board or Jane Addams's work at Hull House. She had cautiously built herself a firm and favourable reputation as a writer for the daily press, and had more recently achieved fame as a persuasive speaker in the public sphere.

Moreover, Spence was ready to help other women achieve similar goals. Charlotte Perkins Gilman remembered, more than thirty years later, a 'strong, liberal-minded woman, Miss Catherine Spence of Scotland [sic]', who took Gilman's first published book with her to England. There Spence left the volume of satirical verses with a publisher who later brought out the edition which founded Gilman's transatlantic reputation.[16] Campaigners like Susan B. Anthony were bound to meet Catherine Spence with delight, for not only could she tell of having met such pioneers of suffrage campaigns in England as Barbara Leigh Smith, Rosamond Davenport Hill and Frances Power Cobbe, but she could also boast of an active Women's Movement in South Australia, proclaim her own credentials as vice-president of the South Australian Women's Suffrage League, and bring tidings of an optimistic struggle there for the vote. She gave 'fourteen paid lectures chiefly for Women's Clubs' during her time in North America, speaking on 'Equal Suffrage mostly',[17] and found when she travelled on to Britain that she 'had been so much associated with the suffragists in America, with the veteran Susan B. Anthony at their head, that English workers in the cause gave me a warm welcome'.[18] While she was in England renewing her friendship with the Davenport Hill sisters and meeting Millicent Garrett Fawcett, who was to become president of the National Union of Women's Suffrage Societies three years later,[19] the suffrage workers at home in South Australia marshalled their energies for what turned out to be the last stage of their campaign. For that struggle, Catherine Spence had ensured attention and support from across the world.

Just as changes in the economic order of South Australian society were, by the 1890s, polarising labour and capital and giving rise to the formation of political parties to contest the interests of each, so changes in the patriarchal social order were altering the boundary between the separate spheres of women and men and leading to the formation of organisations to protect and promote the rights of women. Spence had discussed some of these changes as early as 1878, in the articles which the *Register* republished as the pamphlet *Some Social Aspects of South Australian Life*. At that time those changes were only beginning. They were of three kinds, all interrelated, each of them integral to the changes which also produced the general polarisation of labour and capital in the colony. One was demographic; another concerned the labour of working-class women; the third included changes in domestic production and widening employment opportunities for middle-class women.

Spence was writing too early to observe a decline in the birth-rate in South Australia, but by the 1880s it was falling. The birth-rate fluctuated slightly, but between 1880 and 1910, it fell from 38 percent to 26.5 percent.[20] In Adelaide the rate of population growth fluctuated a great deal, clearly reflecting migration at least as much as the birth-rate, but this rate also fell: from 6.8 in 1876 to 1.8 in 1891 and then to 0.03 in 1896.[21] Even as it recovered a little, subsequently, it was clear that the families which formed the core of the domestic sphere were shrinking. The second kind of change was one which Spence discerned when she commented that manufacturing was depriving women of their traditional forms of domestic production, and noted the frivolous extravagances being produced on the newly-invented sewing machines. Writing a century later, Ray Markey has observed that:

> In a very real sense, women were the industrial cannon fodder for manufacturing growth ... cheap female labour was an essential part of the

process of capital accumulation in the developing manufactures, which were inefficiently structured, subject to price and quality competition from overseas, relatively labour intensive, and, unlike other sectors, relied largely on domestic capital formation even prior to the cessation of British capital inflow in the 1890s.[22]

Markey was discussing changes in New South Wales and, secondarily, Victoria. Despite South Australia's continuing reliance upon pastoralism and mining for local capitalist survival, similar developments in manufacturing also appeared there, though on a very small scale, in the late 19th century. Markey's comments are as valid for South Australia as for New South Wales or Victoria.

Spence had commented on a change from domestic to industrial production of pickles and preserves for household consumption. The vines and fruit trees being grown on the outskirts of Adelaide, to the north in the Barossa Valley, and around Renmark near where the Murray crosses the South Australian border, were providing the means for development of a growing industry in preserving fruit. Like many other managers of households in Adelaide in the 1870s, she had probably found that jam could appear on the tea-table with far less effort and little more cost when bought ready-made from a local retailer than when made at home.[23] Workshops established in Adelaide to make biscuits and confectionery and to roll and pack tobacco undoubtedly had the same effect.[24] The jobs made available in such workshops must often have been casual seasonal work, but they were jobs for the unskilled, and since women could be paid more cheaply than men, those jobs offered to working-class women some small alternative to domestic service which was still the principal opening for women needing to earn wages. A job in a jam factory was, unlike domestic service, beyond the confines of the domestic sphere.

In the provision of clothing, the change was both more marked and more complicated. Machinery was introduced into the clothing industry in South Australia in the 1870s and 1880s, encouraging, and encouraged by, a tariff which the local capitalist legislators imposed on imported garments in 1887.[25] Industrialisation led to increasing specialisation of tasks in clothing factories and workshops, together with a breakdown in old apprenticeship systems and abandonment of the 'one man one garment' principle. Such de-skilling generated a demand for cheap female labour. The harsh conditions, long hours and monotonous repetitive work were still attractive when compared with the hours, the personal subservience and indignity common in domestic service. The relative percentages suggest that women moved from one to the other slowly: in 1891, 6.1 percent of South Australia's female population was still employed in domestic service, while those working in factories amounted to only 1.5 percent.[26] Even among those aged between fifteen and twenty this seems to have been so: the percentage employed in domestic service fell from 24 in 1891 to 18 in 1911 while the percentage employed in industry rose only from 13 to 14.[27] Yet the trends suggest a different story: the number of women employed in domestic service in South Australia halved between 1881 and 1911, whereas the number of those employed in factories and workshops trebled between 1876 and 1911.[28] Clothing production was not the only field in which such changes were taking place. Women were finding paid employment in bookbinding, printing, paper-bag making and laundries as well. But the clothing industry, as the second major single employer of women, showed more clearly than any other how working-class women were moving into a sphere of paid employment which was, like that of their brothers, physically removed from anyone's hearth and home.

The figures disguise a further and closely-related development which suggests that the number of women involved in the clothing industry was greater than was generally recognised. Clothing workshops could not always fill their orders and make the profits that their owners wished for simply by taking on cheap female labour. One solution, a well-established tradition in England, was outwork and its inevitable accompaniment, sweated labour. The practice of outwork in the clothing industry increased in Adelaide during the 1880s and 1890s.[29] Apart from the desperate physical suffering of the sweated outworkers, sweating meant that at least one facet of domestic production in working-class households was being locked into a cash economy. This, too, eroded the distance between the public sphere of men and money, and the domestic sphere of women, children and labour performed unpaid, for love.

The third kind of change in the gender order of South Australian society occurred in the middle-class households in which women were having fewer children and were losing their former occupations as jam-makers, bottlers, picklers and unpaid makers of dresses and suits. These women sought a wider sphere for their energies in the charitable penumbra which their activities extended from their domestic worlds into the public sphere. Some joined the Boarding-Out Society, with Catherine Spence and Emily Clark. Some went hospital visiting, or visited the sick and poor in their homes; women of the North Adelaide Baptist Church did this regularly. Some began raising money for charitable causes developing in the late 19th century, like the Children's Hospital, the Ministering Children's League, the District Nurses, or the South Adelaide crèche for children of working women.[30] After 1876, they could if they wished, engage in local politics: legislation passed in that year empowered them to vote in elections to district councils.[31] Their daughters could seek further education at the Advanced School for Girls, even at Adelaide University, and find salaried or fee-paying work as teachers, lawyers and medical practitioners.[32] Only a small minority of South Australia's middle-class daughters were taking advantage of such expanded opportunities in the 1880s and 1890s, but those who did were, just as much as working-class women, moving into a sphere previously accessible only to their brothers.

Further, those who went on to secondary and post-secondary education, and those who gained post-primary training skills as telephonists or typists, were for a time increasingly likely to find salaried employment, like Spence's ward Rose Hood, in an office or instrumentality of the state.[33] For, despite the systematic colonisers' aims, the state had grown in South Australia during the second half of the 19th century, just as it had in Britain and in the other Australian colonies. Free-enterprise capitalism, however rationalised, required an infrastructure to be able to develop, and the early governors' experience had demonstrated the unlikeliness of individual capitalists being willing to provide that infrastructure themselves. This meant that the colony saw no equivalents of the privately-owned monopoly railroad companies which so horrified Spence when she encountered them in the west of the United States.[34] But it meant, too, that those making profits from the colony's development were prepared to submit to taxation to enable the state to build roads, railways, harbours, waterworks, and even the overland telegraph to Darwin Harbour. Further still, local capital was slowly and partly in response to non-capitalist demand, persuaded of the need for basic general levels of hygiene, health care and education. The colony gradually developed foundations for what would become, in the mid-20th century, a potential welfare state. Both tradition and the systematic colonisers' assumptions had regarded the needs for health, education and welfare as most often supplied within the domestic sphere, supplemented by extra-governmental, free enterprise, philanthropy. However free enterprise philanthropy was a minor undertaking in this colony, even when it began developing in the 1870s and 1880s. This meant that the State – the core of the public sphere – was itself of necessity trespassing into the domestic sphere and its traditional penumbra of feminine good works among the poor, the sick, the unemployed and the uneducated. The State Children's Council offers one example: it developed from mixed governmental and philanthropic origins into a body administering not only reformatories, industrial schools and licensed adoption systems, but also new practices of inspecting lying-in homes and establishing the precursors of children's courts. Catherine Spence boasted of these developments across the western world. The Education Board's transformation into a government Department of Education, thwarting Spence's hopes of becoming a member of the voluntary Education Council, furnishes another example. Where mothers had been active in philanthropy, they were, very gradually, losing occupations to daughters who were salaried government servants.[35]

Such changes were, of course, discussed in quite different terminology at the time. The hegemony of liberalism meant that even labour and feminist demands were usually couched in terms of a fundamental 'natural' justice which worked persuasively among a ruling class with strong liberal origins, backed by a predominantly pastoral and mining economy. It also disguised the efforts which an occasionally militant labour movement and a growing feminist movement contributed to those changes.

All three kinds of change, occurring together, brought into stark relief the contradiction between specific experiences of life for women in South Australia in the 1880s and 1890s and a dominant ideology which continued to depict women as 'naturally' relegated to the domestic sphere, a realm entirely separated from and subordinate to the public sphere of men and affairs of state. By themselves, such structural changes would have been necessary, but were not sufficient, causes for the development of an active Women's Movement in South Australia. The contradiction, experienced and recognised by women, like Spence, who had always found the dominant ideology a constraint upon energy, ambition and self-fulfilment, offered clear occasion for action. The emergence of a Women's Movement in South Australia in the 1880s shows Catherine Spence as less alone than she must often have felt. It also shows that women are, quite as much as any generic 'man', present in the making of our history.

Concern about the needs and rights of women had found expression in South Australia, as in the United States and in Britain, in a variety of activities. In the late 1870s there had been a campaign for advanced education for women. In

The New Woman of South Australia: Grand Old Woman of Australia

the 1880s a host of philanthropic ventures concerned specifically with women were established. These included the Young Women's Christian Association, inaugurated in 1884; the formation of the Social Purity League to press for legislation to raise the age of consent and to combat proposals for licensed brothels; the establishment in the same year of the Women's Christian Temperance Union, off-shoot of the body founded in the United States; and more short-lived enterprises including the Young Women's Institute, a residential club for young women working in shops and factories, and Mrs L. M. Corbin's crèche for children of working women. In January 1890 a different kind of organization, the Working Women's Trades Union, was founded as the result of a large public meeting about sweating in the clothing industry, held in the previous year.[36]

Many of these organisations focused their energies comparatively early on the question of female suffrage. Its place on their agendas had been ensured by its discussion in one of the sanctums of the public sphere: in 1885 Edward Charles Stirling introduced into the House of Assembly a motion which read:

Edward Charles Stirling.
Image courtesy of the
State Library of South Australia
SLSA: B11259.

> That in the opinion of this House, women, except while under coverture, who fulfil the conditions and possess the qualifications on which the parliamentary franchise is granted to men, shall like them, be admitted to the franchise for both Houses of Parliament.[37]

Stirling had been in England acquiring degrees and fellowships in natural science and medicine in the 15 or so years since he and his family had travelled there, with Catherine Spence for company, in 1864. His English acquaintances included the Fawcett family, and he was in correspondence with William Woodall, a liberal member of the House of Commons, who introduced into that House measures for extending the franchise to women, twice in 1884, and again in 1885.[38] It was not particularly surprising that, having returned to South Australia and gained a place in the House of Assembly, Stirling should have sought the same there. After all, the traditions established by the colony's founders depicted it as a more liberal society than that of Britain; a thoroughly progressive liberal measure might well stand a better chance there. Arguments against such a measure which appealed to 'natural' inferiorities or inabilities in women did not match up to the evidence. Stirling was teaching physiology at Adelaide University, and in that subject in three out of four years, the prizes had been won by women; 'Speaking … as a teacher of both sexes,' he said, 'he had no hesitation in saying that he could recognize no essential difference in the mental capacity of men and women'.[39] Moreover, there were immediate, local reasons for 'natural' justice requiring such a concession. In November 1884, South Australia had introduced income tax.[40] In February of that year, partly to conform to British legislation, and partly to clear the way for the income tax legislation by blocking off a potential means of avoiding the tax, the colony had passed a *Married Women's Property Act*.[41] Stirling, echoing J. S. Mill's speech to the House of Commons in 1867, demanded that 'taxation and representation should go hand in hand. Did not a woman who owned property pay taxes like the man in a similar position?'[42] The demand was illogical, since Stirling's motion expressly excluded married women. Had Spence been listening, she might have been reminded of her conversation with John Stuart Mill and Helen Taylor nearly 20 years earlier. Mill was, she recalled,

> particularly earnest about woman's suffrage, and Miss Taylor, his stepdaughter, said she thought he had made a mistake in asking for the vote for single women and widows with property and wives who had a separate estate; it would have been more logical to have asked for the vote on the same terms as were extended to men. The Great man said meekly – "Well, perhaps I have made a mistake, but I thought with a property qualification the beginning would awake less antagonism."[43]

Stirling had no need to give the same attention to property qualifications, since those required for men to vote in elections to the Legislative Council would, if extended to women, still have enfranchised only a tiny minority, but he did need to reassure a patriarchal social order of its continuing domination. He excluded married women, he explained, as Mill had, for tactical reasons.

The members of the House of Assembly greeted Stirling's motion with cheers, and voted in its favour, but they also laughed and quipped throughout his speech. It was all a flippant, chivalrous bluff. When Stirling called that bluff the following year, by introducing not a motion, but a bill, for female suffrage, he ran smack into serious opposition from a patriarchal gender order that suddenly felt threatened. One member of the House of Assembly, Ebenezer Ward, 'did not wish to treat the matter seriously, because he could not imagine it to be within the range of practical politics'.[44] A correspondent to the *Register* envisaged Parliament House being furnished with 'suckling rooms' and proclaimed: 'Manhood gives the right to vote, not maidenhood'.[45] The *Register* remarked, as historians have done since, that women had not asked for the measure.[46] The bill was thrown out, and in 1887 Stirling lost his seat.

However that was only the beginning of the story. Support surfaced immediately: a petition in favour of female suffrage was presented during debates on the bill, signed by the president of the United Trades and Labour Council and 28 delegates who represented 3,000 'artisans and mechanics of the colony'. Predictably, their petition also prayed for the removal of the property qualifications in the bill.[47] The labour movement's support was more than an opportunist gesture against the propertied franchise for the Legislative Council. It continued throughout the 1880s and 1890s, warming as the suffragists' commitment to a democratic franchise became clear. Support surfaced a little later among the philanthropic organisations. In 1888, the Social Purity League, having decided that it would have more influence on legislation if women were able to vote, threw its energies into the formation of the Women's Suffrage League. Meanwhile in 1887, the Adelaide Women's Christian Temperance Union opened a Department of Legislation and Franchise, though it was not until 1890 that a presidential report announced cautiously that: 'While we do not desire to be regarded as a suffrage society, we realize the increased power against legalized sin which will come with the granting of womanhood suffrage'. By that time, the Women's Suffrage League was already actively promoting the cause.[48]

A web of personalities, personal influences and connections linked the organisations of the South Australian Women's Movement around the campaign for the vote. Augusta Zadow, an early and influential member of the Working Women's Trades Union, who used the Union's rooms as her base for administering the Distressed Women and Children's Fund during the depression of 1893, became South Australia's first female Inspector of Factories; in 1893 she spoke at gatherings of both the Women's Suffrage League and the Women's Christian Temperance Union, affirming the commitment of the working women she represented to the suffrage campaign. Agnes Milne, a shirt maker who succeeded Zadow as Inspector of Factories in 1896, was also a member of the Temperance Union. Mary Lee, a foundation member of the Social Purity League, honorary secretary of the Women's Suffrage League from the time it was founded, had made the proposal that the Working Women's Trades Union be formed. Mary Colton, co-worker with Emily Clark and Catherine Spence in the Boarding-Out Society, founder and president of the Young Women's Christian

Unbridling the tongues of women

Elizabeth Webb Nicholls.
Image courtesy of the
State Library of South Australia
(1985).

Temperance Union, president of the Social Purity League, succeeded Stirling as president of the Women's Suffrage League in 1892. Elizabeth Webb Nicholls, president of the Women's Christian Temperance Union from 1889, was also on the council of the Women's Suffrage League, and became superintendent of the Temperance Union's Suffrage Department in 1893. By the early 1890s, these links, together with Mary Lee's persuasive platform oratory and the spread of branches of the Temperance Union throughout the colony, had made the South Australian Women's Movement and its campaign for female suffrage a political force in the public sphere which was too strong for anyone to ignore.[49]

The terms on which the suffragists were demanding the vote had diverged considerably from Stirling's beginning. One of Stirling's supporters in 1886, Robert Caldwell, had introduced his own female suffrage bill in 1888. That abolished the distinction that Stirling had drawn between married women and single women and widows, but it had retained Stirling's property qualifications, and it raised the minimum age for the franchise to twenty-five. The Women's Suffrage League took only two meetings to determine that the age limit should be abolished, along with the property qualifications. Caldwell kept trying, but he would not drop the offending property qualifications. By 1891 the bill that he proposed to introduce, yet again, was so distant from the demands of the Women's Suffrage League and its support-

Mary Lee.
Image courtesy of the
State Library of South Australia
SLSA: B70647.

ers that the League disowned him. Mary Lee sought an audience at a meeting of the United Trades and Labour Council to explain that 'the League did not approve of Mr Caldwell's Bill and still demands women's suffrage without any qualifications whatever'.[50] Reassured, the Trades and Labour Council reaffirmed its support. By the beginning of 1894, the democratic temper of the suffrage campaign had won for it, as well, support from the radical Reform Movement.[51] Since allegiance from the newly-formed United Labour Party and the more widespread agitation for sweeping democratic change that the Reform Movement generated had brought the Liberal Kingston government to power in 1893, the political temper of the suffragists was bound to find favour in government circles.

It had also enticed Catherine Spence into their ranks. Spence had not been involved in the early mobilisation of the suffrage campaign. During 1887 she had been entirely taken up with nursing her mother. Grief at her mother's death, followed by her sister Jessie's, overshadowed 1888. In 1889, since her nephew Charles Wren and his wife were to move into Mrs Spence's house, she moved herself and Ellen Gregory into the 'little community' that they set up with Rose Hood and her three children, in a smaller house Spence owned in East Adelaide.[52] Spence might have hesitated to join the suffrage struggle, even if she had not been so wholly occupied with loss and disruption in her family and household. At the end of her life, she observed:

> For myself, I considered electoral reform on the Hare system of more value than the enfranchisement of women, and was not eager for the doubling of the electors in number, especially as the new voters would probably be more ignorant and apathetic than the old. I was accounted a weak-kneed sister by those who worked primarily for woman suffrage, although I was as much convinced as they were that I was entitled to a vote, and hoped that I might be able to exercise it before I was too feeble to hobble to the poll.[53]

She may, too, have founded the strongly evangelical tenor of many of the Women's Christian Temperance Union's arguments less than wholly congenial. The assumptions lying behind those arguments was that women were not only in essence, entirely different from men, but also better – higher-minded, less selfish and more virtuous. Elizabeth Nicholls's speaking manner, in consonance with her message, was 'inspirational'. Spence's attitude to the question of difference between men and women had taken shape from the doctrines of the church she had joined in her early thirties. They were grounded in Enlightenment rationalism, which regarded the differences between women and men as socially constructed, rather than being innate or 'natural'.[54]

Nevertheless, the suffrage campaign's growing strength proved irresistible. She attended a meeting of the Women's Suffrage League for the first time in 1891. The suffragists must have been pleased to have won such a prize; they invited her to preside over the meeting.[55] By May of that year she had agreed to become one of the

League's vice-presidents, and in June she joined a deputation from the League to the premier, Thomas Playford. In May 1892 her address to the League's annual meeting won her applause as enthusiastic as any that she encountered in her campaign for effective voting. In July of that year, she led another female suffrage deputation to the government.[56] She was hooked. She told a drawing-room meeting in December 1892: 'The women's suffrage movement in this province has ... become too strong for me to keep outside of it any longer. I must take hold of it and endeavour to guide it somewhat'.[57] That report suggests some measure of Spence's charisma, for rather than irritation at her self-importance, the surviving record reports only delight in Spence's support. She did not attempt to direct, or even 'guide' the suffrage campaign. Rather she offered it substantial support. She agreed to urge the Women's Suffrage League's interests during her effective voting campaign, and the League authorised her to enrol members and collect subscriptions.[58] She was a powerful recruit. No other woman in South Australia could so justly assert, as she did, that she 'had taken her full share in colonial life', and that 'Australian politics were the very breath of her nostrils'.[59] Parliamentarians referred to her as 'a well-known authority on political subjects', and averred that she had 'an acquaintance with the principles of government that few men could claim to attain'.[60] The press stood solidly behind her. In April 1893, the *Advertiser* remarked that Miss Spence's 'arguments are thoughtful and sober and her language entirely free from the screeching hysteria that has so often brought ridicule and contempt on the cause of "women's rights"'.[61] At the end of her life Spence observed:

> I do not claim any credit for its [female suffrage's] success in South Australia and the Commonwealth, further than this – that by my writings and my spoken address I showed that one woman had a steady grasp on politics and sociology.[62]

Spence had left for the United States before the election which, in the middle of 1893, brought the Kingston ministry to power. She could have heard from a distance of the suffrage bill which a former Premier, J. A. Cockburn, introduced that year. That bill excluded Caldwell's provisions about property qualifications, but Kingston added to it a provision requiring a referendum, and the bill failed. Kingston had opposed female suffrage while it appeared likely to strengthen the power of the Legislative Council, but the redoubled efforts of the suffragists, together with the support they had won in the labour movement and in the Reform Movement, must have persuaded him that female suffrage would strengthen his government, and perhaps assist his efforts to curtail the Legislative Council's power. The female suffrage bill introduced in 1894 was a government measure.[63] Since the bill was a constitutional amendment, it required a two-thirds majority in both Houses of Parliament. Having gained that in the Legislative Council, for months it lay in the House of Assembly while the government waited for a propitious time to pick it up again. That opportunity finally arrived in December 1894, the same month in which Catherine Spence arrived back in Adelaide.

The suffragists had been extremely busy. There may have been only a minority who were publicly active in the cause, but others, Mary Lee maintained, 'made speeches at their own fireside'.[64] In March the activists in the Women's Suffrage League began circulating a petition. The Women's Christian Temperance Union took it up, using its widespread branches for distribution. Indeed the Temperance Union excelled itself: with only 1,540 members it claimed responsibility for 8,000 of the signatures on the petition and signatures continued to roll in. By the time G. C. Hawker presented the petition in a great roll, to the House of Assembly, it bore 11,600 names.[65] The *Register*'s belief that women did not want the vote was confounded. The petition arrived in Parliament House in August, while the bill was still waiting for the government to attend to it again. Impatience and enthusiasm mounted as, slowly, the day for decision drew closer. By December, it was at its peak. When Spence landed at Port Adelaide on 12 December 1894, she was caught up in it immediately. The suffragists made a grand occasion of her return, crowding into the 'large room' of the Café de Paris to hear her describe her meetings with the suffragists in the northern hemisphere, and to re-instate her in the forefront of their campaign. She joined wholeheartedly in their excitement, announcing that she 'had always been in favour of women's suffrage', and she listened with embarrassment, wrote Jeanne Young, to 'the avalanche of eulogium' which overwhelmed her.[66] Only a few days later, on 17 December, the bill was up for debate. Women deluged parliamentarians with telegrams and filled the galleries of the House of Assembly. After a debate that seemed interminable, lasting into the small hours of the next morning, the division bells were rung and the votes cast. The Constitutional Amendment Bill was passed, making South Australia the first of the Australian colonies to allow women to vote.[67]

In March the next year, Spence received a letter bearing 29 signatures from the National Council of Women of the United States, congratulating her and the women of South Australia on their successful campaign.[68] In August 1895, the labour movement once again demonstrated its support for the feminist cause in a move which the historian, Helen Jones, has discovered recently. Taking advantage of a clause added to the suffrage bill in committee, in an attempt to wreck it, unions nominated both Spence and Mary Lee for selection as candidates for the election to the House of Assembly in 1896. They both declined the honour. Mary Lee did not want to be bound 'by pledge or obligation to any party whatever', and nor did Catherine Spence whose effective voting campaign had established that fact publicly.[69] But how warmed Spence must have felt at such a signal mark of favour from the people who stood most firmly for democracy in South Australia.

At the gathering in the Café de Paris, Spence observed: 'When women receive the right to vote then work would only just begin'.[70] She was not alone in recognising that institutionalising formal political equality between women and men would highlight rather than eliminate the continuing social subordination and economic inequality of women. The boundary between the sphere of domestic and public life might have shifted but it had not removed the boundary between the separate spheres of women and men, nor the domination that the world of men enjoyed over the world of women; that was, indeed still is, sustained by a widespread belief that while the economic order may change, a society's patriarchal social order is grounded in immutable biological difference, and therefore may not alter.[71] A petition arguing against female suffrage in 1894 had mustered 2,000 signatures asserting that women are 'not fitted by nature' to vote.[72] The belief that women are similarly unfit for particular kinds of work is still with us.[73] For the activists of the Women's Movement in South Australia in the decades on either side of the turn of the century, there seemed to be three avenues for further action. One was to offer to women opportunities to learn as much as their brothers had learned about events and procedures in the public sphere, so that they could vote responsibly and independently. Another was to form organisations which would promote solidarity among women and work for change in matters which particularly concerned women. The third was to undertake activities which, in themselves, would provide women with ways of learning independence and self-determination. For the last 15 years of her life, Spence worked strenuously for all three.

Initially the first appeared the most urgent. Women knew little and cared less about public matters because, Spence explained, they 'had been kept out of politics'.

Now that they were called upon to do something entirely outside their traditions and education, they were 'tormented with doubts and difficulties of a domestic, social and ethical character'. The newly-enfranchised voters of South Australia were to go to the polls for the first time in 1896. In March that year, Spence wrote an article for the *Register* headed 'A Few Plain Words to the Women Electors of South Australia' in which she concentrated on the immediate need for information, indicating ways of forming preferences for candidates, and giving simple instructions about filling in voting papers. She also warned her readers against dependence on the advice of husbands, fathers and brothers, and against yielding to a candidate's solicitations without finding out more about him.[74] It was sensible and timely advice, though it probably underestimated the political education that women had given themselves through the suffrage campaign; the press was to observe, with patronising approval, the small number of informal votes cast.[75]

Economic considerations loomed large in Adelaide in an election only three years after the financial crisis sweeping Australia had become most acute in South Australia. Kingston had been brought to power amid unemployment and poverty. He was returned to power in 1896, but his majority may not have been as large as it could have been. Writing nearly half a century later, in 1944, Dorothy H. Paynter reported that:

> A number of women in Adelaide wished to vote, but dared not to do so. Their husbands were employed by certain large firms whose directors were not pleased with events.
>
> It was tacitly understood that employees' wives were expected not to vote, and it was significant that none of them even enrolled. Some of these women knew that their husbands worked too hard and that their wages were too low.
>
> They knew that their homes were poor, and sometimes unhealthy, and they wished to vote for the men who, they believed, had these matters at heart. But they knew also that though one job was easily lost, another was not easily found, and a poor home was better than none. Winter was coming on, and political independence would be small compensation if the children were cold and hungry.[76]

If Dorothy Paynter was right, then the woman inhibited from voting had no need of anyone's advice about how to vote: their political understanding was already acute. However, their numbers were probably relatively small: F. W. Holder, treasurer in Kingston's government, declared that the percentage of women who registered was 'very high'. Of those enrolled, the percentage who went to the polls in 1896 was marginally higher (66.44%) than the percentage of men who voted (66.33%).[77]

Spence continued to offer educational opportunities for potential voters, delivering lectures on subjects as diverse as the anarchist Prince Kropotkin, finance in South Australia, and Susan B. Anthony.[78] Her conviction that women should learn to participate in public life, for their own benefit and for that of the whole society, never wavered. She urged acceptance of political responsibility upon the old scholars of 'Ladies' schools' and nurses alike.[79] But she also complained that South Australian women were not voting 'as women', but as their husbands and fathers voted.[80] She saw the remedy for such dependence in organisation.

At first she was content to support the bodies springing up in the wake of the victory of 1894. In August 1895, she addressed the Women's League, the body formed by members of the now defunct Women's Suffrage League, on the need for solidarity among women, as women, 'apart from all considerations of class and party'.[81] However her acquaintance with the international women's movement, and her growing friendship with feminists in other Australian colonies who looked to South Australia and to Spence as a 'Pioneer Woman' for support, led her to decide that the multifarious activities of the local feminists would be strengthened by affiliation with a central body, a national council of women. The International Council of Women formed in London in 1888, through the national councils affiliated with it, provided a means of co-operating in specific enterprises for organisations that were not otherwise connected.[82] Some South Australians had attempted to found a national council of women as early as 1889, but they had failed. It was 1902 before a public meeting in Adelaide formed a council, with Spence as one of its vice-presidents, and that was after councils had been established in New South Wales, Victoria and Tasmania.[83] Spence believed that the council would give South Australian women impetus for further work, as well as organisation.[84] In 1905 she argued for federation of the state councils 'for the purpose of interaction and combined action'. She urged, as well, inclusion of delegates from associations of teachers, university graduates and nurses, and for smaller subscriptions which would admit less financially comfortable women to membership.[85] Despite her efforts, the South Australian council of women faded out of existence about five years later. The South Australian Council of Women that would achieve recognition in the future was not formed until 1920.[86] It may well have been that failure that prompted Spence to endorse and follow an example being set in Victoria, by Vida Goldstein. In 1909, at the age of 84, she chaired a meeting called to form a Women's Non-party Political Association, a body dedicated to 'removal of all social, economic and other inequalities which still existed between women and men'.[87] That Association, like many of the inequalities it confronted, still exists, though its spiritual descendants in the Women's Electoral Lobby of the 1970s and 1980s have not often recognised it.

Catherine Spence's insistence upon women constituting themselves a political force for change, *as women*, undoubtedly did seem, and may still seem to some, either Utopian or unrealistic, or both. The 1896 elections in South Australia had clearly shown women divided by class and interest, like men. Similar divisions appeared in 1903 in Victoria when the Women's Federal Political Association invited Vida Goldstein to stand for election to the Federal Senate as a *women's* candidate: the Women's Christian Temperance Union refused her support and a breakaway group of Labour women went off to campaign for Labour candidates.[88] Yet in 1901, Spence joined an enterprise which clearly demonstrated the possibility of women working together despite differences in the economic class to which they belonged. This was the Co-operative Clothing Company, formed in premises in Blyth Street, Adelaide. The company was Agnes Milne's idea. She discussed it with a number of working women, and then approached Catherine Spence whose support for co-operation and for self-determination for women was well known. The proposal was to form a company exclusively of women, some of whom would simply own £1 shares in the company, some of whom would be both shareholders and operatives in the factory. The enterprise would be managed by one of the workers who would be appointed secretary-manager, and by monthly meetings of the shareholders constituting a board of management.[89] Spence leapt at the idea: 'I was sure of finding many sympathisers among my friends'.[90] Even before the company was ready to open its factory, its workers and investors had an inspiration, which might have owed something to the grand-daughter of the Scottish wheat-grower who won prizes for his use of new technology a century earlier. They electrified the plant, making the factory the first clothing establishment in Adelaide to use electric power. At its opening in February 1902, after the speeches, Miss Spence 'switched on the electric power and the watchers marvelled at the buttonhole machine and the speed of sewing; one member of Parliament "turned out yards of work in a twinkling"'.[91]

No less remarkable was the list of names of shareholders. These ranged from five people who designated themselves 'Lady' (including Spence who probably considered that she had earned the label by buying eight shares, the largest single holding) through 30-odd who, in 1906, listed themselves as 'housewife' or engaged in 'household duties', to an array which included a grocer, a baker, a domestic servant, a weaver, four machinists, two tailoresses and a dressmaker. All of the workers in the factory held shares, and associates in the suffrage struggle helped: Elizabeth Webb Nicholls invested; the secretary of the Working Women's Trades Union held three shares; Agnes Milne held five.

Catherine Spence became chairman [sic] of the board of the company and attended its monthly meetings for the rest of her life, even when her week's activities included, as well, three days at the Destitute Asylum, a meeting of the State Children's Council, a 'Students meeting', and four visits to introduce some travellers from the United States to South Australia's social services. Surely Lucy Morice was not the only person to marvel at her aunt's energy. Spence worried about the Co-operative Clothing Company: it was threatened by competition from larger firms and merchants lowering their prices for finished goods.[92] Yet the company and its factory – an exclusively women's venture, crossing the boundaries between capital and labour with great success – managed to continue beyond Spence's lifetime. Not until 1913 did competition from the larger clothing manufacturers, also introducing electrically-powered machinery, and incidentally rendering sweating no longer profitable, compel the company to go into liquidation.[93]

All three kinds of activity testified to the continuing commitment and activism of the Women's Movement in South Australia. Their legislative victories had not been major triumphs: chief among them was the *Married Women's Protection Act* of 1896, which enabled women to apply for a court's protection if their husbands had subjected them to cruelty, adultery, desertion or neglect for as long as six months.[94] Even in the wake of the female suffrage legislation of 1894, it was clear that the road forward for women stretched a long way. However, just as links between individuals and organisations in South Australia in the suffrage struggle had contributed to its coherence and success, so links formed nationally and internationally strengthened the Women's Movement across the world.

The New Woman of South Australia: Grand Old Woman of Australia

Catherine Helen Spence in Rose Scott's garden, Sydney 1902. Image courtesy of the State Library of South Australia SLSA: B6759.

Catherine Spence had already spun some connecting threads during 1893 and 1894. She fostered and extended these through her copious international correspondence, and by nurturing the work of younger feminists in Australia who looked to her as a symbol of what they could attempt. When she and Jeanne Young went to Sydney to extend their campaign for effective voting, Rose Scott 'paved the way for her successful public meeting by a reception' at her house at Point Piper. Scott was campaigning vigorously for the vote in New South Wales. Spence spoke beside her on suffrage platforms, and she and Jeanne Young joined her in making 'Mafeking Day' a day of mourning for 'death and desolation' rather than a celebration of anyone's victory in the Boer War.[95] Spence watched, with admiration, the efforts of Vida Goldstein and the suffragists in their protracted struggle in Victoria. She sent on to Goldstein letters from her correspondents in England and the United States, and occasionally contributed articles to the *Woman's Sphere*, the monthly which Goldstein edited for almost five years at the beginning of the 20th century.[96] She encouraged her nieces to take up responsibilities in the public sphere. Eleanor Wren, to whose upbringing she had contributed during a fairly conservative stage of her own development, was to become the 'matriarch' of the Melbourne Unitarian congregation in the 1920s.[97] Lucy Morice, who had become a strong labour supporter by 1905,[98] continued to see her aunt regularly. They collaborated in the formation of the Kindergarten Union, the formation of the Women's Non-Party Political Association, and in the work of the Co-operative Clothing Factory. Lucy provided the hospitality for Vida Goldstein when she visited Adelaide; and for one of Goldstein's opponents in the split in the Victorian suffragists ranks in 1903, Lillian Locke, who was visiting Adelaide to set up a new union to be called the Women's Employment Mutual Association.[99] Spence was undoubtedly both fond and proud of Lucy Morice.

The successors in whom she seems to have placed most hope, however, were friends formed outside her circle of kin. Jeanne Young inherited her mantle as prophet of the effective vote, and also, after consultation with Eleanor Wren, the task of completing her autobiography, a labour of considerable skill. She was to become, as well, Spence's first biographer.[100] It is largely from Jeanne Young and another successor, Alice Henry, that we learn the flavour of Spence's last years. She remained robust and energetic. She told Alice Henry, in passing, that she seemed to stand the heat better than most of her friends; she was writing that letter during a heatwave which brought three successive days with temperatures over 100 degrees Fahrenheit from which her sister-in-law was fleeing to Mt Lofty. The greatest concession that Spence made to the temperature was to decide not to go to church that Sunday.[101] However despite her energy, and the multitude of occupations that she undertook, she could relax among her friends. Jeanne Young reported a cheerful conversation during a week at Victor Harbour, again writing as though she were Spence.

> I remember one day being asked whether I was not sorry I never married. 'No,' I replied, 'for, although I often envy my friends the happiness they find in their children, I have never envied them their husbands.'[102]

Alice Henry, a Victorian born more than 30 years later than Spence, had, as a writer for the *Argus*, suffered for nearly 20 years from constraints upon her work almost identical to those which had confined Spence. She turned for advice to the 'Grand Old Woman of Australia', a title she was subsequently to give Spence, and won from her, not only sympathy but affection. Henry left Australia in 1905 as a delegate from the Melbourne Charity Organisation Society, first for Europe and England, then for the United States.[103] Spence sent her five pounds to help with her travelling expenses, writing:

> Oh my dear friend I shall go with you on this interesting itinerary … You are so much more like minded with me than Vida Goldstein or any others to whom I have bidden God Speed.[104]

Alice Henry ended up in Hull House, on an invitation from Jane Addams that was undoubtedly prompted by Spence's letters.[105] Her stay there led to her appointment as secretary of the Chicago branch of the National Women's Trade Union League and, later, as editor of the League's journal.[106] She remained in that post, with another Australian – Miles Franklin – as her assistant, until 1915, five years after she and all Spence's other friends, admires and supporters had mourned the Grand Old Woman's death.

Catherine Spence died on 3 April 1910, the proofs of her unfinished autobiography lying, corrected, beside her bed. Writing about her shortly afterwards, Rose Scott proclaimed:

> To live in hearts we leave behind is not to die! The shadows of time will no doubt eventually dim the vision we now hold of that vivid personality, but her works will live after her, and be the most fitting monument to her memory. Energetic, helpful, courageous, with broad human sympathy

> guided by a lofty sense of duty and reasoning powers of no mean order, she was an ideal pioneer.

It was a fitting tribute. 'An ideal pioneer', or, as Jeanne Young celebrated her, 'a "Pioneer Woman" of the world, opening new paths for her sisters to tread'. It would be easy, in the late 20th century, to underestimate both the courage of pioneer women like Catherine Spence, and the extent of their achievements. It is salutary to recall that it was little more than a decade before Spence's death that Beatrice Webb, visiting Australia, exclaimed in irritation at the women of Sydney who thought it 'unwomanly' to take an interest in public affairs. It was still necessary at the beginning of this century for Vida Goldstein's monthly journal to carry the motto: 'I am a human being and nothing is outside my sphere'. True, that is a claim we still have to make. But we make it today in a social order which has been significantly shaped by the struggles of the women who set Catherine Spence in the forefront of their campaigns. The patriarchal ordering of gender relations into the public world of men and the domestic world of women was never the same after the struggles in which they engaged. The claims that we make now, we make from vantage points which their work won for us. And their work drew inspiration, and strength, from the remarkable battle that Catherine Spence had waged already, for decades before they were born, to wrest from patriarchal provincialism a hearing for the voices of women. All of us who speak, and expect to be heard, today, owe a tribute to Catherine Spence.

Endnotes

Introduction

1. C.H. Spence, *An Autobiography*, reprinted from the *Register*, Adelaide, 1910, reproduced by LBSA, Australiana Facsimile Editions, no.199, Adelaide, 1975, pp.16-17.
2. *Catherine Helen Spence 1825-1905*, pamphlet reprinted from the *Register*, Adelaide, 1905, p.33; *Advertiser,* 10 October 1969.
3. See J.B. Hirst, *Adelaide and the Country 1870-1917*, Melbourne, 1973, pp.60-61.
4. T. Stevenson, 'Population Statistics', in W. Vamplew, E. Richards, D. Jaensch & J. Hancock, *South Australian Historical Statistics*, Kensington, 1984.
5. Hirst, op. cit., ch.1.
6. Spence, *Autobiography*, p.21.
7. *Register*, 31 October 1925; advertisement, *Australian*, 12 June 1971; E. Dorothea Proud, *Welfare Work : Employer's Experiments for Improving Working Conditions in Factories*, London, 1916; Helen Jones, 'The Catherine Helen Spence Scholarship – A Summary', typescript kindly lent me by Helen Jones, to whom I am grateful.
8. *Advertiser*, 10 October 1969.
9. LBSA, *Bibliography of Catherine Helen Spence*, compiled by Elizabeth Gunton, Adelaide, 1967.
10. H.M. Green, *A History of Australian Literature pure and applied*, 2 vols., Oxford, 1934, vol, i, pp.200-207; G. Blainey, *A Land Half Won*, South Melbourne, 1980, ch.17.
11. James Boswell, *The Life of Samuel Johnson, Ll.D.*, London, 1791, account of 31 July 1763.
12. G.M. Young, 'Portrait of an Age' in *Early Victorian England*, 2 vols., Oxford, 1934, vol. ii, p.415.
13. Cf. Edward Thompson, 'Solitary walker', review of Claire Tomalin, *The Life and Death of Mary Wollstonecraft*, *New Society*, 19 September 1974; A. Scott & R. First, *Olive Schreiner*, London, 1980, Introduction.
14. *Advertiser*, 17 March 1893.

15 See Catherine Hall, 'The butcher, the baker, the candlestickmaker: the shop and the family in the Industrial Revolution' and 'The home turned upside down? The working-class in cotton textiles 1780-1850', both in E. Whitelegg et al (eds), *The Changing Experience of Women*, Oxford, 1982; C. Pateman, 'Women, Nature, and the Suffrage', *Ethics*, vol.90, no.4 (July 1980).
16 See B. Cass, 'Women's Place in the Class Structure', in E.L. Wheelwright & K. Buckley (eds) *Essays in the Political Economy of Australian Capitalism*, 3 vols., Sydney, 1976-8, vol.iii.
17 J. Cooper, *Catherine Spence*, Melbourne, 1972, is a useful introduction and feminist view of Spence, but the size of Oxford University Press's series on notable Australians prevents a full reinterpretation of her life and historical period.
18 Melbourne, 1937.
19 J.F. Young, *Catherine Helen Spence a study and an appreciation*, Melbourne, 1937, Preface.
20 *Ibid.*, pp.13, 48.
21 *Ibid.*, p.13; L.S. Morice, 'Auntie Kate', typescript in SAA, p.2.
22 Quoted in Young, op. cit., p.48. Jeanne Young's daughter-in-law, Mrs. Courtney Young, told me in 1970 that Jeanne Young mislaid the diary in about 1935. My searches have not discovered it.
23 Young, *op. cit.*, pp.27-28; this niece was Eleanor Wren.
24 Spence, *op. cit.*, p.18.
25 Young, *op. cit.*, p.28.
26 Morice, *op. cit.*, p.7; H. Cook, 'Catherine Helen Spence', typescript in SAA, p.3; recollection of Mrs. Marjorie Caw.
27 Morice, *op. cit.*, p.1.
28 Spence, *op. cit.*, p.42.
29 *Ibid.*, p.45.
30 Young, *op. cit.*, pp.16, 13.
31 See [C.H. Spence], 'Hand Fasted – A Romance by Hugh Victor Keith' (pseud.) MS., SAA, typescript ANL, first pub. Ringwood, 1984, H. Thomson (ed.).
32 Morice *op. cit.*, pp. 2, 3.
33 *Ibid.*, pp.4, 7.
34 Spence, *Autobiography*, p.68.
35 L.S. Morice, 'The Life and work of Catherine Helen Spence', in L. Brown *et al*, (eds), *A Book of South Australian Women in the first Hundred years*, Adelaide, 1936, p.138.
36 Cook, 'Catherine Helen Spence', p.1.
37 Morice, 'Auntie Kate', p.3.
38 Cook, *op. cit.*, p.3.
39 Spence, *Autobiography*, pp.68-9.
40 Cook, *op. cit.*, p.3.
41 Conversation with Lucy Spence Morice's son, Mr. Patrick Morice.
42 Morice, 'Auntie Kate', *passim*.
43 (Spence), *Autobiography*, p.79. Jeanne Young wrote the last seven chapters of Spence's autobiography after Spence's death, see Spence, *Autobiography*, pp.3-4. Reference to that portion of the work will be given as (Spence), *Autobiography*.
44 Young, *Spence*, p.80.
45 *Ibid.*, p.11.
46 *Ibid.*, pp.14-15, 16, 193-4, 16.
47 Recollection of Miss Phyllis Crompton.
48 Young, *op. cit.*, pp.186-7.
49 *Ibid.*, pp.15, 32.

Endnotes

50 Morice, 'Auntie Kate', p.4; (Spence), *Autobiography*, p.93.
51 Young, *op. cit.*, p.176.
52 B. Harte & W. Aesop, *Fables*, London, n.d., inscribed 'Edith Cook from C. H. Spence 12.82', kindly lent to me by the recipient's daughter, Mrs. Marjorie Caw.
53 Spence, *Autobiography*, p.57; Young, *Spence*, p.154.
54 (Spence), *Autobiography*, pp.90, 80, 83.
55 Cook, *op. cit.*, p.2.
56 Spence, *Autobiography*, pp.1, 27-8, 46, 55; C.H. Spence, Some recollections of the Life of Helen Brodie Spence – widow of David Spence, n.d. MS., SAA. On 17 December 1983, that house – 9 Trinity Street, College Park – was sold by auction for $220,000. The adjacent block, which had comprised part of the house's grounds, was sold for $160,500.
57 Spence, *Autobiography*, pp.31, 32.
58 *Ibid.*, p.67.
59 *Ibid.*, p.68.
60 C.H. Spence, 'A Week in the Future', *Centennial Magazine*, vol.i (1888), p.388.
61 See L. Z. Bloom, 'Heritages: Mother-Daughter Relationships in Autobiographies', in Cathy N. Davidson & E. M. Broner (eds), *The Lost Tradition: Mothers and Daughters in Literature*, New York, 1980, pp.291-2.
62 Jeanne F. Young, Introductory, in Spence, *Autobiography*.
63 Morice, 'Auntie Kate', pp.3, 5, 6-7.
64 *Ibid.*, pp.6-7; Spence, *Autobiography*, p.68; (Spence), *Autobiography*, p.97.
65 Last will and testament of Catherine Helen Spence, dated 4 March 1895, typescript held by *Australian Dictionary of Biography*, Canberra.
66 Spence, *Autobiography*, pp.18, 24, 67, 68; (Spence), *Autobiography*, pp.89, 97 ; Morice, 'Auntie Kate', p.6.
67 Spence, *Autobiography*, p.20.
68 *Ibid.,*, pp.29, 26, 22.
69 *Ibid.*, pp.28, 37, 39.
70 Cook, *op. cit.*, p.2.
71 *Ibid.*; W.J. Sowden, 'Our Pioneer Press The Register The Observer and the Evening Journal A History', typescript in SAA, p.194.
72 (Spence), *Autobiography*, p.70; Alfred Cridge, *Proportional Representation*, San Francisco, n.d., Bancroft Library, Berkeley University.
73 N. Palmer (ed), *Memoirs of Alice Henry*, Melbourne, 1944, p.12; Miles Franklin, 'Rose Scott: some aspects of her personality and work', in F.S.P. Eldershaw (ed), *The Peaceful Army, A Memorial to the Women of Australia,* Sydney, 1938, p.101; (Spence), *Autobiography*, p.86; Morice, 'Auntie Kate', p.5; and see Janice N. Brownfoot, 'Women's Organisations and the Woman Movement in Victoria c. 1890 to c. 1908', BA Hons thesis, Monash University, 1968, pp.28, 43-5.
74 Spence, *Autobiography*, p.19.
75 *Ibid.*, pp.23, 24, 30, 37, 41, 42-3, 66; (Spence), *Autobiography*, pp.33-4; C.H. Spence 'George Eliot', *Melbourne Review*, I, 2; C.H. Spence, lecture on the Writing of George Eliot, MS., ML; her novel, *Handfasted*, has some marked similarities to Butler's *Erehwon*; C.H. Spence, 'A Californian Political Economist', *Victorian Review*, vol. iv, 1881; her short story, *A Week in the Future*, Sydney, 1889, derives much from Bellamy's *Looking Backward*; Young, *op. cit.*, p.12.
76 Anna Davin, 'Women and History' in Michelene Wandor (comp.), *The Body Politic: Writings from the Women's Liberation Movement in Britain, 1969-1972,* Stage 1, London, 1972, p.224.

1 Acquiring a room of her own

1. Family tree in C.H. Spence's handwriting, uncatalogued MS., SAA.
2. Spence, *Autobiography*, pp.7-16.
3. C.H. Spence, Some recollections of the Life of Helen Brodie Spence – widow of David Spence, n.d. MS., SAA, p.1.
4. Spence, *Autobiography*, pp.10-11.
5. *Ibid.*, p.31.
6. *Ibid.*, p.32.
7. *Ibid.*, p.45.
8. Spence family tree, MS., SAA; Spence, 'Helen Brodie Spence', p.98; Spence, *Autobiography*, p.16.
9. Spence, *Autobiography*, p.8.
10. *Ibid.*, p.11; Spence, 'Helen Brodie Spence', p.62 ; see Brian Abel Smith and Robert Steven, *Lawyers and the Courts: A Sociological Study of the English Legal System 1750-1965*, London, 1967.
11. Spence, 'Helen Brodie Spence', pp.62-7; P. Hume Brown, *A History of Scotland*, 3 vols., Cambridge, 1911, vol. iii, pp.318-19; Spence, *Autobiography*, p.7.
12. Spence, *Autobiography*, p.10.
13. Spence, 'Helen Brodie Spence', p.88.
14. Spence, *Autobiography*, p.8.
15. W.H. Marwick, *Economic Developments in Victorian Scotland*, London, 1913, p.78; J.M. Gest, *The Lawyer in Literature*, London, 1913, p.78.
16. Spence, *Autobiography*, pp.11-12.
17. Royal Commission on the Ancient Monuments of Scotland, [RCAMS], *An Inventory of the Ancient and Historical Monuments of Roxburghshire*, 2 vols., Edinburgh, 1956, vol. ii, pp.265, 268, 292-3, 306; A.D. Hope, *A Midsummer Eve's Dream: variations of a theme by William Dunbar*, Canberra, 1970, p.56.
18. Spence, *Autobiography*, pp.7-8.
19. RCAMS, *op. cit.*, p.298.
20. Spence, *Autobiography*, p.7.
21. W. Notestein, *The Scot in History*, New Haven, 1947, p.45. Spence observed, 'Mrs. Oliphant says that Jeanie Deans is more real to her than any of her own creations, and probably it is the same with me, except for this one work' (*Gathered In*), Spence, *Autobiography*, p.55; see Walter Scott, *The Heart of Midlothian*, London, 1818.
22. Spence, *Autobiography*, p.11.
23. *Ibid.*, pp.9, 12, 10, 7, 10, 12.
24. *Ibid.*, pp.16, 12, 10.
25. *Ibid.*, pp.13, 16.
26. Spence family tree, MS., SAA.
27. Spence, *Autobiography*, p.13. Spence's arithmetic appears shaky ; they may have had to purchase two of the six adult passages.
28. D. Pike, *Paradise of Dissent*, Melbourne, 1957, pp.52-3, 75-83, 99.
29. K. Marx, *Capital*, vol. i, B. Fowkes (trans), Harmondsworth, 1976, part 8, ch.33.
30. Pike, *op. cit.* chs. iii, v, vi; M. Roe, '1830-50', in Frank Crowley (ed.), *A New History of Australia*, Melbourne, 1974.
31. Pike, *op. cit.*
32. C.H. Spence, *Some Social Aspects of South Australian Life*, Adelaide, 1878, p.2.

33 Spence, *Autobiography*, p.14.
34 Pike, *op. cit.*, chs. viii-x.
35 C.H. Spence, *The Laws We Live Under*, Adelaide, 1880, p.20.
36 Spence, *Autobiography*, p.17.
37 Pike, *op. cit.*, pp.238-241.
38 Spence, *Autobiography*, p.17.
39 Pike, *op. cit.*, pp.241, 245.
40 Spence, *Autobiography*, p.17.
41 Spence family tree, MS., SAA; George H. Pitt, *The Press in South Australia*, Adelaide, 1946, pp.59, 14; Spence, *Autobiography*, p.17.
42 Spence, *Autobiography*, pp.17-18.
43 *Ibid.*, p.17.
44 Young, *Spence*, p.42.
45 Spence, *Autobiography*, p.18.
46 *Ibid.*, p.17.
47 Young, *Spence*, p.38.
48 Spence, *Autobiography*, pp.18, 20.
49 Pike, *op. cit.*, p.144; A.G. Austin, *Australian Education 1788-1900*, Melbourne, 1961, p.97.
50 Spence, *Autobiography*, p.18.
51 H. Brown, 'The Development of the Public School System in South Australia, with especial reference to the Education Act of 1851', typescript dated 1940, SAA, p.6; R.J. Nicholas, 'Private and Denominational Schools of South Australia Their Growth and Development', M Ed thesis, University of Melbourne, n.d., pp.44-5.
52 Spence, *Autobiography*, p.18.
53 *Ibid.*, pp.19-20; Spence family tree, MS., SAA.
54 Spence, *Autobiography*, p.24.
55 *Ibid.*
56 *Ibid.*, p.27.
57 Pike, *op. cit.*, ch.xviii; D. Pike, 'South Australia: A Historical Sketch', in Rupert J. Best (ed.), *Introducing South Australia*, Melbourne, 1958, pp.8, 12.
58 Spence, *Autobiography*, p.20 ; Spence family tree, MS., SAA.
59 Spence, *Autobiography*, pp.21, 65 ; Spence family tree, MS., SAA.
60 Spence, *Autobiography*, p.27 ; Phillip Mennell, *Dictionary of Australian Biography*, London, 1862; Pike, *op. cit.*, pp.446-450.
61 Spence, *Autobiography*, p.27.
62 *Ibid.*, p.24 ; see P. Cook, 'Faction in South Australian Politics – 1857-1861', BA Hons thesis, University of Adelaide, 1966, p.18.
63 Spence, *Autobiography*, p.28 ; Mennell, *Dicitonary of Australian Biography*.
64 Pike, *Paradise of Dissent*, ch.xix.
65 Spence, *Autobiography*, pp.28, 61 ; Mennell, *op. cit.*
66 Spence, *Autobiography*, p.61 ; Pike, 'South Australia, A Historical Sketch', p.13.
67 Spence family tree, MS., SAA.; Spence, *Autobiography*, p.28.
68 Spence family tree, MS., SAA.
69 Pitt, *The Press in South Australia*, p.59; Pike, *Paradise of Dissent*, pp.396, 454.
70 Spence family tree, MS., SAA.; Spence, *Autobiography*, p.68.
71 Spence family tree, MS., SAA.; Spence, *Autobiography*, p.46.
72 Spence, *Autobiography*, pp.23, 46, 28, 68.

73 *Ibid.*, p.19.
74 Information from Mrs A.A. Abbie and Mrs M. Caw; W.J. Sowden, 'Our Pioneer Press the Register, The Observer, and the Evening Journal. A History', typescript dated in ink 1926, SAA, pp.82, 103-105; Pike, *op. cit.*, p.395.
75 Spence, *Autobiography*, p.19.
76 *Ibid.*
77 Young, *Spence*, pp.47-8.
78 C.H. Spence, *Clara Morison*, (first pub. London, 1854), Adelaide, 1971, p.214.
79 Young, *Spence*, p.45.
80 E. Showalter, *A Literature of Their Own*, London, 1977, p.21; see also K. Alford, *Production or Reproduction? An economic history of women in Australia, 1788-1850*, Melbourne, 1984, p.219.
81 H. Brown, *op. cit.*, p.24; Pike, *Paradise of Dissent*, p.489.
82 Spence, *Autobiography*, p.22.
83 Young, *Spence*, p.48; Spence, *Autobiography*, p.23.
84 Pike, *Paradise of Dissent*, p.114; M. Hardy, 'The History of Education and Religion in South Australia 1837-1856', University of Adelaide, 1915, p.3; Sowden, *op. cit.*, p.4.
85 J.K. Ramsay, 'Culture and Society in South Australia 1857-1866', BA Hons thesis, University of Adelaide, 1963, pp.49-54; Pike, *op. cit.*, p.504.
86 Spence, *Autobiography*, p.20.
87 Virginia Woolf, *A Room of One's Own*, first pub. 1929, St. Albans, 1977, pp.6, 37-9.
88 Spence, *Autobiography*, p.23; P.M. Last, 'A paper of the life and work of Sir Edward Charles Stirling, FRS., read before the Australian Medical Students Society on Tuesday June 15, 1949', *Australian Medical Students Society Review*, November, 1949.
89 Spence, *Autobiography*, p.23.
90 *Ibid.*
91 Last, *op. cit.*
92 Spence, *Autobiography*, p.29.
93 Clippings in Charles Davies' collection, 'Biography, Obituary, Births, Marriages and Death', vol.ii, SAA.
94 J.B. Hirst, *Adelaide and the Country*, pp.40, 43, 45.
95 Spence, *Autobiography*, pp.55, 68.

2 The line of least resistance

1 Spence, *Autobiography*, p.56.
2 Frederick Sinnett, 'The Fiction Fields of Australia', first published *Journal of Australia*, 1 (July-December 1865), republished and edited by Cecil Hadgraft, University of Queensland Press, 1966; included in J. Barnes (ed.), *The Writer in Australia: A Collection of Literary Documents 1856 to 1964*, Melbourne, 1969.
3 E. Showalter, *A Literature of Their Own*, pp.18, 75, 3.
4 Spence, *Autobiography*, p.26.
5 *Ibid.*, pp.28, 45; C.H. Spence, Lecture on the Love Letters of Robert Browning and Elizabeth Barrett Barrett [sic], n.d., ML.
6 C.H. Spence, lecture on the Writing of George Eliot, n.d., ML; C.H. Spence, 'George Eliot's Life and Work', *Melbourne Review*, X, 39, 1885, p.220.
7 (Spence), *Autobiography*, pp.83-4.
8 Spence, *Autobiography*, pp.15, 25, 38.

Endnotes

9   (C.H. Spence) A Colonist of 1839, 'Why Do Women Wilt', *Register*, 11 December 1889; *Voice*, 9 December 1892; Spence, *Autobiography*, p.55.

10   C.H. Spence to Alice Henry, n.d., quoted in Kay Daniels and Mary Murnane (eds), *Uphill All The Way A Documentary History of Women in Australia*, St. Lucia, 1980, p.281; see also (Spence), *Autobiography*, p.92.

11   Quoted in Showalter, *A Literature of Their Own*, p.55.

12   G. Johnston, *Annals of Australian Literature*, Melbourne, 1970.

13   Spence, *Autobiography*, p.34.

14   *Ibid.*, p.22.

15   See advertisements in the *Telegraph*, 22 February 1864, 10 August 1864.

16   C.H. Spence to the editor *Cornhill Magazine*, 4 March 1878, holograph letter, ML; Spence, *Autobiography*, p.55; see also B.L. Waters and G.A. Wilkes, 'Introduction' in Catherine Helen Spence, *Gathered In*, Sydney University Press, 1977.

17   Spence, *Autobiography*, p.63.

18   *Ibid.*, p.22; M. Crompton, *Passionate Search: A Life of Charlotte Brontë*, London, 1955, pp.148-9.

19   Spence, *Autobiography*, p.22. The publishers, J.W. Parker and Son, went out of business in the early 1860s. Some of their work was taken over by Macmillan: see Charles Morgan, *The House of Macmillan (1843-1943)*, London, 1943, p.65. Macmillan and Company responded to my inquiry about a manuscript which would show the extent to which *Clara Morison* had been abridged with astonishment that anyone might expect them to store such material.

20   Spence, *Autobiography*, p.23.

21   *Ibid.*, p.25.

22   Spence to the editor of *Cornhill Magazine*, 4 March 1878; Spence, *Autobiography*, p.63.

23   Spence, *Autobiography*, p.23; W. Birkett, 'Some Pioneer Australian Women Writers', in F.S.P. Eldershaw (ed.), *The Peaceful Army: a memorial to the pioneer women of Australia 1788-1938*, Sydney, 1938, p.114.

24   F. Sinnett, 'The Fiction Fields of Australia', pp.204, 203, 204, 199-200.

25   H.M. Green, *History of Australian Literature*, 2 vols, Sydney, 1961, vol.i, pp.204-205.

26   E. Morris Miller, *Australian Literature from its beginnings to 1935*, Melbourne, 1940, p.406.

27   J. Barnes, 'Australian Fiction to 1920', in Geoffrey Dutton (ed.), *The Literature of Australia*, Harmondsworth, 1964, p.140.

28   H.G. Turner & A. Sutherland, *The Development of Australian Literature*, Melbourne, 1898, p.79.

29   Green, *op. cit.*, vol.i, p.202.

30   Miller, *op. cit.*, p.406.

31   P. Despasquale, *A Critical History of South Australian Literature 1836-1930*, Warradale, 1978, pp.78, 86.

32   [C.H. Spence] A Colonist of 1839, 'The Unknown Public', n.d., galley proofs, ML.

33   Spence, *Autobiography*, p.64.

34   *Ibid.*, p.23.

35   Joseph Furphy to J.F. Archibald, 4 April 1897, printed in J. Barnes (ed.), *op. cit.*, see also G.A. Wilkes, *The Stockyard and the Croquet Lawn: Literary Evidence for Australia's Cultural Development*, Port Melbourne 1981, pp.73-4, 98-9.

36   (C.H. Spence) A Colonist of 1839, 'Dialect – A Protest', galley proofs, ML.

37   'The Australian in Literature', *Register*, 22 November 1902; the article is anonymous, but it is among Spence's papers in printed form, marked 'C.H.S.' in her handwriting, ML; (Spence), *Autobiography*, p.97.

38 Simone de Beauvoir, *The Second Sex,* H.M. Parshley (trans. and ed.), first published 1953, Harmondsworth, 1972.
39 Spence, *Autobiography,* p.93.
40 S. Sheridan, 'Ada Cambridge and the Female Literary Tradition', in S. Dermody, J. Docker & D. Modjeska (eds), *Nellie Melba, Ginger Meggs and Friends: Essays in Australian Cultural History,* Malmsbury, 1982, p.166.
41 D. Modjeska, *Exiles At Home: Australian Women Writers 1925-1945,* London, 1981, p.121.
42 Spence, *Autobiography,* p.26.
43 M. Franklin, *Laughter, Not For a Cage*, Sydney, 1956, pp.61-63. Franklin believed that Spence was 'generally known' as Helen Spence, but there is no evidence to support this view.
44 E. Moers, *Literary Women*, New York, 1976, p.67.
45 *Ibid.*
46 C.H. Spence, *Mr. Hogarth's Will*, 3 vols., London, 1865.
47 Franklin, *op. cit.,* p.66.
48 Anonymous letter to Smith, Elder & Company, 1 August 1853, in Catherine Spence's handwriting, MS., ML.
49 Spence, *Autobiography*, p.22.
50 *Ibid.,* p.28.
51 *Ibid.,* p.26.
52 J.F. Young, *Spence*, p.103.
53 Spence, *Autobiography*, p.28.
54 V.K. Daniels, 'History and Literature: A Study of the Novels of C.H. Spence', BA Hons thesis, University of Adelaide, 1962, p.39. I am indebted to Kay Daniels for sending me a copy of this thesis.
55 C.H. Spence, *Clara Morison*, Adelaide, 1971, p.92.
56 *Ibid.,* pp.252-3.
57 Daniels, *op. cit.,* p.22.
58 The Author of 'Clara Morison', *Tender and True: A Colonial Tale,* London, 1862, p.82.
59 *Ibid.,* p.202-3.
60 *Ibid.,* p.231.
61 Catherine Ellen [sic] Spence, *The Author's Daughter*, 3 vols., London, 1868, vol.i, p.35.
62 Spence, *Gathered In*, p.62.
63 Quoted in Young, *Spence,* p.60; Spence, *Autobiography,* p.55.
64 Quoted in Showalter, *op. cit.,* p.133.
65 Quoted in Showalter, *op. cit.,* p.135.
66 Spence, *Autobiography,* p.55.
67 Showalter, *op. cit.,* p.28.
68 Franklin, *op. cit.,* p.53.
69 Green, *op. cit.,* p.203.
70 Spence, *Mr. Hogarth's Will*, pp.72-75.
71 (C.H. Spence), 'Hand Fasted – A Romance by Hugh Victor Keith', MS., SAA, Typescript, ANL, pp.82, 177, 76, 276, 330.
72 Spence, *Clara Morison,* p.245.
73 Showalter, *op. cit.,* pp.106, 122.
74 Spence, *Autobiography,* p.22.
75 *Ibid.,* p.23.
76 *Ibid.,* p.25.

77 A.E. Anton, ' "Handfasting" in Scotland', *Scottish Historical Review*, xxxvii, 24, p.90.
78 Spence, 'Hand Fasted', p.57.
79 Spence, *Autobiography*, p.63.
80 Spence, 'Hand Fasted', p.450.
81 C.H. Spence, 'The Place of Religion in Fictitious Literature', *Victorian Review*, ii, 9, p.359; Frances Power Cobbe, 'The Morals of Literature', *Fraser's Magazine*, July 1864, p.131.
82 Daniels, *op. cit.*, pp.22, 33-46.
83 *Ibid.*, pp.58-9.
84 See chapter 3, *infra*, pp.76-9.
85 Daniels, *op. cit.*, pp.46, 66.
86 Charlotte Perkins Gilman, *Herland*, serialised in the *Forerunner*, 1909-1916, first pub. London, 1979.

3 Faith and enlightenment

1 C.H. Spence, *An Agnostic's Progress from the Known to the Unknown*, London, 1884, p.17.
2 S.W. Carruthers, *Three Centuries of the Westminster Shorter Catechism*, University of New Brunswick, 1957.
3 Spence, *Autobiography*, p.10.
4 *Ibid.*, pp.12, 11, 63, 11.
5 *Ibid.*, p.19.
6 Pike, *Paradise of Dissent*, p.264.
7 *Ibid.*, ch.xi.
8 *Ibid.*, p.256.
9 *Ibid.*, p.274.
10 Spence, *Autobiography*, pp.28, 23.
11 *Ibid.*, pp.28, 27.
12 Family tree of the descendants of Thomas Wright Hill and Sarah Lee, parents of Matthew Davenport, Edwin, Rowland, Arthur, Caroline and Frederic, MS. kindly lent to me by Mrs. C. Barham Black; *Remains of the late Thomas Wright Hill, Esq. FRAS together with notices of his life, etc.*, London, 1859; Rosamond & Florence Davenport Hill, *The Recorder of Birmingham: A Memoir of Matthew Davenport-Hill; with selections from his correspondence*, London, 1879; see also entries for Matthew Davenport, Edwin and Rowland in the *Dictionary of National Biography*, vol. 9.
13 'Clark, John Howard', *Australian Dictionary of Biography*, Melbourne 1969, vol. 3.
14 W.J. Sowden, 'Our Pioneer Press', p.155; *Argus*, 31 May 1878.
15 Eric Gunton, 'Hazelwood Cottage, of Hazelwood Park', *South Australian Homes and Gardens*, June 1949, p.80.
16 'Clark, Caroline Emily', *Australian Dictionary of Biography*, vol. 3; Gunton, *op. cit.*, p.80.
17 *Argus*, 31 May 1978; *Register:* 18 August, 12 November, 19 December 1856; Howard Clark to 'My dear Meadows', 8 September 1857; Howard Clark to 'My dearest Lucy', 22 November [1857]; P[?]. M. Martineau to Howard Clark, 10 Aprl 1865, MSS. kindly lent to me by Mrs. C. Barham Black, South Australia; C. Emily Clark to Lady Windeyer, 31 December 1876, MS., ML; Spence, *Autobiography*, pp.27-8.
18 Spence, *Autobiography*, p.28.
19 Information from Mrs. M. Caw and Mrs. R.N. Beckwith.
20 Manuscript Minutes of the Adelaide Unitarian Congregation [AUC] (later of the Unitarian Christian Church Committee [UCCC]) including reports of general meetings of the congregation, 3 vols., June 1854 to October 1856, SAA, minutes for 27 June, 11 July, 14 August

and 21 August, 1854; undated memorandum; Rev. John Crawford Woods, BA, 'Rambling Recollections', 3 vols., MS, SAA, vol. 1, pp.107-8.

21 Dorothy Scott, *The Halfway House to Infidelity. A History of the Melbourne Unitarian Church 1853-1973,* Melbourne, 1980, pp.1-3. I am grateful to David Hilliard for drawing my attention to this book.

22 Spence, *Autobiography*, p.28.

23 *Register*: 2 May, 28 May, 5 July, 2 August, 4 September, 12 September, 17 September, 27 September, 1 October, 3 December, 1856, advertisements.

24 S.H. Mellone, *Liberty and Religion. The first century of the British and Foreign Unitarian Association,* London, 1925, pp.67, 12-14, 70; H. McLachlan, *The Unitarian Movement in the Religious Life of London*, London, 1934, pp.21, 19-20, 48-49, 178-182; *Register*, 5 July 1856, advertisement; Woods, *op. cit.,* pp.61-62.

25 Minutes of AUC, minutes for 8 June 1857.

26 Rev. John Crawford Woods, BA, 'Unitarian Opinion Concerning the Bible: what it is and what it is not', *1st Series Unitarian Belief No. 6*, Adelaide, 1881, p.62; 'The Unitarian Belief Concerning Salvation', *1st Series Unitarian Belief No.4*, Adelaide, 1881, pp.33-34; Woods, 'Unitarian Opinion Concerning the Bible', p.59.

27 Spence, *Autobiography*, p.63.

28 Rev. J. Reid, *In Memoriam. The Rev. John Crawford Woods, B.A.*, Adelaide, 1906, letter iii.

29 Her brother, John, who shared her change of faith, attended a general congregational meeting in November that year, see pencil name at end of list in Minutes of AUC, minutes for 16 November, 1856; Spence, *Autobiography*, p.28.

30 Spence, *Autobiography*, p.63.

31 C.H. Spence, sermon on The Three Reverences, 24 November [no year], MS, SAA, p.3.

32 Spence, *Autobiography*, p.28.

33 Woods, 'The Unitarian Belief Concerning Salvation', p.42.

34 See R.V. Holt, *The Unitarian Contribution to Social Progress in England*, London, 1938; Jo Manton, *Mary Carpenter and the Children of the Streets,* London, 1976; Ethel E. Metcalfe, *Memoir of Rosamond Davenport-Hill*, London, 1904; Scott, *Halfway House*, pp.59, 67-8.

35 C.H. Spence, sermon on the Christian Church, 7 December 1897, MS., SAA, p.24.

36 For the calculations establishing the Unitarians' minority even in the districts where most of them lived, see S.M. Eade [Magarey], 'A Study of Catherine Helen Spence 1825-1910', MA thesis, Australian National University, 1971, pp.113-14 and Appendix B; Minutes of AUC, first annual report.

37 *Genealogy of the family of Francis Clark and Caroline Hill,* unpublished, n.d., kindly lent to me by Mrs. C. Barham Black; Unitarian Christian Church [UCC], *Annual Reports* for 1865, 1870, 1882, 1890-2, 1895-1900, 1907, 1911; M.E. Crompton, 'Pioneers and the Centenary in the Unitarian Christian Church, Adelaide', MS., kindly lent to me by Miss M.E. Crompton; John Howard Clark, *The Heir of Linne A Drawing-Room Burlesque*, Adelaide, 1869; tickets for entertainments given by the Association for Mutual Improvement in connection with the Unitarian Christian Church, SAA; notebook containing minutes of proceedings of social meetings held during 1870, kindly lent to me by Miss M.E. Crompton.

38 Trust Deed of the Unitarian Church of South Australia, SAA; *Register,* 26 December 1856.

39 Trust Deed; Janet K. Cooper [Ramsay], 'The foundation of culture in Adelaide. A study of the First Colonists' Transplantation of Ideas and Art: 1836-1857', MA thesis, University of Adelaide, 1970, pp.21-2; John Tregenza, *Professor of Democracy*, Melbourne, 1968, p.39.

40 *Library Record of Australasia*, i, 4, p.113.

Endnotes

41 'John Howard Clark', *Library Record of Australasia,* i, 4, p.113-115; J.H. Clark, lectures in notebooks, MS., kindly lent to me by Mrs C. Barham Black; *Register:* 16 October 1856, 21 February 1857, 18 December 1858, supplement, 13 June 1878; *Argus,* 31 May 1878; Minutes of the Adelaide Philosophical Society, 10 January 1853 to 25 August 1853, MS., SAA, minutes for 10 January, 31 January 1853; Minutes of Royal Society of South Australia, November 1880 to May 1902, MS., SAA, minute for 2 November 1880.

42 Pike, *Paradise of Dissent,* p.510.

43 David Hilliard, 'The Unitarians in South Australia: an historical note', *Unitarian Quest,* May 1982, p.7. I am grateful to David Hilliard for sending me a copy of this article.

44 See Eade [Magarey], *op. cit.,* Appendix A.

45 A. Simpson & Son Limited, *'Today not Tomorrow' A Century of Progress,* Adelaide, 1954; *Observer,* 15 December 1888.

46 See Eade [Magarey], *op. cit.,* Appendix A.

47 Margaretta Greg, 1853, quoted in Ivy Pinchbeck, *Women Workers and the Industrial Revolution,* London, 1969, quoted in Alford, *op. cit.,* p.223; Mrs. Ellis, *The Daughters of England, their position in society, character & responsibilities,* London, 1842, p.3.

48 S.M. Crompton, 'A Pioneer Church', typescript kindly lent to me by Miss M. E. Crompton; Eade [Magarey], *op. cit.,* Appendix A.

49 Information from Mrs. M. Caw and Mrs Rosa Moore; Morice, 'Auntie Kate', p.2.

50 Crompton, 'Pioneers and the Centenary in the Unitarian Christian Church'.

51 Information from Mrs. M. Caw, daughter of Edith Hubbe, née Cook; Alison Mackinnon, 'Less for Fashion than for Substance: The Advanced School for Girls, 1879-1908', M Ed thesis, University of Adelaide, 1980, pp.44-46.

52 Olive Banks, *Faces of Feminism,* Oxford, 1981, pp.7-8, 28-9.

53 Spence, sermon on Human Responsibility, verso p.8.

54 C.H. Spence, sermon on Egoism and Altruism, 21 November 1897, MS., SAA, p.1.

55 Spence, *An Agnostic's Progress,* pp.49-51.

56 Woods, 'Rambing Recollections', vol. i, pp.133, 139-40, 142; John Crawford Woods, 'A Sketch of the Origin and History of the Unitarian Christian Church, Adelaide, South Australia', *Month by Month,* i.

57 Scott, *Halfway House,* pp.56, 81.

58 Spence, *Autobiography,* p.53.

59 Scott, *Halfway House,* pp.57-8.

60 Spence, *Autobiography,* p.53 ; C.H. Spence, sermon on the texts: Genesis v, 22 and Luke xvii, 5, 24 November 1878, MS., SAA; thanks are given to Miss Spence for taking services by the Committee of the Melbourne Unitarian Church in their Annual Reports for 1891, 1893, 1896, 1900, 1901.

61 C.H. Spence, sermons, MS., SAA.

62 Mrs. Webster's speech, *Addresses delivered in connection with the Opening of the New Unitarian Church, Grey Street, East Melbourne,* Melbourne, 1887, p.7; Martha Webster, *The Rising Faith a Sermon. Preached at the Unitarian Church, Eastern Hill, Sunday 23rd June, 1897,* Melbourne, 1895, p.7.

63 Spence, sermon on the Christian Church, p.14.

64 Reid, *In Memoriam,* letter iii.

65 Spence, *Autobiography,* p.63.

66 There is a sensitive discussion of this work, comparing it with Bunyan's in R.F. Walker, 'Catherine Helen Spence, Unitarian Utopian', *Australian Literary Studies,* May 1971. However, the links that Walker makes between *An Agnostic's Progress, Handfasted,* and Spence's short story

A Week in the Future, in order to make his article a contribution to discussion of the legend of the 1890s, seem to me strained.

67 Woods, 'Rambling Recollections', vol. 3, p.12; C.H. Spence, sermon on text 'Righteousness exalteth a nation, but sin is a reproach to any people', n.d., MS., SAA; Spence, sermon on Egoism and Altruism.
68 'Miss C.H. Spence at the Unitarian Church', *Quiz and the Lantern*, 9 May 1895. I am grateful to David Hilliard for sending me a copy of this article, too.
69 Woods., *op. cit.,* vol. 3, p.12.
70 Morice, *op. cit.,* p.5.

4 Edging out of the domestic sphere

1 See R.V. Holt, *The Unitarian Contribution to Social Progress in England,* London, 1938.
2 Rosamond & Florence Davenport Hill, *The Recorder of Birmingham: A Memoir of Matthew Davenport-Hill; with selections from his correspondence,* London, 1976, pp.103-4; Susan Magarey, 'The Reclaimers: A Study of the Reformatory Movement in England and Wales 1846-1893', PhD thesis, Australian National University, 1975.
3 Florence Hill, *The Boarding-out System distinguished from Baby-farming and Parish Apprenticeship,* a paper read before the National Association for the Promotion of Social Science 1869, London, 1869; E.E. Metcalfe, *Memoir of Rosamond Davenport-Hill,* London, 1904, pp.63-65; Florence Davenport Hill, *Children of the State; the Training of Juvenile Paupers,* London, 1868.
4 Frances Power Cobbe, *Essays on the Pursuits of Women,* London, 1863; Manton, *Mary Carpenter,* pp.148-152; Spence, *Autobiography,* p.37.
5 Hester Burton, *Barbara Bodichon 1827-1892,* London, 1949 (I am grateful to Mandy Leveratt for lending this book to me); Spence, *Autobiography,* p.37.
6 See F.K. Prochaska, *Women and Philanthropy in 19th Century England,* Oxford, 1980, Conclusion.
7 Spence, *Autobiography,* p.37; C.H. Spence, Paper describing a visit to England in 1865-6, MS., SAA.
8 Elizabeth Windschuttle, 'Feeding the Poor and Sapping their Strength: the Public Role of Ruling-Class Women in Eastern Australia, 1788-1850', in Elizabeth Windschuttle (ed.), *Women, Class and History: Feminist Perspectives on Australia 1788-1978,* Melbourne, 1980.
9 Margaret Barbalet, *Far from a low gutter girl: the forgotten world of state wards: South Australia 1887-1940,* Melbourne, 1983, p.191.
10 Kay Daniels, 'Catherine Spence', in History Teachers' Association of New South Wales, *Women and History*, New South Wales Education Department, 1975, pp.62-3.
11 See Ian Gough, *The Political Economy of the Welfare State*, London, 1979, particularly pp.11-15.
12 For example, Elizabeth Wilson, *Women & the Welfare State*, London, 1977, pp.120-122; Martin Durham, 'The Mothers Defence League, 1920-1921: A Case Study in Class, Patriarchy and the State', paper presented to History Workshop Conference 16, Sheffield, 5-7 November 1982; Cora Baldock & Bettina Cass (eds), *Women, Social Welfare and the State*, Sydney, 1983, Introduction.
13 See Barbalet, *Far from a low gutter girl*, p.205.
14 Pike, *Paradise of Dissent*, pp.231-2; Governor Grey to Lord Russell, 7 June 1841, Despatch No. 6 and enclosure 3, *Papers Relative to the Affairs of South Australia*, London, 1843; Pike, *Paradise of Dissent*, pp.359-60, 363.
15 G.N. Hawker, 'Movements for Civil Service Reform in South Australia', BA Hons thesis, University of Adelaide, 1963, pp.4, 42, 71.

16 The argument of this paragraph was suggested in part by J.B. Hirst, 'Centralization Reconsidered: the South Australian Education Act of 1875', *Historical Studies*, xiii, 49 and Hirst, *Adelaide and the Country*, chs. 1, 3.
17 Pike, *op. cit.,* p.80.
18 C.H. Spence, *State Children in Adelaide: a History of Boarding Out in its Development,* Adelaide, 1907, pp.7, 8; Pike, *op. cit.,* pp.318, 319; SA Ordinance No.11 of 1843; SA, *Government Gazette*, 24 August 1848.
19 SA, *Government Gazette*, 22 February 1849; Report of the Destitute Board, SA, *Government Gazette*, 17 January 1850; *Register*, 19 January 1850.
20 SA, *Government Gazette*, 20 June 1850.
21 Rosamond and Florence Davenport Hill, *What We Saw in Australia*, London, 1875, p.141.
22 [SA], 26 & 27 Vic., 1863, no.3; SA, *Government Gazette*, 7 April 1864.
23 SA Parliament, *Debates*, 16 February 1866, c.1073.
24 SA Parliament, *Papers*, no.9; SA Parliament, *Debates*, 1866, cc.376-7.
25 F.P. Cobbe, 'The Philosophy of the Poor-Laws', *Fraser's Magazine*, September 1864, republished as pamphlet, London, 1865.
26 Ivy Pinchbeck & Margaret Hewitt, *Children in English Society Volume ii*, London, 1973, pp.522-523.
27 *Register,* 14 March 1866; *Observer*, 17 March 1866; C.E. Clark, 'The Boarding-Out Society', in Spence, *State Children*, p.17; Boarding-Out Society, *Report*, Adelaide, 1873; C.E. Clark, 'Report of the Initiation and Progress for the Movement for Boarding out the Children of the State in the Province of South Australia', MS., SAA.
28 SA Parliament, *Debates*, 13 September 1866, cc.375-6; Boarding-Out Society, *Report*, 1873, pp.3-4; [Victoria] 27 Vic. 1864, no.216; [SA] 30 Vic. 1866-7, no.12.
29 [SA] 35 & 36 Vic. 1872, no.26.
30 *Register*, 17 August 1870 ; Constance M. Davey, *Children and their Law-makers*, Adelaide, 1956, p.4.
31 'Report of the Committee of the Legislative Council on Destitute Establishments', *Register*, 28 October 1867; see also Rosemary Byerley, 'The Treatment of children in State Institutions in South Australia, 1867-1885', BA Hons thesis, University of Adelaide, 1967.
32 SA Parliament, *Debates*, 17 July 1876, c.104 ; SA Parliament, *Papers*, 1867, no.50; SA Parliament, *Debates*, 23 July 1867, c.156, 31 July 1867, c.231.
33 SA Parliament, *Debates*, 8 January 1869, c.1376, 1 October 1869, c.484, 24 April 1872, c.608, 25 April 1872, c.655; Clark, 'The Boarding-Out Society', p.19; Davey, *Children and their Law-makers*, p.7.
34 Boarding-Out Society, *Reports,* 1873, pp.3-4, 1873-86, rule 8 (printed in each annual report); Clark, 'Initiation and Progress of the Movement for Boarding out', p.3.
35 Boarding-Out Society, *Reports,* 1873-86, rule 5, lists of subscribers; for minimum and maximum numbers of visitors, see *Report*, 1886, *Report*, 1877.
36 Boarding-Out Society, *Reports,* 1873-86, rule 2; Lucy Webb, 'Our Viceregal Ladies', in L. Brown *et al.* (eds.), *A Book of South Australian Women in the first Hundred Years,* Adelaide, 1936, p.86; entry for Henry Ayers and John Cotton in *Australian Dictionary of Biography*, vol. iii; entry for Samuel Davenport in Mennell, *Dictionary of Australasian Biography*. Barbalet observed that Spence was probably the poorest member of this group, p.265, n.48.
37 Boarding-Out Society, *Reports,* treasurer's reports, 1878, p.5, 1879, p.8, 1884, p.3; SA Parliament, *Papers*, 1885, vol.4, no.228, pp.236, 245.
38 Barbalet, *op. cit.,* pp.202-204.

39   *Ibid.*, p.204.
40   [SA]11 & 12 Vic. 1848, no.8.
41   Boarding-Out Society, *Report,* 1878, p.4.
42   Barbalet, *op. cit.,* p.xii.
43   See Prochaska, *Women and Philanthropy, passim.*
44   SA Parliament, *Papers,* 1885, vol.4, no.228; SA *Government Gazette,* 9 December 1886.
45   Last, 'A paper on the life and work of Sir Edward Charles Stirling'; W.G.K. Duncan & R.A. Leonard, *The University of Adelaide 1874-1974,* Adelaide, 1973, p.34.
46   SA Parliament, *Papers,* 1889, no.108; Spence, *State Children,* pp.30-31.
47   Victorian Parliament, *Papers,* 1892-3, vol.4, no.60, p.511; Spence, *State Children,* p.29.
48   SA Parliament, *Papers,* 1896, no.81 ; [SA] 58 & 59 Vic. 1895, no.641; Spence, *op. cit.,* p.48.
49   *Charity review:* i, 1, pp.4-5; i, 2, pp.7-9; v, 2, pp.5-8; *Women's Sphere,* March 1901, pp.59-60; Spence, *Autobiography,* p.69; *Register,* 4 April 1893; C.H. Spence, 'Care of Children in Australia' in J.H. Finley (ed.), *International Congress of Charities Correction and Philanthropy,* Chicago, 1893, pp.291-3; C.H. Spence, 'Charity in South Australia', *Proceedings of the first Australasian Conference on Charity held in Melbourne from 11 to 17 November, 1890,* Melbourne, 1890; C.H. Spence, untitled sermon headed 'Melbourne – Sunday evening', 8 May, no year, MS., ML; C.H. Spence, address on National Council of Women, n.p., n.d., MS., ML; Spence, *State Children.*
50   See Barbalet, *op. cit.,* p.205. I am indebted to John Tregenza for first drawing my attention to the exaggerations in Spence's claims.
51   Minutes of the Destitute Board: 21 January 1897, minute 419; 23 December 1897, minute 466, MS., SAA; (Spence), *Autobiography,* p.83; Cook, 'Spence', p.2.
52   SA Parliament, *Papers,* 1885, no.288, p.237 ; C.H. Spence, 'National or Compulsory Providence', *Proceedings of the Second Australasian Conference on Charity,* Melbourne, 1892, pp.77-85.
53   C.H. Spence, note headed 'the Decline in the Birthrate', unpublished, n.d., MS., ML.
54   C.H. Spence, *The Elberfeld System of Charity: a Study of Poverty,* Adelaide, 1906.
55   Gareth Stedman Jones, *Outcast London,* Oxford, 1971, pp.260-261; Spence, *Elberfeld System.*
56   Daniels, 'Catherine Spence', pp.59-63.
57   See appendices, Magarey, *'A Study of Catherine Helen Spence'.*
58   Boarding-Out Society, *Report,* 1878, pp.7-8.
59   *Ibid;* Spence, *State Children,* pp.85-6.
60   C.H. Spence, Address to the National Council of Women, 30 May 1905, MS., ML.
61   *'State Children' Convention,* Adelaide, 1907, p.9.

5 Learning for the future

1   See, for example, C.H. Spence, evidence to Commission on the working of the Education Acts, SA Parliament, *Papers,* 1882, no.27, p.143.
2   Spence, 'A Week in the Future', *Centennial Magazine,* 7, (1888), pp.657, 659, 660.
3   SA Ordinance no.14, 1846; Ordinances nos. 10 and 11, 1847; SA *Government Gazette,* 7 August 1851.
4   SA Ordinance no.20, 1851.
5   Douglas Pike, 'The History of Education in South Australia', in E.L. French (ed.), *Melbourne Studies in Education 1957-1958,* Melbourne, 1958; A.G. Austin, *Australian Education 1788-1900,* Melbourne, 1961, pp.159-60.
6   Young, *Spence,* p.48.

Endnotes

7   Letter signed 'C.H.S.', *Register,* 30 December 1856; C.H. Spence to Anthony Forster (then editor of the *Register*), 1856, submitting letter for publication, MS., ML.
8   Spence, *The Laws We Live Under,* p.10.
9   Spence, evidence to Commission on the working of the Education Acts, SA Parliament, *Papers,* 1882, no.27, p.143.
10 C.H. Spence, *Address to Women's League,* 7 February, no year, MS., ML; *Register,* 31 October 1905.
11 Spence, *Autobiography,* p.37; C.H. Spence, Paper describing a visit to England in 1865-6, MS., SAA.
12 Florence Fenwick Miller, 'William Ellis and his work as an Educationalist', *Fraser's Magazine,* February 1882; John Lawson and Harold Silver, *A Social History of Education in England,* London, 1973, pp.294-5.
13 Spence, *Autobiography,* p.39.
14 H.G. Turner, *A History of the Colony of Victoria,* 2 vols., London, 1904, vol. ii, p.165.
15 SA Parliament, *Debates,* 14 August 1873, c.143; 10 December 1873, cc.1411-1417; *Register:* 26 July 1873; 26 September 1873.
16 *Register:* 29 August; 1 September; 5 September; 9-12 September; 4 October; 6 October; 11 October; 14 October; 27 October; 31 October; 4 November; 7 November; 8 November; 14 November; 2 December; 9 December 1873.
17 G.E. Saunders, 'John Anderson Hartley and Education in South Australia', BA Hons thesis, University of Adelaide, 1958, pp.15, 16, 17.
18 *Register,* 28 July 1874.
19 *Register,* 1 September 1874.
20 *Register,* 2 February 1875.
21 *Register,* 4 November 1905.
22 *Register,* 1 September 1874; 3 March 1879.
23 C.H. Spence, *Heredity and Environment Delivered before (and printed at the request of) the Criminological Society of South Australia, 23 October 1897,* Adelaide, 1897, p.7.
24 [SA] 38 & 39 Vic., 1875, no.11; 41 & 42 Vic., 1878, no.122.
25 Saunders, *op. cit.,* pp.20, 22.
26 Spence, *Autobiography,* p.54; Cook, 'Spence', p.2.
27 Committee of Enquiry into Education in South Australia 1969-1970, *Education in South Australia,* Adelaide, 1971, p.12.
28 Tregenza, *Professor of Democracy.*
29 C.H. Spence to Professor Pearson, 2 November 1877, MS., La Trobe Library.
30 Spence, *Autobiography,* p.57.
31 *Ibid.*
32 Mackinnon, 'Less for Fashion than for Substance: The Advanced School for Girls, 1879-1908', p.90.
33 Spence, *Autobiography,* p.57 ; Craufurd D.W. Goodwin, *Economic Enquiry in Australia,* Durham, 1966, p.592.
34 Spence, *The Laws We Live Under,* p.97.
35 Spence, *Autobiography,* p.58.
36 Young, *Spence,* p.152.
37 Spence, *The Laws We Live Under,* p.8.
38 R.J. Nicholas, 'Private and Denominational Schools of South Australia. Their Growth and Development', M Ed thesis, University of Melbourne, n.d., pp.83-6, 89-92, 200; Saunders, 'John Anderson Hartley', p.6.

39 C.H. Spence, *Some Social Aspects of South Australian Life*, Adelaide, 1878, p.10.
40 Norman MacKenzie, *Women in Australia*, Melbourne, 1962, p.33.
41 *Register*, 9 October 1879.
42 All of the information and quotation in this paragraph is drawn from Mackinnon, 'Less for Fashion than for Substance'. Alison should not be held culpable for what I have made of the information she presented.
43 *Register*, 18 September 1879.
44 Spence, *Autobiography*, p.58.
45 Mackinnon, *op. cit.*, p.46.
46 Cook, 'Spence', p.2.

6 Round woman in her round hole

1   C.H. Spence, 'George Eliot's Life and Works', *Melbourne Review*, 10 (1885), p.223.
2   Sowden, 'Our Pioneer Press', pp.97-100; George H. Pitt, *The Press in South Australia 1836 to 1850*, Adelaide, 1946, p.16.
3   Spence, *Autobiography*, p.22.
4   Cooper, 'The Foundation of Culture in Adelaide', pp.141-2.
5   Pitt, *The Press in South Australia*, p.59; Spence, *Autobiography*, p.21.
6   Spence, *Autobiography*, p.56; Cooper, 'The Foundation of Culture in Adelaide', pp.149-50; Sowden, 'Our Pioneer Press', p.27.
7   Spence, *Autobiography*, pp.21, 23.
8   John Barnes, note in John Barnes (ed.), *The Writer in Australia: A Collection of Literary Documents 1856 to 1964*, Melbourne, 1969, p.31; Sowden, 'Our Pioneer Press', p.160; Frederick Sinnett, 'The Fiction Fields of Australia', first pub. *Journal of Australia*, 1 (July-December 1865), republished and edited by Cecil Hadgraft, St. Lucia, 1966, included in Barnes (ed.), *The Writer in Australia*.
9   Spence, *Autobiography*, p.24; *Telegraph*, 22 February 1864, advertisement.
10 Spence, *Autobiography*, p.26; anon., 'An Australian's Impressions of England', *Cornhill Magazine*, xii (January 1866).
11 Spence, *Autobiography*, p.25; Edward Wilson, 'Principles of Representation', *Fortnightly Review*, iv, 2 (January 1866).
12 Olive Banks, *Faces of Feminism*, Oxford, 1981, part 1.
13 Spence, *Autobiography*, pp.43, 45; C.H. Spence, Paper describing a visit to England in 1865-6, MS., SAA, pp.E-G.
14 Spence, *Autobiography*, p.45; C.H. Spence, Lecture on the Love Letters of Robert Browning and Elizabeth Barrett Barrett [sic], n.d., MS., ML.
15 Spence, *Autobiography*, pp.52-3, 42; see entries for Turner, Martin and Sutherland in F. Johns, *Australian Dictionary Of Biography*; unsigned 'To Our Readers', *Melbourne Review*, i, 1 (1876); C.H. Spence, 'George Eliot', *Melbourne Review*, i, 2 (1876).
16 Spence, *Autobiography*, p.55.
17 Sowden, 'Our Pioneer Press', pp.27, 28, 160-2, 178-9, 181; Spence, *Autobiography*, p.55.
18 C.H. Spence, 'Graduated Succession Duties', *Melbourne Review*, ii, 8 (1877); 'S' 'Australian Federation and Imperial Union', *Fraser's Magazine* (October 1877); *Register*, 27 October 1877; Spence, *Autobiography*, p.55.
19 Spence, *Autobiography*, p.55.
20 *Ibid.*, pp.25, 26, 52, 56, 61 ; Morice, 'Auntie Kate', p.3.
21 Spence, *Autobiography*, p.55.

22　*Ibid.,* p.55-56.
23　*Ibid.,* p.56.
24　Undated clippings, ML.
25　C.H. Spence, 'Honoré de Balzac: a psychological study', *Melbourne Review*, iv, 16 (1879).
26　Spence, 'George Eliot', p.162.
27　Spence, 'George Eliot's Life and Works', p.243.
28　[C.H. Spence] A Colonist of 1839, 'Why Do Women Wilt', *Register,* 11 December 1889.
29　*Voice,* 9 December 1892.
30　Spence, 'An Australian's Impressions of England', p.111; C.H. Spence, 'The Democratic Ideal', MS. and annotated clippings, ML.; Spence said that this article had appeared in the *Register*, and that she planned to give it as a lecture in the United States in 1893, see *Observer*, 8 April 1893.
31　Spence, 'An Australian's Impressions of England', p.113; *Register*, 16 January 1871.
32　Tregenza, *Professor of Democracy*, pp.92, 97-8; C.H. Pearson, 'On Property in Land', *Melbourne Review*, ii, 6 (1877).
33　Spence, 'Graduated Succession Duties', pp.443-4, 446, 448.
34　C.H. Spence to C.H. Pearson, 2 November 1877.
35　Spence, *Some Social Aspects of South Australian Life*, p.4.
36　C.H. Spence, 'A Californian Political Economist', *Victorian Review*, iv, 20 (1881), pp.139-40, 146.
37　Goodwin, *Economic Enquiry in Australia*, p.110; *Observer,* 26 July 1890.
38　Spence, 'The Democratic Ideal', pp.6, 7, 8, 11, 4.
39　[C.H. Spence] A Colonist of 1839, 'Machinery versus Manual Labour', *Register*, 14 December 1887.
40　Spence, *Some Social Aspects of South Australian Life*, p.3.
41　*Ibid.*
42　*Ibid.,* pp.7, 5, 10, 8, 12, 11.
43　*Ibid.,* pp.7, 5, 19, 8, 12, 11.
44　*Register*, 14 December 1887. The Danish-American Socialist, Lawrence Grönlund, wrote a book called *The Co-operative Commonwealth* published in 1884.
45　Spence, *A Week in the Future.*
46　C.H. Spence A Colonist of 1839, 'A Fortnight on the Village Settlements', galley proofs in ANL, clippings in ML; there is an account of the village settlements in L.K. Kerr, 'Communal settlements in South Australia in the 1890s', MA thesis, University of Melbourne, 1951.
47　C.H. Spence, 'Australian answers to some American problems', lecture headed 'Boston, 8 December 1893', MS., SAA, p.6.
48　C.H. Spence, Lecture on the Nationalization of Health, n.d., MS., ML.
49　Spence, 'The Democratic Ideal', p.8; C.H. Spence, 'An Australian's Impressions of America', *Harper's New Monthly Magazine*, July 1894, p.251.
50　Spence, 'The Democratic ideal', p.8.
51　Spence, *Some Social Aspects of South Australian Life*, p.13.
52　Spence, 'George Eliot's Life and Works', pp.218-19; Spence, *Autobiography*, p.44.
53　Spence, *Some Social Aspects of South Australian Life*; H.G. Turner, *Melbourne Review*, iv, 13 (1878), p.110.
54　H.G. Turner, 'Dialogue on Woman's Rights, 10 December 1871', MS., La Trobe Library.
55　Spence, *The Laws We Live Under*, pp.110, 113.
56　'The Australian in Literature', anonymous leader, *Register*, 22 November 1902, clipping marked 'C.H.S', ML.

57 Spence, *An Agnostic's Progress*, pp.157, 159-60.
58 Spence, *Autobiography*, p.56.
59 B.S. Roach, 'Literature, Art, and Music', *The Centenary History of South Australia*, Adelaide, 1936, p.352.
60 Spence, *Autobiography*, p.55.

7 Prophet of the effective vote

1 Spence, *Autobiography*, p.45.
2 *Catherine Helen Spence 1825-1905*, reprinted from the *Register*, 31 October 1905, p.29.
3 Spence, *Autobiography*, p.23.
4 *Report of meeting on 'Proportional Representation', or effective voting, held at River House, Chelsea on Tuesday, July 10th 1894*, p.6.
5 Spence, *Autobiography*, p.45.
6 Enid Lakeman, *How Democracies Vote. A Study of Majority and Proportional Electoral Systems*, London, first published 1955, 3rd and revised edition 1970, p.108; Hill was secretary to the first board of the Colonization Commissioners, see Pike, *Paradise of Dissent*, p.171.
7 *Southern Australian*, 30 October 1840.
8 Spence, *Autobiography*, p.24.
9 J.S. Mill, 'Recent Writers on Reform', *Fraser's Magazine*, April 1859; Spence, *Autobiography*, p.23.
10 Mill, 'Recent Writers on Reform', pp.489, 500, 503, 502.
11 SA Parliament, *Papers*, 1859, vol.i, p.67 ; Cook, 'Faction in South Australian Politics', pp.112, 115 ; Edwin Hodder, *History of South Australia*, London, 2 vols., vol.i, p.319; Spence, *Autobiography*, p.24.
12 Spence, *Autobiography*, pp.23, 24.
13 See, for example, *Argus*: 2 September; 3 September; 5 September 1859; Spence, *Autobiography*, p.24.
14 SA Parliament, *Debates*, 3 May 1861, c.48 ; 1 August 1861, cc.557, 652-4.
15 *Register*, 30 August 1861.
16 *Register*, 31 August 1861, 9 September 1861.
17 [SA] 14 & 15 Vic., 1861, No.20; see also J.B. Stephenson, 'The Electoral Districts of South Australia and Population as the Bases of Representation 1851-1882', BA Hons thesis, University of Adelaide, 1952.
18 Thomas Hare, *A Treatise on the Election of Representatives, Parliamentary and Municipal*, London, 1859; Lakeman, *How Democracies Vote*, p.268.
19 Mill, 'Recent Writers on Reform', p.505.
20 Hare, *A Treatise on the Election of Representatives*, 4th edition, 1873, p.150.
21 C.H.S., *A Plea for Pure Democracy. Mr Hare's reform bill applied to South Australia*, Adelaide, 1861, p.5; Spence, *Autobiography*, p.24.
22 Spence, *Plea for Pure Democracy*, p.5.
23 *Ibid.*, pp.i, 24.
24 Spence, *Autobiography*, p.24.
25 *Argus* : 5 September, 6 September, 11 September, 18 October, 28 October 1861 ; Lakeman, *How Democracies Vote*, p.224.
26 This point is made forcefully by R.B. Walker, echoing Peter Cook, in his article, 'Catherine Helen Spence and South Australian Politics', *Australian Journal of Politics and History*, xv, 1, p.36. This helpful article is marred by a number of misprints. In the text: p.40 'R.C. Butler'

should be 'R.C. Baker'; p.42 'Crawford Vaughan' should be 'J.H. Vaughan'. In the footnotes: n.9 '1860' should be '1861'; 'Pecunosius' was David Spence not John Brodie Spence, see Spence, *Autobiography,* p.65. The discussion of technicalities on p.39 suggests possible confusion between the Droop quota and the Gregory principle, see below.

27 Spence, *Autobiography*, p.24; Emily Clark to Henry Parkes, 22 April 1862, MS., ML; Spence, Paper describing a visit to England 1865-1866.
28 Spence, *Autobiography*, p.37.
29 *Ibid.,* pp.41-2; Spence, Paper describing a visit to England, p.28.
30 SA Parliament, *Papers*, 1871, vol.2, No.137 ; G. Hoag and G.H. Hallett, *Proportional Representation*, New York, 1926, pp.179-80; Stephenson, 'Electoral Districts of South Australia', pp.94, 109-16; J. Pernica, 'Electoral Systems in New South Wales to 1920 with special reference to Proportional Representation', M Ec thesis, University of Sydney, 1958, p.25.
31 Stephenson, 'Electoral Districts of South Australia', p.113.
32 Spence, *Autobiography*, pp.67-8.
33 *Report of Meeting on Proportional Representation*, pp.6-7.
34 G.D. Combe, *Responsible Government in South Australia*, Adelaide, 1957, p.123; F.S. Wallis, 'History of the South Australian Labour Party, 1882-1900 (summary account of the Minutes of United Trades and Labour Council)', typescript, SAA, pp.6-12, 13-15, 24, 28-30; Smeaton, *The People in Politics*, pp.10-11, 25-8; E.L. Batchelor, *The Labour Party and its Progress. A lecture delivered at the Democratic Club, Adelaide, on March 5th 1895*, Adelaide, 1895, p.4; J.I. Craig, 'A History of the South Australian Labour Party to 1917', MA thesis, University of Adelaide, 1940, pp.40-57; R.L. Reid, 'The Price-Peake Government and the formation of political parties in South Australia', typescript, SAA, p.6.
35 Craig, 'History of the South Australian Labour Party', pp.60, 62; H.T. Burgess (ed.), *The Cyclopedia of South Australia*, 2 vols., Adelaide, 1907, vol.ii, p.167; *Observer*, 18 January 1896; Walker, 'Catherine Helen Spence and South Australian Politics', p.40.
36 *Observer*, 30 May; 6 June; 13 June; 20 June; 4 July; 5 September 1896; Reid, 'The Price-Peake Government', pp.9, 3.
37 Reid, 'The Price-Peake Government', p.6; Craig, 'History of the South Australian Labour Party', p.63; P.G. Peter, 'Militancy and Moderation. A Comparative Study of the Trade Union Movements in New South Wales and South Australia in the 1880s', BA Hons thesis, University of Adelaide, 1959, p.78; see also L.E. Kiek, 'The History of the South Australian Labour Unions', MA thesis, University of Adelaide, 1948, pp.80-82; Wallis, 'History of the South Australian Labour Party', p.10; ANL program in Burgess (ed.), *Cyclopedia of South Australia*, vol.ii, p.167.
38 *Observer*: 26 July 1890, 1 August 1891, 30 July 1892, 7 October 1893, 14 October 1893, 21 July 1894; *Voice*: 9 December 1892, 31 August 1894, particularly 15 September 1893.
39 *Voice*: 7 April; 12 May; 7 July; 22 September 1898; *Observer*, 1 August 1891.
40 *Observer*: 26 July 1890; 7 October 1893; 17 August 1895; *Voice*: 15 September 1893; 22 September 1893; J. Medway Day, *Wages. A paper read before the Society for the Study of Christian Sociology in Adelaide on July 7, 1892*, Adelaide, 1892, pp.3-4.
41 *Observer*: 16 September; 23 September 1893; 15 December 1894; *Voice*: 15 September; 22 September 1893; 6 April 1894; *Mt. Gambier Baptist Church Jubilee Souvenir, 1864-1914*.
42 *Observer*: 1 August 1891; 9 December 1893; 1 July 1893; *Voice*: 29 September 1893; 28 April 1893.
43 Day, *Wages*, p.3; *Voice*, 9 July 1893; *Observer*, 9 June 1894.
44 *Observer*, 11 July 1891; *Voice*, 12 January 1894.
45 *Voice,* 19 January 1894.

46 *Voice*, 15 September 1893; Wallis, 'History of the South Australian Labour Party', pp.28, 29.
47 Spence, *Autobiography*, p.45.
48 *Ibid.*
49 *Ibid.*
50 *Proceedings of the Second Australasian Conference on Charity*, Melbourne, 1892.
51 On Strong, see A.G. Austin (ed.), *The Webb's Australian Diary 1898*, Melbourne, 1965, p.132.
52 Spence, *Autobiography*, p.68.
53 *Ibid.*
54 C.H. Spence, *Effective Voting One vote, one value,* reprinted from the *Advertiser*, 9 February 1893, p.1; see also *Observer*: 27 February; 7 May; 18 June; 20 August 1892; *Voice*: 16 December 1892; 3 February 1893.
55 *Register*, 1 July 1892; *Observer:* 9 July; 16 July; 20 August 1892; *Voice,* 17 March 1893.
56 Spence, Autobiography, p.68; *Observer,* 8 April 1893.
57 *Observer,* 27 February 1892; Spence, *Effective Voting One vote, one value*, p.5; see also C.H. Spence, *Effecting Voting a National Right*, reprinted from the *Century*; the copy in the ANL has 'My last manifesto' written on it in Spence's handwriting.
58 *Observer*, 27 February 1892.
59 *Voice,* 2 June 1893.
60 Elsie Birks to Vivian?, 5 April 1896, SAA. I owe both the quotation and this reference to Bruce Scates of Monash University, to whom I am most grateful. His PhD thesis on 'Radicalism in the labour movement, south-eastern Australia, 1887-1898', will undoubtedly illuminate the general context of the Reform Movement in South Australia.
61 *Register*, 23 February; 28 February 1892; Lakeman, *How Democracies Vote*, p.138; Hoag and Hallet, *Proportional Representation*, p.180.
62 J.F.H. Wright, *Mirror of the Nation's Mind. Australia's Electoral Experiments*, Sydney, 1980, p.99.
63 *Voice*, 17 March 1893; *Report of Meeting on Proportional Representation*, p.4.
64 Spence, *Effective Voting One vote, one value,* pp.1-2; Wright, *op. cit.,* p.116, in relation to the method used in elections to the Australian Senate.
65 *Observer,* 19 October 1895; C.H. Spence, *Effective Voting: Australia's Opportunity. An Explanation of the Hare System of Representation*, Adelaide, 1898, p.19; Lakeman, *op. cit.*, p.131; Wright, *op. cit.,* p.115, in relation to the method used in Tasmanian elections.
66 For example, schedule, A Bill for An Act to amend 'The Electoral code, 1896', Legislative Council no.22, 1902.
67 Colin Mason, Foreword, in Wright, *op. cit.,* p.13.
68 Joan Rydon, 'Electoral Methods and the Australian Party Systems 1910-1951', *Australian Journal of Politics and History,* ii, 1.
69 *Voice*, 16 December 1892.
70 *Advertiser*, 17 March 1893.
71 *Miss C.H. Spence, the electoral reformer*, reprinted from *Register*, 4 April 1893; SA Parliament, *Papers*, 1893, no.123; Young, *Spence*, p.17; *Voice*, 21 April 1893.
72 Spence, *Autobiography*, p.69; 'The Principles of Representation (By Alfred Cridge, San Franciso)', *Observer*, 4 January 1892; Alfred Cridge, *Proportional Representation, including its relations to the Initiative and Referendum,* San Francisco, n.d.; Alfred Cridge, *Voting not Representation a demand for Definite Democracy And Political Evolution*, n.d., both pamphlets in Bancroft Library, Berkeley University, California.
73 *Voice*: 23 June 1893; 8 June 1894.
74 C.H. Spence to John from Rockville Centre, Long Island, New York, 15 September 1893, MS., ML.

75 C.H. Spence to John, n.d., (internal evidence, USA, 1893).
76 *Voice:* 21 July, 20 October 1893; Hoag and Hallet, *Proportional Representation,* pp.187-8; *Proportional Representation Review*, Chicago, September 1893, pp.2-5; (Spence), *Autobiography*, p.73; *Australian Woman's Sphere*, March 1901, p.60.
77 C.H. Spence to Spence family from Brooklyn Boston, 25 January 1894; C.H. Spence to John from Washington Square, 13 February 1894, MS., ML.
78 *Voice*: 8 June 1894; 20 October 1893; *Report of Meeting on Proportional Representation*; (Spence), *Autobiography*, pp.76, 77; *Observer*, 15 December 1894.
79 For example, C.H. Spence, *Proportional Representation Success in Belgium*, reprinted from *Advertiser*, 19 September 1900; C.H. Spence, 'How Should We Vote', clipping c.1901, Guardbook of newspaper cuttings on proportional representation, SA Public Library; C.H. Spence, 'Proportional Representation', *Proceedings of the Australasian Association for the Advancement of Science*, 11th meeting, 1907, p.633.
80 *Observer*, 15 December 1894.
81 *Voice:* 27 April; 4 May; 11 May; 17 August 1894; 22 December 1893; 19 January 1894; *Observer*, 18 May 1895; *Register*, 22 April 1899; Combe, *Responsible Government in South Australia*, pp. 130, 134.
82 J. Quick and R.R. Garran, *The Annotated Constitution of the Australian Commonwealth,* Sydney, 1901, p.159; (Spence), *Autobiography*, pp.80, 90; C.H. Spence, *Federal Convention Elections and Effective Voting,* reprinted from *Weekly Herald*, Adelaide, 1897; *Effective Voting Hare-Spence Method. Defective Voting, Scrutin de Liste*, Adelaide, 1896 (place and date added in pencil) ; R.C. Baker, *A Manual of Reference to Authorities for use of Members of the National Australian Convention*, 1891 (Baker was an influential leader of the ANL); *Observer:* 23 January; 13 March; 17 July 1897.
83 Young, *Spence*, p.80; *Observer*: 23 January, 13 March 1897; (Spence), *Autobiography*, p.81; Spence, *Federal Convention Elections and Effective Voting*.
84 SA Parliament, *Debates*, 24 July 1900, p.192; *Australian Woman's Sphere*, October 1900; SA Parliament, *Debates*, 14 November 1900, p.859, 21 November 1900, p.924; John Playford, 'Australian Labour Party Personnel in the South Australian Legislature 1891-1957', typescript, Adelaide, 1957, SAA; SA Parliament, *Debates*, 8 August 1900, p.296.
85 *Observer*: 19 October 1895; 9 June 1900.
86 SA Parliament, *Debates*, 15 August 1905, p.50; 27 September 1905, pp.347, 349-50; Hon. A.H. Peake, MP, *Objections to Proportional Representation*, n.d.; SA Parliament, *Debates*, 14 November 1900, p.860; 27 September 1905, p.347.
87 *Catherine Helen Spence 1825-1905*, p.23.

8 The New Woman of South Australia: Grand Old Woman of Australia

1 See Robin Gollan, 'American Populism and Australian Utopianism', *Labour History,* November, 1965.
2 Richard J. Evans, *The Feminists: Women's Emancipation Movements in Europe, America and Australasia 1840-1920*, London and New York, 1977, p.56. Like other feminist historians, I have decided to use the terms 'Women's Movement' and 'feminist' in this chapter, even though such usage is anachronistic. The 19th century usually used the term 'woman movement' to designate the multiplicity of groups and activities concerned with protecting or advancing the rights of women. By translating that into 'the Women's Movement' I am endeavouring to draw attention to similarities and continuities between the 19th century and the multitude of groups, organisations and activities that constitute the Women's Movement today. The words 'feminist'

and 'feminism' did not enter popular political discourse until the end of the 19th century. But it would seem to be historically purist to a fault to eschew terms which describe an ideology – 'a distinct and identifiable body of ideas and aspirations, commonly known as the 'rights of women', the 'condition of women' question, the 'emancipation of women' and so on' – which had existed for at least a century before that. See Linda Gordon, *Woman's Body, Woman's Right: A Social History of Birth Control in America*, Harmondsworth, 1977, p.xiv; Barbara Taylor, *Eve and the New Jerusalem: Socialism and Feminism in the Nineteenth Century*, London, 1983, p.x.

3   C.P Gilman, *The Living of Charlotte Perkins Gilman*, New York, 1975, pp.142-3, 144-5, 167-8.
4   (Spence), *Autobiography*, p.70.
5   Meredith Tax, *The Rising of the Women: Feminist Solidarity and Class Conflict, 1880-1917*, New York and London, 1980, p.62.
6   Allen F. Davis, *American Heroine: The Life and Legend of Jane Addams*, Oxford, 1973, pp.49-50, 53, 57, 63-4; Tax, *The Rising of the Women*, pp.60, 93, 96.
7   (Spence), *Autobiography*, p.76; C.H. Spence to A. Hare, 12 January, 1906, SAA.
8   Evans, *The Feminists*, pp.47, 49, 54; Tax, *The Rising of the Women*, pp.165-6.
9   *Australian Woman's Sphere*, March 1901, p.60.
10 Aileen S. Kraditor (ed.), *Up From The Pedestal: Selected Writings in the History of American Feminism*, New York, 1968, p.159.
11 (Spence), *Autobiography*, p.72. Tubman's name is mistakenly printed as 'Tribman'.
12 Dale Spender, *Women of Ideas and What Men Have Done To Them: From Aphra Behn to Adrienne Rich*, London, 1983, p.362.
13 (Spence), *Autobiography*, p.72.
14 See Kraditor (ed.), *Up From The Pedestal*, p.98.
15 (Spence), *Autobiography*, p.73.
16 Gilman, *The Living of Charlotte Perkins Gilman*, pp.169-70.
17 C.H. Spence to Rose Scott, 20 September 1902, Scott papers, ML., quoted in Helen Jones, 'Women's Education in South Australia; Institutional and Social Developments, 1875-1915', PhD thesis, Adelaide University, 1980, p.248.
18 (Spence), *Autobiography*, p.75.
19 Ray Strachey, *The Cause: A Short History of the Women's Movement in Great Britain*, London, 1978, pp.105, 287; (Spence), *Autobiography*, p.76.
20 Stevenson, 'Population statistics', in Vamplew *et al.*, *South Australian Historical Statistics*, Kensington, 1984, tables 1-3.
21 Pavla Miller, 'Schooling and Capitalism: Education and Social Change in South Australia, 1836-1925', PhD thesis, University of Adelaide, 1980, table II, p.391. I am grateful to Pavla Miller for this reference.
22 Ray Markey, 'Women and labour, 1880-1900', in Elizabeth Windschuttle (ed.), *Women, Class and History: Feminist Perspectives in Australia 1788-1978*, Melbourne, 1980, pp.89, 91.
23 David J. Gordon, *Handbook of South Australia*, Adelaide, 1908, p.176.
24 Edna Ryan & Anne Conlon, *Gentle Invaders: Australian Women at Work 1788-1974*, Melbourne, 1975, pp.42-3.
25 Helen Jones, 'Women at Work in South Australia, 1889-1906', *Journal of the Historical Society of South Australia*, 2 (1976). I am grateful to Ian Davey for this reference.
26 Jones, 'Women's Education in South Australia', p.179.
27 Miller, 'Schooling and Capitalism', table 23, p.402.
28 Jones, 'Women's Education in South Australia', p.179.
29 *Ibid.*, pp.180-196; Daniels and Murnane (comps), *Uphill all the way*, pp.170-178.

30 Jones, 'Women at Work in South Australia', p.4.
31 [SA], 39 & 40 Vic., 1876, no.43, clause 187.
32 See Jones, 'Women at Work in South Australia', pp.5-6.
33 *Ibid.,* p.4.
34 C.H. Spence, 'An Australian's Impressions of America', *Harper's New Monthly Magazine* (July 1894), p.251
35 Miller, 'Schooling and Capitalism', table 13 (a), p.393 shows that the number of civil servants increased from 480 in 1857 to 1,890 in 1890 and then to 3,306 in 1900. Jones, 'Women at Work in South Australia', p.5, points out that the majority of school teachers at the turn of the century were women, most of them employed by the Education Department. See also F.K. Prochaska, *Women and Philanthropy in Nineteenth Century England*, Oxford, 1980, conclusion.
36 For more information about all of these organisations, and for a more detailed account of the suffrage campaign, see the careful and comprehensive research in Jones, 'Women's Education in South Australia', chapters 4-6.
37 SA Parliament, *Debates*, 22 July 1885, c.319.
38 Last, 'A paper on the life and work of Sir Edward Charles Stirling, F.R.S.', *Adelaide Medical Students' Society Review*, November 1949; Foundation members of the Adelaide Club 1863-1864, typescript, SAA; Constance Rover, *Women's Suffrage and Party Politics in Britain 1866-1914,* London, 1967, p.219.
39 SA Parliament, *Debates*, 22 July 1885, c.323.
40 [SA] 47 & 48 Vic. 1884, No. 323.
41 [SA] 45 & 47 Vic. 1883-4, No. 300.
42 SA Parliament, *Debates*, 22 July 1885, c.326.
43 Spence, *Autobiography*, pp.41-2.
44 SA Parliament, *Debates*, 22 September 1886, c.1079.
45 Quoted in Jones, 'Women's Education in South Australia', p.234.
46 For an account of the historiography of the suffrage campaign in South Australia, see Jones, *op. cit.,* appendix F.
47 Jones, *op. cit.,* p.235.
48 *Ibid.,* pp.236-45.
49 *Ibid.,* chapters 4 and 5.
50 *Ibid.,* chapter 5.
51 *Voice*: 26 January; 20 April 1894.
52 Spence, *Autobiography*, pp.67-8.
53 *Ibid.,* p.41.
54 Jones, 'Women's Education in South Australia', p.243; Banks, *Faces of Feminism,* Oxford, 1981, pp.7-8, 28-9.
55 *Observer*, 28 March 1891.
56 Women's Suffrage League of South Australia, *Annual Report,* Adelaide, 1891; *Register*, 3 June 1891; 9 July 1892; *Observer*: 21 May 1892; 16 July 1892.
57 *Voice*, 9 December 1892.
58 *Ibid.,* Women's Suffrage League, *Report*, July 1894.
59 *Register*, 3 June 1891.
60 SA Parliament, *Debates*, 26 August 1891, c.896; 14 August 1894, c.886; E.J. Wadham, 'Women's Suffrage in South Australia 1883-1894', BA Hons thesis, University of Adelaide, 1952, p.66.
61 *Advertiser*, 17 March 1893.

62 Spence, *Autobiography*, p.41.
63 Jones, 'Women's Education in South Australia', p.255.
64 Quoted in Jones, *Ibid.*, p.266.
65 *Ibid.*, p.260.
66 *Observer*, 22 December 1894; (Spence), *Autobiography*, pp.77-78.
67 Jones, 'Women's Education in South Australia', p.261; see also Pat Corbett, 'Women's Suffrage; Myths, Fantasies, Evidence', typescript, Politics Department, Adelaide University, 1984. I am grateful to Pat Corbett for giving me an early draft of this article.
68 May Wright Sewell, Susan B. Anthony, et al. to C.H. Spence, 1 March 1895, MS., SAA.
69 Jones, 'Women's Education in South Australia', p.274.
70 *Observer*, 22 December 1894.
71 See Carole Pateman, 'Women, Nature and the Suffrage', *Ethics*, vol.90, no.4, July 1980.
72 Jones, 'Women's Education in South Australia', p.252.
73 See, for example, Ann Game and Rosemary Pringle, *Gender At Work*, Sydney, 1983.
74 C.H. Spence, 'The Approaching Elections: A Few Plain Words to the Women Electors of South Australia', reprinted from the *Register*, 24 March 1896.
75 *Register*, 10 June 1896.
76 D.H.P., 'Women here Had First Vote 48 years ago', *Mail*, 22 April 1944, Newspaper cuttings vol.2, SAA, p.257. A note on the clipping gives the author's name as Dorothy H. Paynter.
77 Jones, 'Women's Education in South Australia', pp.279-80.
78 C.H. Spence: lecture entitled 'Memoirs of a Revolutionist', 1905, MS., ML; lecture entitled 'Finance in South Australia', fragment, n.d., MS., ML; lecture entitled 'Susan Brownell Anthony Born 1820 Died 1906', n.d., MS., ML; lecture entitled 'Miss Anthony Voted Once', n.d., MS., ML.
79 C.H. Spence, *Address to the Old Scholars' Association of Ladies' Schools on the 13 April, Banqueting Room, Town Hall,* Adelaide, n.d. the copy in the ANL has '1894' written on it in pencil, but internal evidence suggests 1904; C.H. Spence, 'Political Responsibilities', *Australasian Nurses Journal*, 15 November 1906, p.360.
80 C.H. Spence, lecture on the National Council of Women, n.d., ML.
81 *Observer*, 31 August 1895.
82 Janice Brownfoot, 'Women's Organisations and the Woman movement in Victoria c.1890 to c.1908', BA Hons thesis, Monash University, 1968, p.54.
83 *Register*, 12 September 1902.
84 Spence, lecture on the National Council of Women, pp.8-9.
85 C.H. Spence, lecture entitled 'National Council of Women', 30 May 1905, MS., ML.
86 Information from Miss Ruth Gibson, National Council of Women, Adelaide.
87 Vivienne Szekeres, 'A History of the League of Woman Voters in South Australia 1909-1976', BA Hons thesis, University of Adelaide, 1976, pp.3-4, 9.
88 Christine Fernon, 'Women's Suffrage in Victoria', *Refractory Girl*, no.22 (May 1981), pp.21-2.
89 *Woman's Sphere*, 10 March 1902, quoted in Daniels and Murnane (comps.) *Uphill all the Way*, p.180.
90 (Spence), *Autobiography*, p.94.
91 Jones, 'Women's Education in South Australia', p.221. All of the account of the Co-operative Clothing Factory is drawn from Jones, pp.218-225.
92 C.H. Spence to Alice Henry, 12 May (1905), MS., SAA.
93 Jones, 'Women's Education in South Australia', pp.218-225.
94 See Szekeres, 'A History of the League of Woman Voters', p.10.

Endnotes

95 (Spence), *Autobiography*, pp.91, 92-3, 86-7 ; Women's Political Education League, President's address, August 1904, 5 November 1906, pamphlets, ML.
96 (Spence), *Autobiography*, p.100; *Woman's Sphere*: December 1900, March 1901; C.H. Spence to Alice Henry, 23 November 1906, MS., SAA.
97 Scott, *The Halfway House to Infidelity*, p.63.
98 C.H. Spence to Alice Henry, April 1905, MS., SAA.
99 (Spence), *Autobiography*, pp.98, 100; Morice, 'Auntie Kate', p.5; Jones, 'Women's Education in South Australia', pp.222, 224, 209-10.
100 (Spence), *Autobiography*, Introductory, pp.3-4; Young, *Spence*, *passim*.
101 C.H. Spence to Alice Henry, 9 December 1904, MS., SAA.
102 (Spence), *Autobiography*, p.85.
103 Alice Henry, 'Memoirs', typescript, Melbourne, 1944; Alice Henry, 'Grand old woman of Australia: C.H. Spence', *Survey*, no.24, 16 April 1910; Diane Kirkby, 'Alice Henry and the Women's Trade Union League: Australian reformer, American reform', in M. Bevege, M. James, C. Shute (eds.), *Worth Her Salt: Women at Work in Australia*, Sydney, 1982, p.246.
104 Spence to Alice Henry, 9 December 1904?
105 C.H. Spence to Alice Henry, 12 January 1906, MS., SAA.
106 Kirkby, 'Alice Henry', pp.246-254.
107 Quoted by Jeanne Young, (Spence), *Autobiography*, p.4.
108 A.G. Austin (ed.), *The Webb's Australian Diary 1898*, Melbourne, 1965.

Bibliography

The most comprehensive bibliography of the works of Catherine Spence is still that compiled by Elizabeth Gunton, of the Research Service of the Public Library of South Australia, and printed in 1967. Since I have documented my text fully, I have not listed again, here, all the works of Spence that I consulted. Readers who wish to pursue them further will find them, and more, in E.J. Gunton, *Bibliography of Catherine Helen Spence* LBSA, Adelaide,1967.

Those of Catherine Spence's works that I have listed here, are the few I found that were not itemised in Gunton's bibliography, and those which have been published or re-printed since that bibliography was printed. The remainder of the bibliography given here consists of other primary and secondary source material consulted.

This statement, in itself an historical observation, was accurate at the time when this book was published. Since then, however, any Bibliography concerning Catherine Spence must be headed by Barbara Wall's 'Catherine Helen Spence: a bibliography', State Library of South Australia home-page/South Australiana/Catherine Helen Spence/Barbara Wall

1 Works of Catherine Spence

a. Novels

Clara Morison: a tale of South Australia during the gold fever, first pub. 2 vols., J.W. Parker, London, 1854, repub., Rigby, Adelaide, 1971, with introduction and glossary by Susan Eade [Magarey].

Gathered In, first printed *Observer* 3 September 1881 – 18 March 1882. First pub., Sydney University Press, 1977, with introduction by B.L. Waters and G.A. Wilkes.

Handfasted, Penguin, Ringwood, 1984, edited with preface and afterword by Helen Thomson.

Periodical articles

'Australian Federation and Imperial Union', *Fraser's Magazine,* October 1877, signed 'S'.

'A Federal Outlook on Charity', *Charity Review*, i, 1, March 1900.

'Mother State and her little ones: Children's Courts of Justice and Infant Life Protection', *Charity Review*, v, 2, June 1904.

'Our Library: State Children in Australia: A History of Boarding-Out and its Developments', *Charity Review,* viii, 2, June 1907.

Pamphlets & broadsheets

Effective Voting One vote, one value, reprinted from the *Advertiser*, 9 February, 1893.

Effective Voting. Hare-Spence Method. Defective Voting. Scrutin de Liste, Adelaide, 1896.

Published addresses

Heredity and Environment. Delivered before (and printed at the request of) the Criminological Society of South Australia, 23 October 1897, Adelaide, 1897.

Sermons

Sermon with no title, headed 'Melbourne, Sunday evening 8th May', no year, MS, ML.

Sermon on text: James I, 27, 21 October 1900.

Newspaper Articles

b. Located among Spence's papers

Article entitled 'State Children Association, England. Report for three years 1904, 1905, 1906', headed 'Article sent to Register and declined', MS., ML.

'A Fortnight on the Village Settlements', by C.H. Spence. A Colonist of 1839, galley proofs in ANL, clipping MS., ML.

'The Democratic Ideal', MS. In MS. 202/3, annotated clippings with no indication of paper, MS., ML.

'Dialect – a Protest', by C.H. Spence a Colonist of 1839, galley proofs, MS., ML.

Bibliography

'The Dignity of Labour and Thrift' by a Colonist of 1839, clipping, MS., ML.

'The Drink Question/Continuation, Prohibition, or Regulation?' by C.H. Spence – A Colonist of 1839, galley proofs in ANL.

'The Unknown Public'. By a Colonist of 1839, clipping in MS., ML.

c. Located in the press

'Review of *'The Silent Sea'* by 'Antarlo' [Catherine Martin], *Voice,* 9 December, 1892, signed 'C.H.S.'

'Children and the State in South Australia', *Woman's Sphere*, March 1901.

'Australia's Opportunity', *Woman's Sphere*, March 1901.

'The Australian in Literature', *Register*, 22 November 1902, anonymous, but clipping marked 'C.H.S.' in MS., ML.

Lectures

Finance in South Australia, fragment, n.d. MS., ML.

Is Free Trade the Best Policy for South Australia?, n.d. MS., ML.

Love Letters of Robert Browning and Elizabeth Barrett Barrett [sic], n.d., MS., ML.

Memoirs of a Revolutionist, 1905, MS., ML.

Miss Anthony Voted Once, n.d., MS., ML.

National Council of Women, typescript, 30 May 1905, MS., ML.

The Nationalization of Health, n.d., MS., ML.

Robert Browning, n.d., MS., ML.

Susan Brownell Anthony, Born 1820 Died 1906, n.d., MS., ML.

Address to Women's League, 7 February, no year, MS., ML.

The writing of George Eliot, n.d., MS., ML.

Notes

Poem headed 'July 1866' in C.H. Spence's handwriting, SAA.

On the Decline in the Birthrate, n.d., MS., ML.

Family tree of the descendants of David Spence and Helen Brodie in C.H. Spence's handwriting, n.d., SAA.

Letters

To Anthony Forster [then editor of the *Register*] submitting letter on religious education in schools for publication, dated 1856, MS., ML.

To C.H. Pearson, 2 November 1877, MS., La Trobe Library.

Holograph letter to the Editor, *Cornhill Magazine,* 4 March 1878, MS., ML.

To John Spence, from Rockville Centre, Long Island, New York, 15 September 1893, MS., ML.

To John Spence, n.d., [internal evidence U.S.A. 1893], MS., ML.

To Spence family, from Brooklyn, Boston, 25 January 1894, MS., ML.

To John Spence, from Washington Square, 13 February 1894, MS., ML.

To Mr Sowden [then editor of the *Register*], 14 March [1910], the year and a note that Catherine Spence died at about 3 o'clock [but on 3 April] have been added in another hand, MS., SAA.

2 Other primary sources

Manuscript

Adelaide Philosophical Society, Manuscript Minutes (become Minutes of the Royal Society of South Australia in November 1880), January to August 1853, 1880-1902, MS., SAA.

Adelaide Unitarian Congregation, Manuscript Minutes (later of the Unitarian Christian Church committee, including reports of general meetings of the congregation), 3 vols., June 1854-October1868, in the possession (1969) of Mrs. Rosa Moore, Port Willunga, South Australia.

Catalogue of books held by the South Australian Institute 1864-1884, 3 vols, MS., SAA.

Clark, Caroline Emily, letter to Henry Parkes, 22 April 1862, Parkes Correspondence, ML.

–, letter to Lady Windeyer, 31 December 1876, MS., ML.

–, Report of the Initiation and Progress of the Movement for boarding out the Children of the State in the Province of South Australia, MS., SAA.

Clark, John Howard, lectures, letters and journals. MS. in the possession of Mrs. C. Barham Black, Unley Park, South Australia.

Cook, Harriet, Catherine Helen Spence, n.d., typescript, SAA.

Destitute Board Records, MS., SAA.

Destitute Persons Department, Ledger of Children boarded out 1855-67, MS., SAA.

Destitute Board, Manuscript Minutes, vols., 10-19, 1889-1910, MS., SAA.

Garran, Robert, Manuscript Diary, MS., ANL.

Henry, Alice, 'How South Australia Cares for Children', *Sydney Morning Herald*, 9 April, 1904.

–, 'A Children's Court of Justice', *Argus*, 12 September, 1903.

Hill, Florence Davenport, 'A Court of Justice for Children', letter to the editor, the *Times*, 27 October, 1907, drawing attention to the children's court in South Australia.

Morice, Lucy Spence, 'Auntie Kate', n.d. typescript, SAA.

Scott, Rose, Address to the Feminist Club, 12 April 1921, typescript, ML.

Sewell, May Wright, Susan B. Anthony *et al.*, to C.H. Spence, 1 March 1895, MS., SAA.

State Children's Department, Correspondence, 1889 ff., MS., SAA. [There are thirty boxes of letters; I made only a random selection of the letters for the years 1889-1892.]

Turner, J.G., Dialogue on Women's Rights, 10 December 1871, MS., La Trobe Library.

Sowden, W.J., Our Pioneer Press The Register The Observer and the Evening Journal. A History, n.d., typescript, SAA.

Unitarian Christian Church, Manuscript Minutes relative to the establishment of a Unitarian Christian Church in Adelaide, 1854, in the possession (1969) of Miss M.E. Crompton, Heathpool, South Australia.

–, notebook containing manuscript minutes of proceedings of social meetings held on 23 February, 2 March, 23 March, 30 March, 6 April, 1870, in the possession (1969) of Mrs. Dora Harris and Miss M.E. Crompton, Heathpool, South Australia.

Women's Political Asociation, Manuscript Minutes, partial copy supplied (1970) by Mrs N. Jones, League of Women Voters of South Australia, Adelaide.

Woods, Rev. John Crawford, Rambling Recollections, 3 vols., MS., SAA.

Newspapers, newspaper cuttings & newspaper articles

Anon., 'Miss C.H. Spence at the Unitarian Church', *Quiz and the Lantern*, 9 May, 1895.

Davis, Chas., MD, collected Biography, Births, Marriages and Deaths clippings, SAA.

Guardbook of newspaper cuttings on Proportional Representation, South Australian Public Library.

Guardbook of newspaper cuttings about C.H. Spence, South Australian Public Library.

Adelaide Observer, references selected from 1850, 1866-67, 1890-1910.

Argus, references selected from 1856, 1857, 1859, 1861, 1878.

Australian Woman's Sphere, monthly, Melbourne, I-V, 1-55, La Trobe Library, vols. I-II only consulted.

Inquirer, 20 January 1900.

South Australian *Register*, references selected from 1859-1910.

Southern Australian, references selected from 1839-40.

Voice, weekly, ed. J. Medway Day, Adelaide, 9 December 1892 – 31 August 1894.

Woman's Voice, weekly, M.S. Wolstenholme. (ed.), Sydney, August 1894 – December 1895, ML.

Articles & periodicals

Anon., 'John Howard Clark', *Library Record of Australasia*, I, 4.

Clark, Caroline Emily, 'The Boarding-out Society', in C.H. Spence, *State Children in Australia: a History of Boarding Out and its Developments,* Adelaide, 1907.

Cobbe, F.P., 'The Morals of Literature', *Fraser's Magazine*, July 1864.

See note, 'The Philosophy of the Poor Laws', *Fraser's Magazine*, September 1864.

Mill, J.S., 'Recent Writers on Reform', *Fraser's Magazine*, April 1859.

Miller, F.F., 'William Ellis and his work as an Educationalist', *Fraser's Magazine,* February 1882.

Pearson, C.H., 'On Property in Land', *Melbourne Review*, ii, 6.

Proud, Cornelius, 'How Woman's Suffrage was won in South Australia', *Review of Reviews*, 20 January 1895.

Rinder, Samuel, 'A Californian Political Economist – A Reply', *Victorian Review*, iv, 22.

Sinnett, Frederick, 'Fiction Fields of Australia', *Journal of Australasia,* i, July to December 1865.

Woods, John Crawford, 'A Sketch of the Origin and History of the Unitarian Christian Church, Adelaide, South Australia', *Month by month*, i, 10.

Proportional Representation Review, Chicago, September 1893.

Representation, monthly journal of the British Proportional Representation Society, 1-19, February 1908 – November 1910.

Pamphlets

Addresses delivered in connection with the Opening of the New Unitarian Church, Grey Street, East Melbourne, by Chief Justice Higinbotham. Mrs. Webster, et al., Melbourne, 1887.

Batchelor, E.L., *The Labour Party and its Progress. A lecture delivered at the Democratic Club, Adelaide, on March 5th 1895,* Adelaide, 1895.

Boarding-Out Society, *Reports,* Adelaide 1873-1886, bound collection, South Australian Public Library.

Catherine Helen Spence 1825-1905, reprinted from the *Register,* 31 October 1905.

Clark, John Howard, *The Heir of Linne A Drawing-Room Burlesque,* printed for private circulation, Adelaide, 1869, in the possession (1969) of Mrs. C. Barham Black, Unley Park, South Australia.

Cridge, Alfred, *Proportional Representation,* San Francisco, n.d., Bancroft Library, University of California Berkeley.

–, *Proportional Representation, including its relations to the Initiative and Referendum,* San Francisco, n.d., Bancroft Library, University of California Berkeley.

Voting not Representation a Demand for Definite Democracy and Political Evolution, n.d., Bancroft Library, University of California Berkeley.

Day, J. Medway, *Wages: a paper read before the Society for the Study of Christian Sociology in Adelaide on July 7, 1892,* Adelaide, 1892.

Dependent Children, Interstate Congress of Workers, Adelaide, May 1909, Adelaide, 1909, in SAA.

Mackellar, Hon. Charles K., MLC, *The Child, The Law, and The State: being a short account of the progress of reform of the laws affecting children in New South Wales, with some suggestions for their amendment and more humane and effective application,* Sydney, 1907.

Melbourne Unitarian Church, *Annual Reports* for 1880-1882, in the possession (1969) of Miss M.E. Crompton, Heathpool, South Australia.

–, *Annual Reports,* 1886-1901, Victorian Public Library, missing those for Melbourne Unitarian Church, 1888, 1894, 1895, 1897-99.

Nanson, E.J., M.A., *Electoral Reform. An exposition of the theory and practice of proportional representation,* Melbourne, 1899.

Peake, Hon. A.H., MP, *Objections to Proportional Representation,* n.p., n.d., [almost certainly Adelaide, ?1905].

Report of meeting held on 'Proportional Representation', or effective voting, held at River House, Chelsea, on Tuesday, July 10th, 1894. Addresses by Miss Spence, Mr. Balfour and others, London, 1894.

'State Children' Convention, held at the Prince of Wales Theatre, University of Adelaide, Tuesday, November 19th, 1907, Adelaide, 1908.

South Australian Woman Suffrage League, *Annual Report,* Adelaide, 1891.

Turner, Martha [later M. Webster], *The Sacrament of Life A Sermon delivered in the Unitarian Church, Melbourne, on 3rd November, 1872,* Melbourne, 1872.

Unitarian Christian Church, *Annual Reports for* 1865, 1870, 1882, 1890-92, 1895-1900, 1902-5, SAA.

Webster, Martha, *The Rising Faith A Sermon Preached at the Unitarian Church, Eastern Hill, Sunday 23rd June 1895,* Melbourne, 1895.

Womanhood Suffrage League of New South Wales, *Reports,* 1892-1901, ML.

Bibliography

Woman Suffrage League of New South Wales, *Womanhood Suffrage, Public Meeting. Protestant Hall, Monday, 4ᵗʰ June, 1900. Speakers – The Hon. Sir William Lyne, Premier of N.S.W. Miss C. Spence and Mrs Young (South Australia), J.S.T McGowen, Esq., MLA, J. Cook, Esq., MLA., J. Thomas, Esq., MLA, Members of Parliament, and others,* broadside, ML.

Women's Political Education League, New South Wales, *President's Address*, August 1904, 5 November 1905, pamphlets, ML.

Women's Suffrage League of South Australia, *Report,* Adelaide, 1894.

Woods, Rev. John Crawford, *Two sermons, on secular, moral and religious education,* Adelaide 1856.

–, *Dr. William E. Channing, A Unitarian both in his life and at his death*, Adelaide, 1877.

–, 'The Unitarian Belief Concerning Salvation', 'The Unitarian Belief Concerning the Soul's Destiny in a Future State', 'Unitarian Opinion Concerning the Bible: what it is and what it is not', *1ˢᵗ Series Unitarian Belief*, nos. 4, 5, 6, Adelaide, 1881, pamphlets, Victorian Public Library.

–, 'Conscience and Human Life', *2ⁿᵈ Series Conscience,* no. 2, Adelaide, 1881, pamphlet, Victorian Public Library.

Parliamentary & other official publications

South Australian Government Gazette, 1848-51, 1864, 1867, 1886.

South Australian Parliamentary Debates, references from 1860-1905.

Papers Relative to the Affairs of South Australia, presented to both Houses of Parliament by Command of her Majesty, London, 1843.

Report of the Board of Education, SA Parliament, Papers, 1860, no. 34.

Despatches on Constitution and Electoral Acts, 1856, SA Parliament, Papers, 1861, vol. 3, no. 164.

Comparative Statement of the Estimated and Actual Revenue and Expenditure … for the year ended 31ˢᵗ December 1866, SA Parliament, Papers, 1867, no. 2.

Statistical Records of South Australia for 1866, SA Parliament, Papers, 1867, no. 9.

Report of Destitute Board on Industrial School at Brighton, SA Parliament, Papers, no. 50.

Comparative Statement of the Estimated and Actual Revenue and Expenditure … for the year ended 31 December 1867, SA Parliament, Papers, 1868, no. 3.

Report of Select Committee of the House of Assembly on the Electoral Districts Bill, SA Parliament, Papers, 1871, vol. 2., no. 137.

Report (No.3) of the Royal Commission on Penal and Prison Discipline. Industrial Schools, Victorian Parliament, Papers, 1972, vol. 3, no. 55.

Second Report of the Commission appointed to inquire into and report upon the working and management of the public charities of the colony, New South Wales Parliament, Votes & Proceedings, 1873-4, vol. 5.

Report of the Board appointed to inquire into the outbreak of inmates of the Reformatory for boys at Jika, on 13 March, 1878, Victorian Parliament, Papers, 1878, vol. 2, no. 21.

Reports of the Committee of Inspectors of Industrial Schools and Reformatory Schools, Victorian Parliament, Papers, 1880-81, vol. 4, no. 101.

Report of the Commission on the workings of the Education Acts, SA Parliament, Papers, 1882, no. 27.

Second and Final Report of the Commission appointed to report on the Destitute Act, 1881, SA Parliament, Papers, 1885.

Correspondence re Resignation of State Children's Council, SA Parliament, Papers, 1888, no. 108.

Reports of State Children's Council for years ended 30 June 1889-1910, SA Parliament, Papers, 1888, no. 94; 1889, no.39; 1890, no.39; 1891, no.39; 1892, no. 28; 1893, no.123; 1894, no. 94; 1895, no.81; 1896, no.81; 1897, no.81; 1899, no.63; 1900, no. 63; 1901, no. 68; 1902, no.82; 1903, no. 64; 1904, no. 64; 1905, no. 64; 1907, no. 59; 1908, no. 55; 1909, no. 70; 1910, no. 66.

Report of the Shops and Factories Commission, SA Parliament, Papers, 1892, no. 37.

Report of the Royal Commission on Charitable Institutions, Victorian Parliament, Papers, 1892-3, vol. 4, no. 60.

Progress Report of the Adelaide Hospital Commission, SA Parliament, Papers, 1895, vol. 2, no. 20.

Bill for an Act to amend 'The Electoral Code, 1896', SA Legislative Council, no. 22, 1902 [Prepared by Mr. J.H. Vaughan], in South Australia Parliamentary Library; bills for proportional representation introduced in 1903-9 were the same.

Report of the Select Committee of the Legislative Council on the Alleged Sweating Evil, SA Parliament, Papers, 1904, no. 71.

Bill for an Act to amend 'The Electoral Code, 1908', SA House of Assembly, no. 6, 1910 [Prepared by Mr. J.H. Vaughan], in South Australian Parliamentary Library.

Education in South Australia: Report of the Committee of Enquiry into Education in South Australia, 1969-70, Adelaide, 1971.

Royal Commission on the Ancient Monuments of Scotland, An Inventory of the Ancient and Historical Monuments of Roxburghshire, 2 vols, Edinburgh, 1956.

Books

Allen, J.H., *An Historical Sketch of the Unitarian Movement since the Reformation,* Christian Literature Co., New York, 1894.

Besant, Annie, *An Autobiography,* Unwin, London, 1st edition 1898, another edition, 4th impression, 1917.

Cobbe, F.P., *Life of Frances Power Cobbe as told by herself,* with additions by the author and introduction by Blanche Atkinson, posthumous edition, Richard Bentley, London, 1904.

Forster, Anthony, *South Australia its progress and prosperity,* S. Low, son and Marston, London, 1866.

Gilman, Charlotte Perkins, *Herland,* serialized in the *Forerunner,* 1909-1916, 1st edition, Women's Press, London, 1968.

Hare, Thomas, *A Treatise on the Election of Representatives, Parliamentary and Municipal,* 1st edition, Longman, Brown, Green, Longman & Roberts, London, 1859.

Hill, Florence Davenport, *Children of the State: the Training of Juvenile Paupers,* Macmillan & Co., London, 1875.

Hill, Rosamund Davenport & Florence Davenport, *What We Saw in Australia,* Macmillan & Co., London, 1875.

Hodder, Edwin, *The History of South Australia from its foundations to the year of its jubilee,* 2 vols, Low, Marston & Co., London, 1893.

Reid, Rev. John, *In Memoriam, The Rev. John Crawford Woods, B.A.,* Whillas & Ormiston, Adelaide, 1906.

Remains of the late Thomas Wright Hill, Esq., F.R.A.S., together with notices of his life, [by himself, with a continuation of the same by his son M.D. Hill], privately printed, London, 1859, in the possession (1971) of Mrs Rosa Moore, Port Willunga, South Australia.

Turner, H.G., *A History of the Colony of Victoria from its discovery to its absorption into the Commonwealth of Australia,* 2 vols, Longmans, London, 1904.

Turner, H.G. & Sutherland, A., *The Development of Australian Literature,* Longmans, Green & Co., London, 1898.

Worsnop, Thomas, *History of the City of Adelaide: From the foundation of the province of South Australia in 1836, to the end of the Municipal year 1877,* Williams, Adelaide, 1878.

3 Secondary Sources

Unpublished theses, papers & family trees

Brown, Henry, The Development of the Public School System in South Australia, with especial reference to the Education Act of 1851, 1940, typescript, SAA.

–, The Life and Work of Sir Richard Davies Hanson (1805-1876), Fred Johns thesis, University of Adelaide, 1938, SAA.

Brownfoot, J.N., Women's Organisations and the Woman Movement in Victoria, c 1890 to c 1908, BA Hons thesis, Monash University, 1968.

Byerley, Rosemary, The Treatment of Children in State Institutions in South Australia, 1867-1885, BA Hons thesis, University of Adelaide, 1967.

Cook, Peter, Faction in South Australian Politics 1857-1861, BA Hons thesis, University of Adelaide, 1966.

Cooper, Janet K. [Ramsay], The foundation of culture in Adelaide. A study of the First Colonist Transplantation of Ideas and Art: 1836-1857, MA thesis, University of Adelaide, 1970.

Corbett, Pat, Women's Suffrage; Myths, Fantasies, Evidence, typescript, Politics Department, University of Adelaide, 1984.

Craig, J.I., A History of the South Australian Labor Party to 1917, MA thesis, University of Adelaide, 1940.

Crompton, M.E., Pioneers and the Centenary in the Unitarian Christian Church, Adelaide, n.d., MS. in the possession (1969) of Miss M.E. Crompton, Heathpool, South Australia.

Daniels, V.K., History and Literature: A Study in the Novels of C. H. Spence, BA Hons thesis, University of Adelaide, 1962.

Durham, Martin, The Mothers Defence League, 1920-1921: a Case Study in Class, Patriarchy and the State, paper presented to History Workshop Conference 16, Sheffield, 5-7 November, 1982.

Eade, Susan [Magarey], A Study of Catherine Helen Spence 1825-1910, MA thesis, Australian National University, 1971.

Family tree of the descendants of Thomas Wright Hill and Sarah Lee, parents of Matthew Davenport, Edwin, Rowland, Arthur, Caroline and Frederick, in the possession (1969) of Mrs. C. Barham Black, Unley Park, South Australia.

Family tree of the descendants of Dr. John Macnee and Ann Dixon, MS. In the possession (1969) of Mrs. C. Barham Black, Unley Park, South Australia.

Foundation members of the Adelaide Club 1863-1864, typescript, SAA.

Ganzis, N., Tom Price, First Labour Premier: A Political Biography, BA Hons thesis, University of Adelaide, 1959.

Genealogy of the family of Francis Clark and Caroline Hill, in the possession (1969) of Mrs. C. Barham Black, Unley Park, South Australia.

Hardy, Mabel, The History of Education and Religion in South Australia 1837-1856, Tinline thesis, University of Adelaide, 1915.

Hawker, G.N., Movements for Civil Service Reform in South Australia. A brief history of the years 1836-1916 with special reference to the Civil Service Commission of 1888, BA Hons thesis, University of Adelaide, 1963.

Henderson, L.M., Vida Goldstein 1869-1949, Biographical notes by her niece, n.d., typescript ANL.

Howe, Renata, The Wesleyan Church in Victoria 1855-1901: Its Ministry and Membership, MA thesis, University of Melbourne, 1951.

Jones, Helen Patricia, Women's Education in South Australia: Institutional and Social Developments, 1875-1915, Ph D thesis, University of Adelaide, 1980.

Kerr, L.K., Communal Settlements in South Australia in the 1890s, MA thesis, University of Melbourne, 1951.

Kiek, L.E., The History of the South Australian Labour Unions, MA thesis, University of Adelaide, 1948.

Mackinnon, Alison, Less for Fashion than for Substance: The Advanced School for Girls, 1879-1908, M Ed thesis, University of Adelaide, 1980.

Magarey, Susan, The Reclaimers: A Study of the Reformatory Movement in England and Wales 1846-1893, PhD thesis, Australian National University, 1975.

Miller, Pavla, Schooling and Capitalism: Education and Social Change in South Australia, 1836-1925, PhD thesis, University of Adelaide, 1980.

Nicholas, R.J., Private and Denominational Schools of South Australia. Their Growth and Development, M Ed thesis, University of Melbourne, 1952.

Pernica, J., Electoral Systems in New South Wales to 1920 with special reference to Proportional Representation, M Ec thesis, University of Sydney, 1958.

Peter, P.G., Militancy and Moderation. A Comparative Study of the Trade Union Movements in New South Wales and South Australia in the 1880s, BA Hons thesis, University of Adelaide, 1959.

Ramsay, J.K., Culture and Society in South Australia 1857-1866, BA Hons thesis, University of Adelaide, 1963.

Reid, R.L., The Price-Peake Government and the formation of political parties in South Australia, n.d., typescript, SAA.

Saunders, G.E., John Anderson Hartley and Education in South Australia, BA Hons thesis, University of Adelaide, 1958.

Stephenson, J.B., The Electoral Districts of South Australia and Population as the Basis of Representation 1851-1882, BA Hons thesis, University of Adelaide, 1952.

Szekeres, Vivienne, A History of the League of Women Voters in South Australia 1909-1976, BA Hons thesis, University of Adelaide, 1976.

Wadham, E.J., Women's Suffrage in South Australia 1883-1894, BA Hons thesis, University of Adelaide, 1952.

–, The Political Career of C.C. Kingston, 1881-1900, MA thesis, University of Adelaide, 1953.

Walker, E.G., The Story of the Franchise, dramatic monologue performed in Adelaide, 23 June, 1944, typescript, supplied by Miss E.G. Walker, Fullarton, South Australia.

Wallis, F.S., History of the South Australian Labour Party, 1882-1900, summary of the minutes of the United Trades and Labour Council, n.d., typescript SAA.

Articles

Anton, A.E., ' "Handfasting" in Scotland', *Scottish Historical Review*, xxxvii, 24.

Baldock, Cora & Cass, Bettina, 'Introduction', in Baldock, C. & Cass, B. (eds.), *Women, Social Welfare and the State*, George Allen & Unwin, Sydney, 1983.

Barnes, John, 'Australian Fiction to 1920', in Dutton, G. (ed.), *The Literature of Australia,* Penguin, Harmondsworth, 1964.

Bloom, Lynn Z., 'Heritages: Mother-Daughter Relationships in Autobiographies', in Davison, C.N. & Broner, E.M. (eds.), *The Lost Tradition: Mothers and Daughters in Literature,* F. Ungar Publ. Co., New York, 1980.

Cass, Bettina, 'Women's Place in the Class Structure', in Wheelwright, E.L. & Buckley, K. (eds.), *Essays in the Political Economy of Australian Capitalism*, vol. iii, Australia & New Zealand Book Company, Sydney, 1978.

Curthoys, Ann, 'Historiography and Women's Liberation', *Arena*, no.xxii, 1970.

Daniels, Kay, 'Catherine Spence', in History Teachers' Association of New South Wales, *Women and History*, New South Wales Education Department, 1975.

Davidge, J.L., 'Builders of the Commonwealth', *Advance Australia*, 1 December, 1928.

Davies, A.F., 'Criteria for Political Life History', *Historical Studies*, xiii, 49.

Davin, Anna, 'Women and History', in Wandor, M. (comp.), *The Body Politic: Writing from the Women's Liberation Movement in Britain,* 1969-1972, Stage 1, London, 1972.

Fernon, Christine, 'Women's Suffrage in Victoria', *Refractory Girl*, no.22.

Gollan, Robin, 'American Populism and Australian Utopianism', *Labour History*, November, 1965.

Gunton, Eric, 'Hazelwood Cottage of Hazelwood Park', *South Australian Homes and Gardens*, June, 1949.

Hall, Catherine, 'The butcher, the baker, the candlestick maker: the shop and the family in the Industrial Revolution', and 'The home turned upside down: The working-class in cotton textiles 1780-1850', both in Whitelegg, E. *et al*, (eds.), *The Changing Experience of Women*, Martin Robertson, Oxford, 1982.

Henry, Marie B., 'The Grand old Woman of Australia', *Sydney Opinion,* i, 5.

Hilliard, David, 'The Unitarian in South Australia: an historical note', *Unitarian Quest*, May, 1982.

Hirst, J.B., 'Centralization Reconsidered: the South Australian Education Act of 1875', *Historical Studies,* xiii, 49.

Jones, Helen, 'Women and Work in South Australia, 1889-1906', *Journal of the Historical Society of South Australia*, 2, 1976.

Kirkby, Diane, 'Alice Henry and the Women's Trade Union League: Australian reformer, American reform', in Bevege, Margaret, James, Margaret, & Shute, Carmel (eds.), *Worth Her Salt: Women at work in Australia*, Hale & Ironmonger, Sydney, 1982.

MacKenzie, N., 'Vida Goldstein: the Australian Suffragette', *Australian Journal of Politics and History*, vi, 1.

Magarey, Susan, 'Radical Woman: Catherine Spence', in Fry, Eric (ed.), *Rebels and Radicals*, George Allen & Unwin, Sydney, 1983.

–, 'Can there be justice for women under capitalism: Questions about "Patriarchy" ', in Broom, Dorothy (ed.), *Unfinished Business*, George Allen & Unwin, Sydney, 1984.

Markey, Ray, 'Women and Labour, 1880-1900' in Windschuttle, Elizabeth (ed.), *Women, Class and History: Feminist Perspectives on Australia 1788-1978*, Fontana Collins, Melbourne, 1980.

Pateman, Carole, 'Women, Nature and the Suffrage', *Ethics* 4.90, pp.564-75, July 1980.

Peterson, M. Jeanne, 'The Victorian Governess: Status Incongruence in Family and Society', *Victorian Studies*, xiv, 1.

Pike, Douglas, 'The History of Education in South Australia', in French, E.L. (ed.), *Melbourne Studies in Education 1957-1958*, Melbourne University Press, Melbourne, 1958.

Roach, B.S., 'Literature, Art and Music', in *The Centenary History of South Australia*, Royal Geographical Society of Australasia, S.A. Branch, Adelaide, 1936.

Roe, Michael, '1830-1850', in Crowley, Frank (ed.), *A New History of Australia*, William Heinemann, Melbourne, 1974.

Rydon, Joan, 'Electoral Methods and the Australian Party System 1910-1951', *Australian Journal of Politics and History*, ii, 1.

Sheridan, Susan, 'Ada Cambridge and the Female Literary Tradition', in Dermody, Susan, Docker, John & Modjeska, Drusilla (eds.), *Nellie Melba, Ginger Meggs and Friends: Essays in Australian Cultural History*, Kibble Books, Malmsbury, 1982.

Thompson, Edward, 'Solitary Walker', review of Claire Tomalin, *The Life and Death of Mary Wollstonecraft*, *New Society*, 19 September, 1974.

Walker, R.B., 'Catherine Helen Spence, Unitarian Utopian', *Australian Literary Studies*, May 1971.

–, 'Catherine Helen Spence and South Australian Politics', *Australian Journal of Politics and History*, xv, 1.

Windschuttle, Elizabeth, 'Feeding the Poor and Sapping their Strength: the Public Role of Ruling-Class Women in Eastern Australia, 1788-1850', in Windschuttle, E. (ed.), *Women, Class and History: Feminist Perspectives on Australia 1788-1978*, Fontana Collins, Melbourne, 1980.

Books

Abel-Smith, Brian & Steven, Robert, *Lawyers and the Courts: A Sociological Study of the English Legal System 1750-1965*, Heinemann, London, 1967.

Alford, Katrina, *Production or Reproduction? An economic history of women in Australia, 1788-1850*, Oxford University Press, Melbourne, 1984.

Austin, A.G., *Australian Education 1788-1900*, Pitman, Melbourne, 1961.

–, (ed.), *The Webbs' Australian Diary 1898*, Pitman, Melbourne, 1965.

Banks, Olive, *Faces of Feminism*, Martin Robertson, Oxford, 1981.

Bibliography

Barbalet, Margaret, *Far from a low gutter girl: the forgotten world of state wards: South Australia 1887-1940,* Oxford University Press, Melbourne, 1983.

Barnes, John (ed.), *The Writer in Australia: A Collection of Literary Documents 1856 to 1964,* Oxford University Press, Melbourne, 1964.

Beauvoir, Simone de, *The Second Sex*, trans. and ed. H.M. Parshley, first published 1953, Penguin, Harmondsworth, 1972.

Blainey, Geoffrey, *A Land Half Won,* Macmillan, South Melbourne, 1980.

Briggs, Asa, *Victorian People: some reassessments of people, institutions, ideas and events, 1851-1867,* Penguin, Harmondsworth, 1965.

Brown, L. *et al* (eds.), *A Book of South Australian Women in the first Hundred Years,* Rigby, Adelaide, 1936.

Burgess, H.T. (ed.), *The Cyclopedia of South Australia,* 2 vols, Adelaide Cyclopedia Co., Adelaide, 1907.

Burton, Hester, *Barbara Bodichon 1827-1891,* Murray, London, 1949.

Carruthers, S.W., *Three Centuries of the Westminster Shorter Catechism,* University of New Brunswick for the Foundation, New Brunswick, 1957.

Combe, G.D., *Responsible Government in South Australia,* Adelaide Government Printer, Adelaide, 1957.

Connell, R.W. & Irving, T.H., *Class Structure in Australian History: Documents, Narrative and Argument,* Longman Cheshire, Melbourne, 1980.

Cooper, Janet [Ramsay], *Catherine Spence,* Oxford University Press, Melbourne, 1972.

Crompton, Margaret, *Passionate Search: A Life of Charlotte Brontë,* Cassell, London, 1955.

Daniels, Kay & Murnane, Mary (comps.), *Uphill all the way: A Documentary History of Women in Australia,* University of Queensland Press, St. Lucia, 1980.

Davey, Constance M., *Children and their Lawmakers,* Griffin Press, Adelaide, 1956.

Davis, Allen F., *American Heroine: The Life and Legend of Jane Addams,* Oxford University Press, London, 1973.

Despasquale, P., *A Critical History of South Australian Literature 1836-1930,* Pioneer Books, Warradale, 1978.

Duncan, W.G.K. & Leonard, R.A., *The University of Adelaide 1874-1974,* Rigby, Adelaide, 1973.

Eisenstein, Z.R., *The Radical Future of Liberal Feminism,* Longman, New York, 1981.

Eldershaw, F.S.P. (ed.), *The Peaceful Army, A Memorial to the Pioneer Women of Australia 1788-1938,* Women's Executive Committee and Advisory Council of Australia's 150th Anniversary Celebrations, Sydney, 1938.

Evans, Richard J., *The Feminists: Women's Emancipation Movements in Europe, America and Australasia 1840-1920,* Croom Helm, London, 1977.

Flexner, Eleanor, *Century of Struggle: The Women's Rights Movement in the United States,* Atheneum, Massachusetts, 1959.

Franklin, Miles, *Laughter, Not for a Cage,* Angus & Robertson, Sydney, 1956.

Game, Ann & Pringle, Rosemary, *Gender at Work,* George Allen & Unwin, Sydney, 1983.

Gest, J.M., *The lawyer in literature,* The Boston Book Co., Boston, 1913.

Gilman, C.P., *The Living of Charlotte Perkins Gilman,* Harper & Row, New York, 1975.

Goodwin, Craufurd D.W., *Economic Enquiry in Australia,* Duke University Press, Durham, N.C., 1966.

Gordon, David J., *Handbook of South Australia*, Adelaide Government Printer, Adelaide, 1908.

Gordon, Linda, *Woman's Body, Woman's Right: A Social History of Birth Control in America*, Penguin, Harmondsworth, 1977.

Gough, Ian, *The Political Economy of the Welfare State*, Macmillan, London, 1979.

Green, H.M., *A History of Australian Literature pure and applied,* 2 vols., Angus & Robertson, Sydney, 1961.

Hall, Alfred (ed.), *Aspects of Modern Unitarianism,* Lindsey Press, London, 1922.

Hannan, A.J., *The Life of Chief Justice Way*, Angus & Robertson, Sydney, 1960.

Hirst, J.B., *Adelaide and the Country 1870-1917,* Melbourne University Press, Clayton, 1973.

Hoag, C.G., & Hallett, G.H., *Proportional Representation*, Macmillan, New York, 1926.

Holt, R.V., *The Unitarian Contribution to Social Progress in England,* Lindsey Press, London, 1938.

Hume Brown, P., *History of Scotland*, 3 vols., Cambridge University Press, 1st edition 1899-1909, another edition 1911.

Johnson, George W., & Lucy A. (eds.), *Josephine Butler: an autobiographical memoir,* J.W. Arrowsmith, Bristol, 1911.

Johnston, Joanna, *Mrs. Satan: the incredible saga of Victoria Woodhull*, Macmillan, London, 1967.

Kamm, Josephine, *Rapiers and Battleaxes: the women's movement and its aftermath*, George Allen & Unwin, London, 1966.

Kraditor, Aileen S. (ed.), *Up From The Pedestal Selected Writings in the History of American Feminism*, Quadrangle/The New York Times Book Co., New York, 1968.

Lakeman, Enid, *How Democracies Vote: A Study of Majority and Proportional Electoral Systems,* Faber, London, 1st edition 1955, 3rd and revised edition, 1970.

Lawson, John & Silver, Harold, *A social history of Education in England*, Methuen, London, 1973.

Mackenzie, Norman, *Women in Australia*, Cheshire, Melbourne, 1962.

Manton, Jo, *Mary Carpenter and the Children of the Streets*, Heinemann, London, 1976.

Marwick, W.H., *Economic Developments in Victorian Scotland*, George Allen & Unwin, London, 1936.

Marx, Karl, *Capital*, 3 vols., vol.1, trans. Ben Fowkes, Penguin, Harmondsworth, 1976.

McLachlan, H., *The Unitarian Movement in the Religious Life of England,* George Allen & Unwin, London, 1934.

Mellone, S.H., *Liberty and Religion. The first century of the British and Foreign Unitarian Association,* Lindsey Press, London, 1925.

Metcalfe, Ethel, *Memoir of Rosamond Davenport-Hill,* Longmans, Green & Co., London, 1904.

Miller, E. Morris, *Australian Literature from its beginnings to 1935,* Melbourne University Press, Melbourne, 1940.

Modjeska, Drusilla, *Exiles at Home: Australian Women Writers 1925-1945,* Sirius Books, London, 1981.

Moers, Ellen, *Literary Women*, Doubleday, New York, 1976.

Bibliography

Notestein, Wallace, *The Scot in History*, Cape, London, 1947.

Palmer, Nettie (ed.), *Memoirs of Alice Henry*, reproduced from type-written copy, Melbourne, 1944.

Pike, Douglas, *Paradise of Dissent: South Australia 1829-1957*, Longmans, Melbourne, 1st edition 1957, 2nd edition 1967.

Pinchbeck, Ivy, *Women Workers and the Industrial Revolution 1750-1850,* Frank Cass, London, 1st edition 1930, new impression 1977.

Pinchbeck, Ivy & Hewett, Margaret, *Children in English Society,* 2 vols., vol.ii, Routledge & Kegan Paul, London, 1973.

Pinney, Thomas (ed.), *Essays of George Eliot*, Columbia University Press, New York, 1963.

Pitt, George H., *The Press in South Australia 1836 to 1850,* Wakefield Press, Adelaide, 1946.

Playford, John, Australian Labour Party Personnel in the South Australian Legislature 1891-1957, duplicated typescript, Adelaide, 1957.

Prochaska, F.K., *Women and Philanthropy in nineteenth-century England,* Clarendon Press, Oxford, 1980.

Quick, J. & Garran, R.R., *The Annotated Constitution of the Australian Commonwealth*, Angus & Robertson, Sydney, 1901.

Rover, Constance, *Women's Suffrage and Party Politics in Britain 1866-1914,* Routledge & Kegan Paul, London, 1967.

Royal Geographical Society of Australasia, South Australian Branch (Inc.), *Proceedings of the Society for the session 1935-6,* vol.37, Adelaide, 1937.

Ryan, Edna & Conlon, Anne, *Gentle Invaders: Australian Women at Work 1788-1974,* Nelson, Melbourne, 1975.

Scott, Ann & First, Ruth, *Olive Schreiner,* Deutsch, London, 1980.

Scott, Dorothy, *The Halfway House to Infidelity: A History of the Melbourne Unitarian Church 1853-1973,* Unitarian Fellowship of Australian and the Melbourne Unitarian Peace Memorial Church, Melbourne, 1980.

Showalter, Elaine, *A Literature of Their Own,* Virago, London, 1977.

Simpson, A & Son Ltd., *'Today not Tomorrow' A Century of Progress*, Simpson, Adelaide, 1954.

Smeaton, T.H., *The People in Politics: A Short History of the Labour Movement in South Australia,* Daily Herald, Australia, 1914.

Spender, Dale, *Women of Ideas and What Men Have Done To Them: From Aphra Behn to Adrienne Rich*, Routledge & Kegan Paul, London, 1983.

Stedman Jones, Gareth, *Outcast London,* Clarendon Press, Oxford, 1971.

Strachey, Ray, *'The Cause' a short history of the women's movement in Great Britain,* Bell, London, 1928.

Tax, Meredith, *The Rising of the Women: Feminist Solidarity and Class Conflict 1880-1917*, Monthly Review Press, New York & London, 1980.

Taylor, Barbara, *Eve and the New Jerusalem: Socialism and Feminism in the Nineteenth Century,* Virago, London, 1983.

Tregenza, John, *Professor of Democracy: The Life of Charles Henry Pearson, 1830-1894 Oxford Don and Australian Radical*, Melbourne University Press, Melbourne, 1968.

Vamplew, Wray, Richards, Eric, Jaensch, Dean & Hancock, Joan, *South Australian Historical Statistics*, Australia 1788-1988: A Bicentennial History, Kensington, 1984.

Wilbur, E.M., *A History of Unitarianism in Transylvania, England and America,* Harvard University Press, Massachusetts, 1952.

Wilkes, G.A., *The Stockyard and the Croquet Lawn: Literary Evidence for Australia's Cultural Development*, E. Arnold, Port Melbourne, 1981.

Wilson, Elizabeth, *Women & the Welfare State*, Tavistock Publications, London, 1977.

Wright, J.F.H., *Mirror of the Nation's Mind: Australia's Electoral Experiments*, Hale & Ironmonger, Sydney, 1980.

Young, G.M. (ed.), *Early Victorian England 1830-1865,* 2 vols., Oxford University Press, London, 1951.

Young, J.F., *Catherine Helen Spence: a study and an appreciation*, Lothian Publishing Co., Melbourne, 1937.

Index

Electronic Index: this book is available from the website as a down-loadable PDF with fully searchable text. Please use the electronic version to complement the index: www.adelaide.edu.au/press.

A

Abercrombie, Liliard, 53, 59, 62
Addams, Jane, xv, 142, 143, 163
Adelaide Children's Hospital, 71
Adelaide Club, 6, 71
Adelaide Co-operative Society, 133
Adelaide Democratic Club, 132, 137
Adelaide Educational Institution, 70
Adelaide *Observer*, xxii, xxiii, 45
Adelaide University, 147, 150
Advanced School for Girls, 19, 72, 93, 103, 104, 147
Advertiser, 132, 135, 154
Allegemeiner Deutscher Verein, 129
Allen, James ('Dismal Jimmy'), xii, 37
American Proportional Representation League, 136
An Agnostic's Progress from the Known to the Unknown, 75
Anthony, Susan B., xv, 136, 142, 143, 144, 158
Anti-Poverty Society, 115

Argus, xxi, 36, 106, 107, 108, 114, 124, 126, 163
Austen, Jane, 44, 49, 50, 55
Australasian, 45
Australasian Charities Conference, 131
Australian Examiner, 106
Australian National League (ANL), 128
A Week in the Future, xxi, xxii, 45, 60, 61, 62, 93, 117, 118
Ayers, Lady, 85

B

Baker, John, 70, 71
Bakewells, the, 19, 32
Bakewell, William, 45
Bank of South Australia, 34, 35
Baptist Church, 37, 129, 146
Barbalet, Margaret, 79, 86
Barnes, John, 47
Barr Smith, Joanna and Robert, 40, 132
Baynton, Barbara, *Bush Studies*, 44
Beare, Catherine, 18

Beare, Lucy (later Duval), 19
Bellamy, Edward, *Looking Backward*, 20, 62, 117
Bentley, Richard & Son, publishers, 46
Birkbeck schools, 96
Birks, Elsie, 133
Birks, J. N., 130
Blackley, W. L., 88
Blainey, Geoffrey, *A Land Half Won*, 8, 121
Blyth, Arthur, 81
Boarding-Out Society, 83, 84, 85, 86, 87, 88, 90, 100, 143, 146, 151
Bonython, Lady, 15
Book Society and Subscription Library, 39
Booth, Rev. William, 74
Boucaut, James, 36
British Proportional Representation Society, 127, 133
Brodie, Alexander (CHS's uncle), 34
Brodie, Mary (CHS aunt), 17
Brontë, Charlotte, 44, 45, 57
Brontë sisters, 43
Brooker, T. H., 138
Brownhill Creek, xii, 29, 30
Browning, Elizabeth Barrett, 44
Browning, Robert, 65, 108
Bunyan, John, *A Pilgrims Progress*, 63, 72
Burra, 33, 34, 55, 126
Butler, Samuel, 20

C

Café de Paris, 155, 156
Caird, Mona, *The Wing of Azrael*, ix, 112
Caldwell, Robert, 152
Calvinism, xi, 27, 36, 63, 67
Carlyle, Thomas, 130
Carpenter, Mary, 67, 77
Charleston, D. M., 129
Church of Scotland, 24, 25, 64, 66

Clara Morison, xx, xxi, 37, 39, 45, 46, 47, 48, 49, 52, 53, 54, 55, 60, 61, 62, 64, 77
Clark, Caroline Emily, 64, 88, 89
Clark, Francis, 65
Clark, Howard, 65, 70, 102, 107, 108, 109, 119, 131
Clark, John Howard, 70, 109
Cobbe, Frances Power, 77, 82, 87, 143
Cockburn, J. A., 154
Colton, Mary, 151
'Columba', 59, 60
'compulsory providence', 88
Constitutional Amendment Bill, 155
Cook, Edith (later Hübbe), 19, 72, 103, 104
Co-operative Clothing Company, 159, 160
Corbin, Mrs L. M., 149
Cornhill Magazine, xxi, 107, 108, 110
Craik, Professor, 126
Cridge, Alfred, xxii, 19, 135, 137
Criminological Society, 99
Cumming, Jessie, 35

D

Daniels, Kay, 4, 53, 55, 61, 79, 95, 98
Daughters of England, 71
Davenant, Miles, 53
Davenport, Mrs, 85
Davidson, *The Old Order and the New*, 130
Davin, Anna, 4, 21
Deans, Jeannie, 26
de Beauvoir, Simone, 9, 48
Despasquale, Paul, 47
Destitute Asylum, 16, 81, 82, 83, 88, 160
Destitute Board, 16, 80, 81, 83, 84, 85, 87, 88
Destitute Persons' Relief and Industrial and Reformatory Schools Act, 1872, 83
Dickens, Charles, xxi, 43, 59
Distressed Women and Children's Fund, 151
Donnelly, *Caesar's Column*, 130

Index

Downer, J. W., 35
Droop, H. R., 133
Duval, Rose and Kitty (her daughter), 19

E

Edgeworth, Maria, 25
Edinburgh, Scotland, 24, 26, 27, 96
Education Act, 94, 97, 99, 100
Education, Board of, 95
Education, Council of, 99, 100
Education, Department of, 148
Effective Voting League, 138
Elberfeld System on Charity, The, 89
Elder, George, 30
Elder, Smith & Company, 40, 107
electoral act amendment bill, 124
electoral reform, 19, 41, 112, 119, 153
Eliot, George, xxi, 11, 20, 44, 57, 73, 77, 105, 108, 111, 112, 118
Elliot, Margaret, 37, 38, 53, 58, 59, 62
Ellis, Sarah, 71
Ellis, William, 96, 102
English Poor Law Board, 83
Enlightenment, 61, 65, 66, 67, 72, 94, 153
Exhibition Building, Adelaide, 83

F

Farmer's and Producer's Political Union (FPPU), 128
Fawcett, Millicent Garrett, 144
Female Refuge, 71
female suffrage, xv, 7, 77, 135, 136, 149, 150, 151, 152, 154, 155, 156, 160
feminism, ix, xii, xv, 7, 9
Finlayson, John Harvey, 109
Franchise Reform Act, 108
Franklin, Miles, xiv, 49, 52, 58, 163
Fraser's Magazine, xxvii, 109, 110, 123

Free Church, 24, 64
Free-Trade and Liberal Association, 139
Frome, E. C., 33

G

Garran, Andrew, 106, 119
Garrison, William Lloyd, xx, 135, 142
Gathered In, 32, 45, 46, 48, 50, 51, 53, 57, 58, 60, 61
Gawler, George, 29
Gearhart, Sally, 62
George, Henry, *Progress and Poverty*, xv, xvii, 20, 115, 130, 133, 135
Gilfillan, John Alexander, 37
Gilles Street, Adelaide, 29
Gilman, Charlotte Perkins, xv, xxii, 20, 44, 62, 141, 143
Gilmour, "Professor", 133
Girls' Literary Association, 76
Girton College, 96
Glasgow, Scotland, 96, 136
Glyde, Lavington, MP, 124
Glynn, P. M., 138
Goldsmith, Oliver, 32
Goldstein, Vida, xxv, 8, 20, 131, 159, 162, 163, 164
Gouger, Robert, 28
Grant, Kerr, 15
Gray, Edith, 53, 58
Green, H. M., 8, 47, 58
Gregory, Ellen Louisa, 18
Gregory, J. B., 134
Grey, George, 30
Grieg, Margaretta, 71
Gunton, Elizabeth, 7

H

Haining, Rev. Robert, 64
Handfasted, xiii, xxi, xxii, xxvi, xxvii, 45, 46, 48, 50, 51, 53, 59, 60, 61, 62
Hardy, Arthur, 70, 71
Hare-Spence system, 134
Hare, Thomas, xvi, 20, 96, 123, 124, 126, 133
Hartley, John Anderson, xviii, xxvi, 19, 97
Hawker, G. C., 155
Hazelwood Park, Adelaide, 65
Henry, Alice, 20, 162, 163
Hickock, E. J., 137
Hill, Edwin, 96
Hill, Florence Davenport, 77
Hilliard, David, 71
Hill, Matthew Davenport, 65, 77
Hill, Octavia, 69, 87, 89, 90
Hill, Rosamond Davenport, 67, 143
Hill, Rowland, 65, 77, 123, 126
Hodges, Minnie, 53
Hogarth, Francis, 50, 53
Holder, F. W., 158
Hood, Rose, 147, 153
Howell, George, 116
Hull House, xv, 142, 143, 163
Humberstone, Mr, 53, 54

I

industrialisation, xvii, 102, 129
industrial school at Magill, 84
industrial schools, 83, 148
International Conference on Charities and Correction, 135
International Congress of Charities, Correction and Philanthropy, 88
International Council of Women, 158

J

James, Henry, 106
Jeffries, Rev. Dr, 129
Johnson, Samuel, 8
Jones, Helen, xii, xiv, xxvi, 156

K

Kay, Misses, 72
Keith, Hugh Victor, 53
Kindergarten Union, 53
Kingston, C. C., 16

L

labour movement, 129, 139, 141, 148, 151, 154, 155
Ladies' Federal Union, 141
Lancaster, Mary, 53, 58
Lancaster, Rose, 38, 53, 56, 59
land legislation, xvii, 109, 110, 113
Land Reform League, xvii, 109, 110, 113
Lane, William, 130
Lee, Mary, xxv, 151, 152, 155, 156
Le Guin, Ursula, xxii, 62
Leigh Smith, Barbara, 77, 96, 143
Lewes, G. H., xxi, 118
Liberal and Democratic Union (LDU), 129
Liberal-Country Party, 139
liberalism, 118, 148
'Lib-Lab' coalition, 129
Lindsay, Allan, 53
Lindsay, Jessie, 47
Lindsay, Mrs, 51, 56, 59
Locke, Lillian, 162
London, x, xvi, 7, 18, 19, 39, 45, 50, 69, 77, 89, 96, 100, 107, 123, 126, 136, 142, 143, 158
London School Board, 69, 77, 143
Longfellow, W. W., 130

Index

Lubbock, Sir John, 133
Ludlow, J. M., 43
lying-in homes, 43

M

Mackinnon, Alison, 103
'MacLeod, Mrs Alick' (Catherine MacKay/Martin), 112
manhood suffrage, 123, 125, 126
Mansfield, Katherine, 9
Maritime Strike, 128
Markey, Ray, 144
Married Women's Property Act, 150
Marshall, Alfred, 116
Martin, Annie, 71, 82, 134
Martin, Arthur Patchett, 109
Martin, Catherine, xv, xxvi, 44
Martineau, James, 74
Martin, E. M., 65
Martin, Henry, 55
Martins, the, 70
Marx, Karl, 28, 130
Masefield, Edward, 53, 56
Medway Day, J., 129
Melbourne Review, xxi, xxvii, 109, 111, 114, 119
Melbourne University, viii, 109
Melrose, Scotland, x, 24, 25, 26, 27, 40
Melville, Jane, 53, 59, 62
Miller, E. Morris, 47
Mill, J. S., 20, 96, 123, 126, 150
Milne, Agnes, 151, 159, 160
Ministering Children's League, 147
Modjeska, Drusilla, 49
Moers, Ellen, 50
More, Hannah, 98
Morgan, Sir William, 71
Morice, Lucy, xii, xiii, 12, 13, 18, 110, 160, 162

Morison, Clara, 38, 39, 50, 58, 59, 64, 74
Morison, J. C., 116
Mr Hogarth's Will, 39, 45, 46, 48, 50, 52, 53, 59, 60, 143
Mundy, Alfred, 33
Murray, Andrew, 30, 36, 107
Musgrave, Lady, 84

N

Nassau, Mrs, Senior, 87
National American Women's Suffrage Association, 142
National Association for the Promotion of Social Science, 77, 131
National Association of Coloured Women, 142
National Council of Women, xxiii, 91, 155
National Defence League, 128
National Union of Women's Suffrage Societies, 128, 144
National Women's Trade Union League, 163
Navelle, Ernest, 137
Neglected and Criminal Children's Act, 83
New England Women's Club, 143
Nicholls, Elizabeth Webb, xxv, 152, 160
Nightingale, Florence, 8
North, Robert, 53, 55

O

Oliphant, Margaret, 44, 57, 59
Orphan School, 84
Oswald, Kenneth, 53, 58
Owen, Robert, 39

P

Pacific Coast Council of the Trades and Labour Federation, 136
Palmyra, 5, 27, 32
Parkes, Henry, 126

Parliamentary Commission on the Destitute, 88
Parr, James Hamilton, 35
Parsons, J. Langdon, 103
patriotism, 130
Paynter, Dorothy H., 157
Peake, A. H., 129
Pearson, C. H., 100, 114
philanthropy, 147, 148
Phinn, Miss, 26, 32, 33, 74
Piercy, Marge, xxii, 62
Pike, Douglas, *Paradise of Discent*, 3, 64
Playford, Thomas, 154
poor relief, 80, 82, 88, 89
preferential voting, 125
Presbyterian Ladies College, 100
Price, Tom, 128, 138, 139
proportional representation, xiii, xiv, xv, xvi, xix, xxiii, 12, 20, 123, 125, 126, 127, 131, 132, 133, 134, 135, 136, 139
Proportional Representation Congress, 136
Proportional Representation Society, 127, 133, 136
Proud, Cornelius, 130
Proud, E. Dorothea, 7

Q

Quiltys, the, 18
Quiz and the Lantern, 75

R

rationalism, 66, 67, 72, 153
Reed, Thomas Sadler, 85
reformatories, 77, 83, 87, 148
Reform Movement, 129, 130, 132, 133, 134, 137, 139, 152, 153, 154
Reginald, Charles, 19, 50, 53
Register, ix, xiii, xiv, xxi, xxii, 2, 70, 82, 98, 100, 102, 105, 106, 109, 110, 111, 113, 114, 119, 120, 121, 124, 125, 132, 135, 144, 151, 155, 157
religious liberty, 64
Representation of the People Act, 127
Royal Commission on Education, 103
Royal Society of South Australia, 70
ruling class, 6, 148
Russ, Joanna, xxii, 62

S

Salvation Army, 74
Sand, George, 44
Saunders, A. T., 130
Schreiner, Olive, ix, 44, 112
Scotland, x, xiv, 16, 24, 25, 27, 32, 33, 34, 50, 57, 64, 66, 108, 123, 143
Scott, Dorothy, 73
Scott, Rose, xii, xiii, xxv, 8, 20, 161, 162, 163
Scott, Sir Walter, 43, 53
Sheridan, Susan, 4, 48
Showalter, Elaine, 39, 58, 59
Simpsons, the, xii, 3, 71
Single Tax, xv, xvii, 115, 129, 133, 135, 137
Single Tax League, 129, 135, 137
Sinnett, Frederick, 43, 46, 107
Smith, Barbara Leigh, 77, 96, 143
Social Purity League, 149, 151, 152
Society for the Study of Christian Sociology, 129
Some Social Aspects of South Australian Life, xxi, xxvi, 119, 144
South Australian Company, 19
South Australian council of women, 158
South Australian Council of Women, 159
South Australian Fabian Society, 129
South Australian Institute, viii, 70, 74, 108, 131
South Australian Mechanics' Institute, 43
South Australian Mining Company, 34

South Australian Political Association, 124
South Australian Proprietary School, 33
South Australian School Society, 33
South Australian Society of Arts, 70
Southey, Robert, Poet Laureate, 44
Spence, David, x, xi, xii, 23, 24, 25, 27, 28, 30, 33, 34
Spence, Helen Brodie, xi, 17
Spence, Jessie, 30
Spence, John, 35, 45, 106
Spencer, Anna Garlin, 142
Spencer, Herbert, 91
Spence, William (father & brother), 24, 34
Stackpole, Henrietta, 106
Starr, Ellen, xv, 142
State Children' Convention, 91
State Children's Council, 87, 88, 90, 91, 121, 128, 135, 148, 160
Stephens, Samuel, 18
Stevenson, Margaret, 105
Stirling, Edward Charles, 40, 87, 149
Stirling, Edward (father), xxiv, 40
Stirlings, the, 19, 40
Stow, T. Q., 33
Strong, Dr Charles, 131
Sutherland, Alexander, 47, 109
Sydney Morning Herald, 106, 127

T

taxation, xvii, 80, 113, 114, 115, 147, 150
Taylor, Helen, 150
Taylor, John, 19, 40, 45, 53, 64, 106
Telegraph, 107
Tender and True, 38, 45, 46, 53, 55, 58, 60, 107
Thackeray, W. M., xxi, 43, 59, 60
The Author's Daughter, 37, 45, 46, 47, 48, 50, 51, 53, 56, 58, 60
The Laws We Live Under, xx, 101, 104, 132

Thompson, J. Day, 129
Times (Adelaide), 37
Torrens Land Act, 113
Tubbins, Mrs, 53
Tubman, Harriet, 142
Turner, George, 137
Turner, Henry Gyles, xxi, 72
Turner, Martha, 72, 73, 75
Twining, Louisa, 87
Tyson, Robert, 136

U

ULP Council, 128
unionism, 102
Unitarian Christian Church, xii, 2, 65, 67, 69, 70, 72, 121
Unitarian Church's Mutual Improvement Society, 108
Unitarian congregation, 19, 65, 67, 72, 90, 162
Unitarianism, 65, 66, 67
United Labour Party (ULP), 128, 152
United Trades and Labour Council (UTLC), 2, 128, 151, 152
University of Adelaide, 15, 87, 103
Utopianism, 129, 132, 133, 137

V

Voice, 130, 134, 137

W

Wakefield, Edward Gibbon, 28
Ward, Ebenezer, 150
Watts, Henry, 33
Way, Samuel (later Chief Justice), 131
Webb, Beatrice, 69, 164
Webster, John, 73
Weekly Herald, xxvii, 137, 138

Weekly Mail, 45, 46, 50, 107
West Terrace, Adelaide, 29
Wheatley, G. E., 129
Whitham, C. L., 72
Whitridge, W.W., 106
Williams, William Smith, 45
Wilson, Edward, 107
Windschuttle, Elizabeth, 79
Withering, Miss, 53, 54, 61
Wollstonecraft, Mary, 8
'woman movement', 6, 7
Woman's Sphere, 162
Woman Voter, 73
Women's Christian Temperance Union, 139, 149, 151, 153, 155, 159
Women's Electoral Lobby, 159
Women's Employment Mutual Association, 162
Women's Federal Political Association, 159
Women's Movement, 141, 142, 143, 148, 151, 152, 156, 160
Women's Non-Party Political Association, 162
Woodall, William, 149
Woods, John Crawford, 65
Woolf, Virginia, 9, 23, 40
working men's clubs, 128
Working Men's Patriotic Association, 129
Working Women's Trades Union, 149, 151, 160
Working Women's Union, 141
Wren, Charles, 153
Wren, Eleanor, xii, xiii, 162
Wren, William, xii, 18, 36

Y

Young, Jeanne, xiii, xx, xxiii, 9, 10, 11, 13, 14, 15, 17, 20, 37, 38, 53, 102, 137, 141, 142, 155, 162, 163, 164
Young Women's Christian Association, 149
Young Women's Institute, 149

Z

Zadow, Augusta, Inspector of Factories, 151

www.ingramcontent.com/pod-product-compliance
Lightning Source LLC
Chambersburg PA
CBHW060510300426
44112CB00017B/2616